THE WILL TO LEAD

Managing with Courage & Conviction in the Age of Uncertainty

NEIL H. SNYDER

ANGELA P. CLONTZ

IRWIN
Professional Publishing
Chicago • London • Singapore

HD
57.7
S692
1997

© Neil H. Snyder and Angela P. Clontz, 1997

⬛▼ Times Mirror
M Higher Education Group

Library of Congress Cataloging-in-Publication Data

Snyder, Neil H. (Neil Harding),
    The will to lead : managing with courage and conviction in an age
of uncertainty / by Neil H. Snyder and Angela P. Clontz.
        p.   cm.
    Includes index.
    ISBN 0-7863-1014-6
    1. Leadership.   2. Leadership—United States—Case studies.
I. Clontz, Angela P.   II. Title
HD57.7.S692   1997
658.4'092—dc20   96–31815

Printed in the United States of America
1 2 3 4 5 6 7 8 9 0 DO 3 2 1 0 9 8 7 6

PREFACE

For more than 45 years, leaders in businesses throughout the United States have been unwilling to do their jobs despite increasing competitive pressure from foreign firms. They have been too content and too anxious to hold on to their positions to make the hard choices that will determine their ability to compete effectively in the next century.

The automobile and steel industries were the first to experience the onslaught of fierce foreign competitors. One by one, established U.S. firms in these industries saw their markets decline slowly at first, and then rapidly as U.S. consumers demonstrated a preference for high-quality and competitively priced products. Leaders in some firms, like Ford Motor Company, had to go to the brink of disaster before they recognized the changing competitive landscape and developed the will to lead. We deal with the Ford experience in detail in chapter 11 of this book.

Leaders in a few U.S. firms did not wait until they had to change before acting. They are clearly the exception to the rule. For example, leaders at Motorola and GE made hard choices and invested heavily in their products and their people to position themselves as two of the best firms in the world. Today they can compete effectively anywhere.

But leaders in most U.S. firms are still reluctant to step up to the plate and make hard choices. It is just a matter of time before they have no choice but to act.

This book is about developing the will to lead and the courage to make changes. Business leaders must take bold steps now to ensure that their companies retain and improve upon their competitive positions. We want to warn you in advance that many of the ideas presented in this book are controversial, but we believe they are correct nonetheless and deserve attention.

THE BEGINNING OF A REVOLUTION

During the 1980s and 1990s, U.S. businesses in numerous industries undertook rightsizing and reengineering programs that brought about a return to profitability and competitiveness in terms of balance sheet and income statement data. But many of them have gone about as far as they can go with these efforts, and now they must find a way to improve the capabilities and productivity of their people if they are to have any hope of competing with the best firms in the world.

On the positive side, U.S. firms continue to be the most productive in the world. But on the negative side, the rate of productivity improvement in the United States lags productivity increases in other countries. Unless U.S. firms change their ways and rethink their assumptions about how to run their businesses, it is only a matter of time before competitors, both here and abroad, catch up with and surpass them.

During this time, businesses in other industrialized nations like Great Britain, Germany, and Japan were content to protect their margins. But things are changing overseas. Businesses and governments in other industrialized nations are taking revolutionary steps to improve their competitiveness, and the gap between them and the best U.S. firms is disappearing rapidly. If leaders in U.S. businesses fail to make hard choices now, it is just a matter of time before their firms will lose momentum and will once again be struggling to catch up.

HOW DID IT BEGIN?

The problems we face today did not come about overnight. They are firmly rooted in a philosophy that developed immediately following World War II and has held great sway ever since. The war was a tremendous economic boom period for U.S. businesses, and after the war U.S. businesses were the only ones in the world with their production capacities intact and a ready market for goods and services.

Following World War II, U.S. consumers had good jobs and lots of money to spend, and businesses were able to sell all they could produce. Quality simply was not an issue. Neither were costs. Consumers were willing to buy anything businesses could produce, and they were not very discriminating. Thus, businesses paid almost no attention to quality, even though now famous quality guru W. Edwards Deming warned of the future pitfalls of ignoring quality and customer satisfaction..

They ignored his pleas, so he went to Japan where he found a receptive audience. U.S. businesses would not understand the cost of this error until the late 1970s and early 1980s when foreign competitors, from Japan and Germany primarily, introduced high-quality products in the United States at competitive prices, and U.S. firms lost market share rapidly.

As we said before, costs were not viewed as terribly important after the war. The production capacities of our foreign competitors were destroyed during World War II. Most of them were preoccupied with the struggle to survive. Thus, the only competitors U.S. firms viewed as serious threats were other U.S. businesses. If they routinely ignored quality, costs, and the efficiency of their operations, they were not at a competitive disadvantage because their competitors were doing the same thing. The failure to pay attention to these issues was the norm, and it became institutionalized in most firms.

To make matters worse, following World War II the U.S. government initiated programs and policies that could not be sustained in a competitive environment. Because of the robust business activity following the war, tax revenues grew rapidly, and government officials assumed the growth in revenue would continue indefinitely. These programs, although intended to create a "Great Society," instead led to excess and abuse and an enormous debt and deficit burden.

Just as important, these government programs ushered in a welfare state, the dependency ethic, and the destruction of the work ethic. Today, these problems stand in the way of our ability to improve productivity in business and government, increase our standard of living, and compete effectively with the best firms in the world.

THE FIRST STEP TOWARD A SOLUTION IS TO RECOGNIZE THE PROBLEM

It took the recessions of the 1970s and 1980s to awaken U.S. firms to the new economic reality and to force them to pay attention to their customers' demands for high-quality products at competitive prices. By then, Japanese and German firms were producing some of the finest products in the world and selling them in the United States at prices below the cost of many U.S. firms. Furthermore, firms in China, Korea, and other countries were finding willing buyers in the United States for their products. If U.S. business leaders had been minding the store and if they had demonstrated the will to lead, they would not have been so unprepared. This should never happen again.

MAKING HARD CHOICES AND PREPARING TO COMPETE IN THE NEXT CENTURY

Today, business leaders face a test that will determine their ability to compete effectively in the next century. Today's problems stem from divisions in the workplace, the destruction of the work ethic, an obsession with harmony, and the fear of change. Lack of money, equipment, and technology are not holding U.S. firms back—it is the capabilities and behaviors of people that present the greatest challenge.

To prosper in the future, business leaders must be courageous and demonstrate the will to lead people to higher performance levels. They must alter their basic assumptions and abandon the philosophies that have made it difficult for them to achieve excellence. They need to focus their attention on building effective teams. The team approach to running businesses we will present in this book is not like the ones we hear so much about today. Our approach combines the best of individual efforts with the best of group efforts and produces results.

Additionally, they must give people responsibility and hold them accountable for producing results. This will not be easy. Today's younger workforce is composed of people who were born and nurtured during a time in our nation's history when we as a nation did everything imaginable to convince them that people are not responsible for their own actions. And following, without responsibility for individual action, they certainly cannot be held accountable no matter what they do.

Finally, leaders must get back to the basics and encourage people to develop their entrepreneurial talents. There is no way we can compete in the global economy unless all our people learn to take actions at every step of the production process and in every job to improve performance. Furthermore, to lead entrepreneurs, leaders must be entrepreneurial. Entrepreneurs do not respect leaders who are not entrepreneurial, and they will not follow for long if our leaders fail to establish work environments that are less bureaucratic and more open to new ideas.

Unless we move aggressively on these three fronts simultaneously, we will not fare well in the next century as we face stiff competition from businesses in every corner of the world. It is our sincere hope that this book will assist business leaders who have the will to lead.

Neil Snyder
Charlottesville, Virginia

Angela Clontz
Charlotte, North Carolina

ACKNOWLEDGMENTS

In the process of writing this book, we talked with hundreds of people about our ideas and got a great deal of useful feedback from them. Several people went above and beyond the call of duty and provided us with assistance and advice that we found essential as we developed our thoughts and conclusions. Margaret Bolen, Mary K. Broecker, Norvin Clontz, Margaret Craddock, Jim Dowd, Mary Hodges, Margaret Howell, Martha Maznevski, Dudley Pettit, Leonard Sandridge, Bruce Scott, Bill Shenkir, David Upton, Jeff Walker, Nancy Walker, and Ellen Whitener were particularly helpful as we went about our work. Katie Snyder, Melanie Snyder, Rebekah Snyder, Lydia Clontz, and Todd Newnam had to make personal sacrifices as we toiled to complete this project, and we want to thank them for their patience and understanding. Without their support, we could not have done our work. We also want to thank the McIntire School of Commerce Foundation for their support.

    We would be negligent and less than honest if we failed to extend a special thank-you to several people who did not agree with some of our conclusions in controversial areas. We know full well that many of the ideas in this book are not universally held, and therefore they are threatening to people who have bought into the doctrine of political correctness hook, line, and sinker. We made a concerted effort to understand their logic and rationale as they explained their perspectives to us. After due consideration, we believe that common sense, logic, and the evidence support our conclusions. We are more convinced now than we have ever been that U.S. businesses and our nation will have a difficult time competing unless our leaders demonstrate the will to lead and challenge some of the fundamental premises underlying decisions made in institutions throughout our society. Radical change is in order, so the road will be bumpy. But those who have the will to lead, conviction, and courage will prevail and get the job done.

CONTENTS

Chapter 7

Teamwork: Leadership from the Top   99

Chapter 8

Making Everyone Accountable   119

Chapter 9

Creating a Risk-Taking Environment   139

Chapter 10

Ted Turner: The Building of an Empire   161

Chapter 11

Jack Welch: Making GE Competitive   177

CHAPTER 1

The Leadership Challenge

The world is in the midst of political and economic changes the likes of which we have never seen. Maps of the world become obsolete before they can be published, and technological developments in many fields occur at such a rapid pace that manufacturers hardly recover their costs before their products are outdated. The Renaissance and Industrial Revolution, although turbulent periods, do not compare with what we are living through today.

To complicate matters for U.S. business leaders, throughout the world market economies are developing that rival, or have the potential to rival, the economy of the United States. Japan and Germany are the most obvious examples of this, but they are not the only ones. Countries like Taiwan, Vietnam, and China, to name only three, have made tremendous progress, and businesses in these and other countries are putting significant pressure on U.S. firms to produce top-quality products at competitive prices. If U.S. business leaders respond inappropriately to these challenges, their firms and our society will suffer.

The economies of these developing countries are bustling; their standards of living are rising; and their productivity is increasing. They all have problems that must be addressed, but we think economic pressures and their

1

desire to join the world's most advanced industrialized nations will motivate them to reconsider their policies in areas that create problems
between them and their trading partners. China, in particular, must deal
with human rights concerns and patent and copyright law violations before
they can assume their place among the economic superpowers of the
world. It would be foolish for leaders in U.S. businesses to ignore the
progress made by businesses throughout the world, including businesses
in developing countries, and fail to take a cold, hard, objective look at the
competitiveness of their own firms.

There is no letup in sight. Business and government actions will continue to alter the competitive landscape in the years ahead. For example,
trading blocks like the European Community (EC) in Europe, the Association of Southeast Asian Nations (ASEAN) in Asia, and Canada, Mexico,
and the United States in North America are changing the way we think
about international competition. These changes have brought about economic and political consolidation as businesses and nations have worked to
find more effective ways to compete. Additionally, they have altered our
concept of national boundaries and have contributed to the rapid growth of
joint ventures between businesses in different nations. As we will see in
chapter 12, this movement is being led by firms like Ford Motor Company,
which is well on its way to becoming a company without a country.

THE WILL TO LEAD

If business leaders do not adjust quickly to the changing world economy
and demonstrate the will to lead, their firms will not survive, or they will be
only marginally successful, at best, and this is not good enough in the competitive world in which we live. To be sure, there are excellent examples of
U.S. firms that are among the very best in the world. For instance, Ford
Motor Company has focused its resources, and today it produces some of
the finest and most affordable products and services available anywhere.
Likewise, Motorola and GE are among the most competitive businesses in
the world, and the quality of their products is second to none.

These firms do business in some of the most competitive and rapidly
changing industries in the world, and their people have learned many
lessons any business can benefit from knowing. For example, their relent-
less pursuit of product and process improvements and their efforts to
develop their people have contributed greatly to their competitive strength.
But most U.S. businesses are struggling to catch up with their competitors,
and many of them never will, unless they are willing to make radical

changes in the way they run their businesses. Stating it as simply as we can, businesses must learn to improve their performance, or they will lose to better prepared competitors.

Barriers to Effective Organizations

Most leadership models describe organizations heading in one clearly focused direction, with all their members working in concert to achieve *one vision* that is identified and communicated by the leader. In reality, leaders often find that people in organizations do not share the same vision. Instead, different groups and individuals advance competing ideas of the future. Even when they begin with the basic ideas embodied in the leader's vision, they may then proceed to adapt that vision to their own "unique perspectives," sometimes with catastrophic results for the organization.

Of course, managers in many U.S. businesses are quite familiar with this phenomenon through their interactions with labor unions. The history of labor-management relations in this country is filled with examples of competing visions clashing and doing great harm to businesses and to individuals. Even in recent years, where increasing competitive pressures have moved these traditional adversaries into closer cooperation, opposing forces have tried to pull them apart again.

A maverick antimanagement group within the UAW, for example, repeatedly attacks union leaders for their support of total quality management programs, especially those calling for greater employee involvement in decision making. This separatism has been reinforced by a recent decision of the National Labor Relations Board. They found that DuPont was in violation of the National Labor Relations Act for having established quality improvement teams without prior consultation with union leaders. In chapter 2, we will examine in greater detail the impact of unions on executive leadership, with particular attention to the role played by unions in the decline of major corporations in the United States. These divisions in the workplace plague business and nonbusiness organizations alike, and their effects have the potential to threaten our nation's competitiveness.

Decay in the Work Ethic

The concept of a "work ethic" is derived from the ideas of Martin Luther and John Calvin, later developed by the sociologist Max Weber, as a set of moral beliefs that emphasized the intrinsic value of work. Widely known as the "Protestant work ethic," these beliefs led workers to exert their best efforts as a moral obligation to themselves, their families, and their communities.[1] For obvious reasons, communities everywhere boast that their local workforces live by these ideas. For years the words "American" and "work ethic" were practically inseparable, and states like Minnesota, California, and Georgia make special efforts to claim that this type of work ethic make them the best places for start-ups and expansions.

Work ethic decay has caused many businesses to seek locations for facilities heretofore not considered. In weighing different locations for possible expansion, executives typically report that they consider the quality of the local workforce as a key issue. For example, a 1990 study in Fortune called "The Best Cities for Business" cited Salt Lake City, Minneapolis–St. Paul, Atlanta, and Sacramento as the areas with the best workers in the United States The study suggested that businesses locating in these areas could expect to find workers with advanced skills and a strong work ethic, leading to easier hiring, lower turnover, and better performance.[2]

However, as business has become more global and competitive pressures have forced firms to control costs to keep prices down, two things have occurred. Businesses consider a far more extensive list of potential sites, and countries around the world are competing on the basis of a strong work ethic and low labor costs. Nations from El Salvador to Vietnam, for example, are all the more competitive for having been recognized for a large supply of workers who can be counted on to work hard and long hours willingly for their employers. Some argue that these workers are being exploited. Nonetheless, they have demonstrated a willingness to work hard to improve their standard of living and are changing the competitive environment as a result. Japan is widely known to have a work ethic so strong that government intervention has been necessary to encourage workers to take earned vacations, to make a two-day weekend a standard part of the workweek, and to reduce overtime.[3]

By contrast, in recent years the more industrialized nations of the world have noted marked declines in the work ethic of their own people. Even Japanese analysts have noted a change in employee willingness to work hard for their employers, especially among younger workers. Nowhere is this trend more evident than in Sweden, however, where industrial production has fallen 15 percent since 1989. According to one recent study, the "Swedish disease" results from a set of government policies that encourage workers not to work. Swedes who are unemployed, sick, or busy caring for their children can receive between 90 percent and 100 percent of their salaries. This gives them little incentive to come to work, resulting in a worker absentee rate as high as 25 percent.[4] While Swedish industry has attempted to counteract this weakness with increasing automation and especially robotics in its factories, the government continues to struggle to change Swedish society to restore the work ethic.

But the disease is not exclusively Swedish. Germany is feeling the effects of a decade of largesse and is now paying the price. At Babcock-Borsig AG, for example, there will be no more anniversary bashes for people who have been with the company for 25 and 40 years; no more free saunas; vacations are being cut from 38 to 30 days a year; and Christmas bonuses are being cut in half and given only to people who actually earned them. The German economy is anemic, and German business leaders are concerned about the declining work ethic in Germany.

According to Hans Westphal, Babcock-Borsig's chairman, "We're in the same situation in the manufacturing industry in Germany now that the Americans were in the early 1980s. Why are we so far behind? Because beginning in 1982 we had a boom period that lasted nearly 10 years. That time was used by American manufacturers to restructure and be more aggressive, while we were riding the wave. We became too fat, too heavy, and we didn't do the homework that we needed to do to be competitive in the future."[5]

Evidence of a decline in the U.S. work ethic is not hard to find either. For example, a 1992 survey of members of the American Management Association reported that 79 percent of respondents believed that U.S. productivity has suffered because of a decline in the traditional American work ethic.[6] A human resources manager who spent two weeks working in a fast-food restaurant to gauge the work ethic of young American workers found that employees typically held a set of beliefs characterized by contempt for customers, poor work habits, widespread employee theft, and an overall orientation to work best described as "taking the system" and "milking the place dry."[7] Part of this problem is a result of these workers not having been properly prepared for work, and part of it is due to the way they are managed. We will deal with the particular needs of Generation X employees in chapter 3.

We believe that, as is the case in Sweden and Germany, U.S. government policies have contributed greatly to this problem. After years of expansion in American welfare programs, an ethic of dependency on "the system" has seriously undermined the U.S. work ethic and has hampered the ability of U.S. firms to compete in the global market. To be sure, there are good examples of people who have moved from welfare dependence to gainful employment due to hard work and persistence, but the system itself provides too few incentives to work. A recent study in the *Journal of Labor Research* argued that reform of this system must include more rewards for people who work and fewer rewards for those who do not, and that welfare caseworkers must continually emphasize to welfare recipients that they have a moral obligation to get a job.[8] These concepts are not new. President Abraham Lincoln offered this warning over 100 years ago: "You cannot build character and courage by taking away a man's initiative and independence. You cannot help a man by doing for him what he should do for himself."

Failure to Hold Individuals Accountable for Their Actions

We believe that there has been a fundamental erosion in the beliefs of American workers, and responsibility for that extends to management as well as to government. For example, one survey of a national sample of the U.S. workforce in 1990 found high levels of cynicism among U.S. workers, expressing low levels of trust and confidence in management. The authors noted that workers bring this cynicism with them to the workplace, but they also argued that this outlook is nurtured in what they call "cynical companies."[9]

Judith M. Bardwick, another writer concerned with the decline of the work ethic, blames management for fostering the same "entitlement" mentality others have noted among welfare recipients. These workers believe they do not have to earn their salaries or benefits with hard work; instead, they think they are entitled to these rewards—these rewards are simply owed to them by virtue of their status as employees. Management is to blame for the spread of this mind-set because they do not hold employees *accountable* for performance. Accordingly, employees stop working hard because their managers no longer require it.[10]

Clearly, anything management does that reduces the perceived connection between performance and rewards will inevitably reduce employee motivation to work. We will argue in chapter 4 that among the most pernicious ways in which this connection is undermined is the continued prominence of affirmative action programs in American industry. Whatever their original intent, these efforts demonstrate to employees on a daily basis that all employment decisions—hiring, promotions, compensation, and termination—are based not on merit but on individual characteristics such as race and gender. Instead, management must focus its efforts today on restoring employee confidence in the old-fashioned belief that hard work, and hard work alone, will bring rewards to those who deserve them.

On the other side of the coin, management must demonstrate its willingness to hold employees accountable for their actions. Far too often managers are unwilling to hold people accountable for their actions because they cannot face the prospect of conflict with others. What if the individual defends his or her actions by blaming others, or by blaming me? They fear that an honest attempt to address performance problems and failures may be interpreted as a personal attack, or worse yet, as "discrimination" against a member of a protected class.

What End Harmony?

Managers motivated by these fears often hide behind a misguided conception of "teamwork" to avoid their responsibility to manage performance. They argue that the team depends on a feeling of goodwill and "harmony" in order to achieve its goals, and any attempt to hold an individual accountable for individual behaviors will spoil that feeling and destroy the team. In fact, nothing could be further from the truth. Individual effort, even in teams, depends on the belief that what I do matters, that my actions are noticed, that my performance makes a difference, and that all members of the team have an equal obligation to perform.

Where managers fail to address poor performance, individuals conclude that results do not matter, and so their own behaviors do not matter, either. When other employees see poor performance unpunished and rewards given for nonperformance-related reasons, they question everything: Is there a vision for this organization? What is really important in this organization? Why should I risk doing anything? Contrary to the expectations and wishes of some managers, teams are *strengthened*, not weakened, when leaders step forward and confront the problems and the people who are responsible for them.

This is true at all levels of the organization, for executives as well as for workers: Behaviors that are unethical, illegal, or otherwise unacceptable cannot be overlooked, dismissed, or lightly forgiven. By the same token, managers responsible for bottom-line results and major projects can no longer be allowed to escape the consequences of their actions simply by blaming tough economic conditions or by moving up to another management position. Nothing is more demoralizing for workers than to watch senior management continually rewarded with raises, large bonuses, and stock options, while the financial disasters for which these same executives are responsible result in layoffs, salary reductions, or demands for union concessions in collective bargaining.

In short, leaders seeking to inculcate values and beliefs in their organizations that will enable them to prosper must find ways to overcome workforce cynicism and to restore trust and confidence and belief in the American work ethic.

The Fear of Change

Leaders who succeed in communicating their vision and values to those whom they must lead face yet a third obstacle in their struggle to lead: fear of change. Even those who are excited by the possibilities of the shared goals they will accomplish, and who commit themselves entirely to the ideals and the behaviors implied by the shared values, still may find themselves unable to *act* because they fear the changes they must face and the personal changes they must make to succeed.

The reasons people fear change are almost as numerous as the types of change that leaders seek to achieve. And as Paul Lawrence noted in a *Harvard Business Review* article 40 years ago, the mere fact of resistance to change is not in itself a problem to be overcome; people may resist change for a number of good reasons, and resistance should be treated less as an obstacle to be overcome and more as a signal of a problem that should be analyzed and resolved.[11]

Along the same lines, in a later *Harvard Business Review* article called "Choosing Strategies for Change," Kotter and Schlesinger argued that change implementation plans must proceed from a complete diagnosis of employee resistance to change. These authors went on to identify four major reasons for resistance: "a desire not to lose something of value; a misunderstanding of the change and its implications; a belief that the change does not make sense for the organization, and a low tolerance for change."[12]

As we are interested here primarily in those cases in which employees understand and support the rationale for the change, we are particularly interested in the first and the last reasons advanced by Kotter and Schlesinger. In our view, resistance to change, or more precisely, the inability to act in support of change, results from two primary fears: the fear of loss and the fear of failure.

It makes good sense that individuals who now have something of value would fear any change that might cause them to lose it. This "something of value" may be concrete, in the sense of a job title, an expense budget, decision-making authority, or other organizational resources; or it may be more abstract—a sense of accomplishment, achievement, superiority, or simply a feeling of security that comes from knowing the current system well. Fear of losing these psychological "possessions" often lies behind professed "rational" reasons for resisting change. Individuals may be only vaguely aware of these reasons, and so it becomes all the more difficult for leaders to respond to and allay these fears, which hobble and retard organizational action.

In the same way, it is natural for people to fear failure and ridicule, particularly as they try to learn and do new things. This is especially true for adults, and for anyone who has become used to success in the activities they have undertaken and mastered in the past. Evidence of this can be found any winter weekend on the "bunny slopes" of any ski resort: As small children whiz by, occasionally fall, and rise again, grown men and women stand awkwardly, grimacing in embarrassment. Struggling to stay on their feet, afraid to fall, afraid to look foolish, many put the poles and skis aside and take refuge in the lodge, giving up rather than taking the risk to learn and then to enjoy a new sport.

The parallel to work is clear: Many people learn not to risk new things because the "fall" is too painful to endure. They fear being seen as a failure, and they fear being ridiculed or possibly punished for having made a mistake. As Edgar Schein has argued, in a world that demands continual change and learning in organizations, leaders must find ways to make people feel safe as they try to learn.[13] In later chapters of this book we will examine the ways in which successful organizations have continued to encourage and support their people in learning and risking new things.

ORGANIZATION OF THIS BOOK

The political and economic challenges we face have created an unprecedented need for quality leaders, and we believe the demand for quality leaders will undoubtedly increase as we approach the next millennium. Chapters 2 through 6 of this book examine obstacles to leadership in American business today.

To prosper in the 21st century, businesses must learn to compete under a different set of rules. The adversarial relationships between business and labor that have caused so many problems over the last 50 years cannot continue. Labor and management must realize that they are on the same team and learn to cooperate to compete effectively. In chapter 2, we will show how they can accomplish this.

Additionally, business leaders must learn to incorporate a new generation of workers who have been raised differently than they were. This group, known as Generation X, has a lot of potential, but they cannot be managed effectively using the antiquated management philosophies of the past. In chapter 3, we will offer suggestions about how to manage Generation X employees effectively.

Furthermore, business leaders must begin to question their own policies and practices, and they must have the courage to change them when logic and the evidence suggest that change is necessary. Affirmative action policies, in particular, have created more problems than they have solved because they undermine the work ethic and reduce the corporate focus on performance. In the competitive world of the 21st century, any policy that effects performance negatively must be scrutinized carefully and revised to reflect the realities of the competitive market. In chapter 4, we will show how affirmative action policies have hurt U.S. businesses and explain how they can be revised to produce more competitive firms.

As they seek to improve the performance of their firms, leaders will encounter resistance, and many of them will be tempted to compromise important principles to maintain harmony, but harmony leads to mediocrity, not excellence. To achieve excellence, leaders must adhere to high standards and adopt a business philosophy that encourages differences of opinion and perspective about how to achieve outstanding results. In the short run, these different views lead to disharmony, but in the long run they lead to a better understanding about products, processes, and customer needs. Ultimately, they contribute to the creation of a firm that is better prepared to compete.

Too many times in the past, leaders have sought the illusion of harmony at the expense of excellence, and their firms have suffered as a result. Ford, General Motors, and Chrysler learned this lesson the hard way in the 1970s and 1980s. Their Japanese and German competitors infiltrated the U.S. market with higher-quality cars that were less expensive in many cases than the cars manufactured by the Big Three automobile producers, and U.S. consumers flocked to them as a result. This should not happen again. In chapter 5, we will show why the indiscriminate pursuit of harmony produces mediocre performance and offer ways to manage creative tension.

Some of the resistance leaders encounter will occur simply because people fear change. Since change is inevitable, leaders must work with their people to embrace it, or they will not be competitive. It is not enough merely to react to changes in the market. The most successful firms in the 21st century will initiate change and force their competitors to respond. In chapter 6, we will show how to introduce change successfully.

Chapters 7 through 9 of this book focus on three initiatives that must be undertaken if U.S. firms are to be competitive in the rapidly changing global market: developing effective teams, promoting accountability, and championing entrepreneurs. To improve the performance of their firms, leaders are beginning to pay attention to the value of groups of employees working together in teams. There is no question that teams can contribute greatly to product and process improvements and to a better bottom line, but many leaders fail to appreciate the importance of individual effort in a team environment. In chapter 7, we will show why team effort does not reduce the importance of individual contributions, and we will explain how to get the most out of people working in teams.

For businesses to excel, every person in the organization from top-level executives to hourly workers must contribute to the firm's overall performance. If they are not held accountable for producing results, the wrong precedent will be set, and the firm's performance will suffer as a result. In chapter 8, we will examine why it is essential to hold people accountable for what they actually do, and we will explain how to do it in a positive and supportive way.

To be competitive in this rapidly changing world, firms must improve their performance continually, and their people must never be satisfied. They must learn to act in a more entrepreneurial way as they look for new and better ways to get their jobs done, and when they do they will inevitably make mistakes. These mistakes are the cost of creativity, and they must be accepted. Unfortunately, many times leaders punish mistakes too harshly, and they offer too few rewards for successes. In chapter 9, we will explain how to develop a more entrepreneurial, creative, and innovative workforce that is motivated to excel.

Chapters 10 through 12 present examples of business success that should encourage the reader and offer ideas for individual improvement. Chapter 10 focuses on Ted Turner, and it demonstrates the power of creativity and ingenuity. Chapter 11 looks at the persistence and determination of Jack Welch at General Electric as he transformed GE into one of the most competitive firms in the world. And chapter 12 examines Ford Motor Company as it went from near bankruptcy in the early 1980s to a shining example of corporate success in the 1990s. At this point, we begin by examining ways to improve labor-management relations.

ENDNOTES

1. Herbert Applebaum, "Work and Its Future," *Futures,* May 1992, pp. 336–350.
2. Patricia Sellers, "The Best Cities for Business," *Fortune,* October 22, 1990, pp. 48–54.
3. Yasuyuki Hippo, "Japan:The Reduction in Working Time—an Unfinished Cultural Revolution," *Futures,* June 1993, pp. 537–550.
4. Paul Klebnikov, "The Swedish Disease," *Forbes,* May 24, 1993, pp. 78, 80.
5. Rick Atkinson, "German Workers Getting Stiff Shot of Reality," *The Washington Post,* February 22, 1994, pp. A1 and A 12.
6. Seymour Martin Lipset, "The Work Ethic, Then and Now," *Journal of Labor Research,* Winter 1992, pp. 45–54.
7. James Sheehy, "The New Work Ethic Is Frightening," *Personnel Journal,* June 1990, pp. 28–36.
8. Robert Rector, "Welfare Reform, Dependency Reduction, and Labor Market Entry," *Journal of Labor Research,* Summer 1993, pp. 283–297.
9. Philip H. Mirvis and Donald L. Kanter, "Beyond Demography: A Psychographic Profile of the Workforce," *Human Resource Management,* Spring 1991, pp. 45–68.
10. Michael A. Verespej, "The 'Psychology of Entitlement':It Must Be Broken," *Industry Week,* April 5, 1993, pp. 35–36.
11. Paul R. Lawrence, "How to Deal with Resistance to Change," *Harvard Business Review,* May–June 1954; cited in *Management of Change,* A Harvard Business Review paperback (Boston: Harvard Business School Publishing Division, President and Fellows of Harvard College, 1991) pp. 77–85.
12. John P. Kotter, and Leonard A. Schlesinger, "Choosing Strategies for Change," *Harvard Business Review,* March–April 1979, p. 107.
13. Edgar H. Schein, "How Can Organizations Learn Faster? The Challenge of Entering the Green Room," *Sloan Management Review,* Winter 1993, pp. 85–92.

2

CHAPTER

Division in the Workplace: Unions

Today business leaders face a workforce that is more diverse and divided than ever before. Diversity in the workplace is the norm, and given demographic changes in the United States, we know tomorrow's workforce will be even more diverse than the present one. Diversity in itself presents no problems. In fact, diversity leads to different perspectives and approaches to problem solving that work together to make businesses more open and competitive. But overemphasis on group affiliation can act as a divider of the organization. While unions once acted as a unifying force to ensure that labor was fairly represented in American business, today many unions act as a drag on U.S. competitiveness. By seeking consistent, nonproductivity-based wage increases and limiting workplace flexibility, unions have put themselves at odds with management's corporate goals and divided the workplace.

This division makes leading an organization difficult, because it is virtually impossible to unite divided groups behind a common goal or vision. The old military maxim, divide and conquer, suggests that the way to destroy an enemy is to divide its ranks. In business, the maxim applies as well. If we allow division in our workforce to persist, we will be conquered. We believe that unions still have an important role to play in the workplace.

In this chapter we will spend some time addressing the changing and increasing skill and education requirements in the workplace. Furthermore, we will discuss the decline in the education system and its failure to meet these changing needs. Clearly, businesses and unions are not responsible for the poor performance of our education system, but businesses depend on an educated workforce and are being forced to take on much of the responsibility to train and educate employees. But the task is becoming harder, and we believe unions should help sponsor these efforts. As skills and education become more critical in both service and manufacturing jobs, unions have a responsibility to improve the employability and productivity of their membership. Union leaders have the resources and infrastructure to make a new, value-adding role for themselves in the workplace. And business leaders are needed to guide this effort. Business leaders must reach out to unions, find common ground, and define the skill and education needs of a more competitive workforce.

FOCUSING ON THE PAST

Unions have been around for a very long time. From medieval trade guilds that controlled quality standards to the more sophisticated unions of the 1950s that pushed for wage, safety, and work-practice regulations, employee organizations have significantly contributed to the development of today's workplace and the prosperity of America. No one can argue that American business went through a period in the late 1800s and early 1900s when workers were often treated unfairly. Unions were instrumental in reversing these patterns and provided workers with a voice in corporate America.

However, we believe that today's unions must evolve and adapt to the changing needs of society and the workplace. American business is under intense pressure from abroad. Unlike the post–World War II decades of unquestioned world leadership and prosperity, America's leadership is not a given. Business leaders are being forced to revise many workplace practices and to change the old ways of thinking and managing. It is time that unions do the same.

The consistent wage increases and inflexible contracts of many unions exert a strain that most U.S. companies cannot withstand. And many do not have to. While the Big Three automakers provide the union with 385,000 UAW members, foreign car makers and their suppliers now employ over 109,000 workers in the United States—92 percent of them nonunion. The ranks of nonunion auto employees continue to grow as Mercedes-Benz and BMW open new plants in the Southeast. To date, the UAW has had little success with its attempts to unionize these foreign-owned plants. An embarrassing 1989 defeat at the Nissan Motor Company plant in Smyrna, Tennessee, dealt a serious blow to the UAW's efforts to attempt other high-profile elections.

The UAW's power and reputation have also been hurt by the ongoing standoff at Caterpillar, which continues to cause division within its organization. Since 1991, Caterpillar has gone without a negotiated contract. Rather than accept the 1991 standard deal taken by Deere & Company, Caterpillar let the union strike and has hired over 700 retirees and temporary employees to pick up the slack. While the standoff caused initial losses, Caterpillar posted record earnings in 1994.[1]

Given the "success" at Caterpillar, Deere & Company sought to take advantage of the weakening in the UAW during its next round of contract negotiations in 1994. After the generous 1991 contract, Deere changed its strategy to one of strong demands and apparent intractability. Asking for 70 percent lower wages for new hires and pay tied to productivity gains, Deere is hoping to enhance its long-term competitive prospects. With one of the oldest average workforces in the nation—the average Deere UAW member is less than eight years from retirement—the company is balking at hiring new workers at the current $22 per hour rate.[2] The UAW can expect pressure from more companies as foreign competitors continue to exert tremendous pressure on U.S. firms, and the public is becoming increasingly disenchanted with unions.

The UAW is not alone in feeling pressure. Between 1975 and 1991, the Steelworkers' union membership declined from 1 million to 500,000; the International Ladies Garment Workers Union fell from 350,000 to 150,000; and the Machinists' union dropped from 800,000 to 500,000 members.[3]

Recent events have only increased the questions surrounding the role unions play in the United States. The 1994–95 baseball strike angered fans and cost owners, players, and city sponsors nearly $1 billion. Not only did baseball financials suffer, but the image of baseball suffered as well. Many Americans, faced with layoffs, pay cuts, and job changes have little patience for a strike dedicated to securing millions more in earnings for a select few.

Employees, both pro- and antiunion, see this behavior and relate it to their own workplaces. No one wins when management and workers are at odds. We believe that today's workers realize the immense competitive pressure facing the nation and are willing to work together with management to secure a healthy future for themselves and their children.

While certainly less powerful than in prior decades, we believe that unions are not maximizing their role in American business. Many unions have fought efforts to change workplace practices to achieve productivity growth. And for logical reasons. Some of these changes rely on improved individual productivity, automation, and displacement of people. This in turn leads to fewer members, lower dues, and less power.

CHANGE WAS INEVITABLE

Despite union barriers, many businesses moved forward with tough workplace changes. And much of America's competitive spurt of the early 1990s was the direct result of downsizing. While painful for companies and individuals alike, many American companies have returned to a period of growth made possible by better-allocated resources. Yet real hourly wages, the hallmark of union performance, have fallen from their 1973 peak. This translates into significant dollars. Based on 1982 levels, real average weakly earnings in 1970 were $298. In 1994, they had fallen to $256, a nearly 15 percent drop.[4]

Some of this phenomenon can be explained by the changing priorities of business leaders. After a rough-and-tumble period in the 1970s and 1980s, corporate profits as a percent of national income have surged, reaching nearly 7 percent, their highest point since the 1970s. To remain competitive, companies have used these funds to buy new equipment, technologies, and systems—at the expense of wage increases for workers. But to warrant real wage increases, worker productivity must improve; and until very recently, the rate of productivity increases in the United States has not kept up with the rate of productivity improvements in many other nations. According to the Bureau of Labor Statistics, from 1979 through 1985 the United States trailed Japan, Germany, and France in productivity measured by growth in output per hour in manufacturing. Only since 1990 has the United States pulled slightly ahead of these rivals by boosting its productivity growth to nearly 3 percent annually.

During the 1980s, many U.S. businesses increased their profitability through layoffs, attrition, and hiring freezes. Now that companies have achieved more appropriate employee bases, the question is, where will companies find future productivity growth and the much-sought-after real wage increases?

We believe real wage increases will come when businesses learn to mobilize their employees and better utilize their skills. And improving skills and productivity is not easy under good conditions. Yet many unions have complicated the already difficult task by fighting innovations such as total quality management, team and employee empowerment, cross-training, education, flexible scheduling, and productivity-based pay increases, which help to develop the skills of their members. These workplace changes and others are essential if U.S. companies are to remain competitive with the most productive firms in the world. We believe unions can play a vital role in improving the quality and wages of the nation's workforce if they are willing to look beyond their traditional roles toward roles that fit the needs of business and society today. It is in each union's interest to consider the role they play carefully, and it is each business leader's responsibility to become actively involved in bringing about the kinds of changes that will enable them to compete effectively.

WORKERS MUST FOCUS ON SKILLS OR LOSE

Today's jobs require a higher level of education and skills. No longer do computers reside in the back office or headquarters. Computers are located on plant floors, in warehouses, in trucks—virtually anywhere transactions take place. Not only do computers require literate operators for entry and retrieval, but they demand people who can analyze information and draw conclusions to solve problems. Even noncomputer environments have manual tracking systems that require the same level of analytical and problem-solving capability to yield benefit.

Labor force participation patterns support this trend toward higher-skilled employees. Kevin M. Murphy, an economist at the University of Chicago, found that labor force participation by prime-age men fell by 1.6 percentage points from the early 1970s to the late 1980s. Murphy reports, "Virtually all of the decline was among the low-wage workers, especially the lowest 10 percent, whose participation rate fell 6.5 percentage points." The Labor Department also reports that over half of the jobs created in recent years have been in relatively high-wage, high-skill occupations. And the pattern yields no evidence of a reversal in favor of the lower-skilled segment.[5]

The debate over NAFTA brought this issue to the forefront. Many blue-collar workers fought against NAFTA and other free-trade initiatives in hopes of preserving low-skill, high-pay jobs. They do not want to face the reality that "the rate and duration of unemployment for blue collar workers have gone up in the last 15 years, and their wages have gone down. Blue collar income has been sinking for 15 years. But if you have a college, and especially if you have a graduate, degree, your income has been increasing." Robert Reich, secretary of labor under President Bill Clinton, continued: "A lot of people haven't got it in their heads how important skills are. Kids don't see the relationship between school and work. That's got to change."[6]

Business leaders would describe a skilled person the way many of us would have described a high school graduate 30 years ago—literate in English and numbers, able to solve logic and mathematics problems, able to interpret basic diagrams and charts. Certainly a large group of the population has or is developing these skills through higher education or job training. But many are not. Union members are not alone in fighting to remain adequately skilled in the changing world. Millions of unrepresented workers face the same challenge. Yet unions have a unique advantage in their ability to organize efforts for and communicate to their memberships. But the efforts must begin.

THE EDUCATION SYSTEM IS NOT HELPING

Business and union leaders cannot ignore the educational patterns in America today. They affect the value and employability of tomorrow's workers and members. Yet statistics suggest that a significant and growing segment of the population is falling behind in basic math and English. According to the National Commission on Excellence in Education in 1983:

- Some 23 million American adults are functionally illiterate by the simplest tests of everyday reading, writing, and comprehension.
- About 13 percent of all 17-year-olds in the United States can be considered functionally illiterate. Functional illiteracy among minority youth may run as high as 40 percent.
- Average achievement of high school students on most standardized tests is now lower than it was 26 years ago.
- There was a steady decline in science achievement scores of U.S. 17-year-olds as measured by national assessments of science in 1969, 1973, and 1977.

- Between 1975 and 1980, remedial mathematics courses in public four-year colleges increased by 72 percent and now constitute one-quarter of all mathematics courses in those institutions.[7]

And more recently, according to the 1994 results from the respected National Assessment of Educational Progress,

- Only one of three 12th graders mastered rigorous reading passages.
- Only 11 percent showed a strong grasp of history.
- The general standards of U.S. schools pale in comparison to those of other industrialized nations. In France, Germany, Israel, and Japan, for example, roughly half of all students take Advanced Placement examinations; one-third pass. Only 6.6 percent of U.S. kids take Advanced Placement exams; 4.4 percent pass.

According to Albert Shanker, president of the American Federation of Teachers, "Very few American pupils are performing anywhere near where they could be performing."[8]

This data is devastating considering that the future will require skills well beyond the basics. As education spending continued to rise dramatically during the 1980s, student performance failed to improve. Since 1960, education spending per public school student has risen from roughly $2,000 to over $5,000 by 1990—and this after adjusting for inflation. At the same time, however, combined SAT scores have fallen from nearly 975 points to approximately 900 points.[9] The downward trend in education must change to meet the needs of tomorrow's workplace.

WORKPLACE NEEDS ARE CHANGING RAPIDLY

And workplace skill requirements are not stagnant—they are changing rapidly. According to *Workforce 2000* by William Johnston, the new jobs being created require higher skills than existing jobs.[10] The percentage of high-skill jobs such as engineers, lawyers, technicians, and teachers will grow from 24 percent to 41 percent of the workforce by the year 2000. Lower-skill jobs such as transport workers, machine setters, hand workers, and helpers and laborers will fall from 40 percent to 27 percent of the job mix.[11] These statistics should alarm all of us. It is frightening to think what can happen if present trends continue.

Peter Drucker also discusses the changing requirements of the nation's workforce and the challenge it poses to the industrial workers who dominated the last 100 years. In his 1994 article "The Age of Social Transformation" he defines a newly emerging dominant group called "knowledge workers." Drucker predicts that

By the end of this century, knowledge workers will make up a third or more of the work force of the United States—as large a proportion as manufacturing workers ever made up, except in wartime. The majority of them will be paid at least as well as, or better than, manufacturing workers ever were. And the new jobs offer much greater opportunities.[12]

He goes on to support the notion of a different mind-set and approach to work that is centered on continuous learning. This type of learning requires a cultural shift much more dramatic than the shift from agricultural to industrial work. Furthermore, these skills are not important just for service industries such as banking, consulting, and entertainment. They are essential in modern manufacturing. Unless union leaders change and actively support skill development for their members, both business and labor will suffer.

UNIONS HAVE NOT RESPONDED BY CHANGING —ONLY ENTRENCHING

Unions now represent only 11 percent of the nation's private-sector workforce, down from the 1953 peak of 36 percent.[13] The decline in union membership is not just a U.S. phenomenon. The same thing is happening throughout the industrialized world as low-cost, nonunion nations expand into Western markets. Some of the decline is driven by the reduction of total jobs among traditionally unionized industries such as autos, steel, and textiles. But another, more problematic trend to unions is the increasing difficulty they face in gaining new members to replace the losses.

Large companies are working hard to fend off unionization—and with success. According to the National Labor Relations Board, unions are targeting the southern United States in an effort to increase their ranks. But southern companies are dedicating resources to fend off these "attacks," leaving unions with only a 20 percent success rate in companies with over 100 employees during 1993 and 1994. However, small companies with fewer than 50 employees have fewer resources to "fight" and are giving unions some hope with a 60 percent victory rate. And unions understand these numbers. Of the 81 union elections in North Carolina, South Carolina, and Georgia in 1993 and 1994, 75 percent took place in companies with fewer than 50 workers.[14] However, this trend does not bode well for union prospects. Each target company requires significant resources and time to organize an election, and these small companies fail to provide a big payoff in terms of membership and dues.

So why are the unions unable to recruit new members? The answer should be obvious. When potential union workers see a 20-year decline in average real wages despite union efforts, they question the wisdom of joining a union at all.

Companies are unable to provide real wage increases unless productivity improvements justify them. If productivity increases do not occur, eventually firms and even countries must find other ways to compete— namely through lower real wages. This problem has plagued Great Britain for more than 100 years. In 1860, a British worker had real wages 2.5 times that of a German worker. Yet by 1980, real wages in Germany had surpassed Great Britain by a 2:1 margin.[15] Britain kept its jobs, but the lack of productivity gains in noncompetitive industries kept real wages low by Western standards. Eventually their competitive advantage had turned into one of exporting cheap labor. This type of competitive advantage cannot lead to improved living standards over the long term. Companies face the same problem—competition on wages is not a battle that any U.S. company should want to fight or even win.

Rather than working to find ways to improve worker productivity or raise employee skill levels, many unions have entrenched and focused their efforts on membership numbers. Faced with declining numbers and tougher barriers from companies, many unions have become more creative in membership initiatives. For example, the International Brotherhood of Electrical Workers is awaiting a Supreme Court ruling on its practice of "salting." Salting involves a union dispatching its own members to work in nonunion companies in the hopes of organizing from within. The union pays any wage and benefit differential to the employee as well as any expenses related to the union campaign.

In this particular case, the union infiltrated Town & Country Electric, and when the planted employee began prounion activities, the company fired him. The company is arguing that it can legally fire the man under federal law because he is an employee of another company and its union.[16] Regardless of the outcome of this case, unions will face more judicial oversight of their activities in the years to come, and their time and money would be better spent on programs that actually improve the competitiveness of their members.

EDUCATION IS THE LONG-TERM SOLUTION

The United States is already facing increasing wage disparity between the "haves" and "have nots." Since 1973, family incomes have risen for the highest 20 percent but fallen for the lowest 20 percent. This growing income disparity is a clear indication of the reduced demand for unskilled workers in the United States. Wages of college graduates, on the other hand, rose by around 30 percent relative to those of people with 12 or fewer years of education. The bottom 10 percent of wage earners, however, have taken a 13 percent cut in real wages since 1979.[17] Many other industrial countries are facing similar pressure. The European Community has kept incomes from diverging by maintaining high minimum wages; but the cost of income equality has been significant—either high, often double-digit unemployment or growing government employment coupled with high deficits. Neither option bodes well for long-term competitiveness.

Another recent study shows the same connection between education and wages. Richard J. Murnane and John B. Willett of Harvard University's Graduate School of Education and Frank Levy of the Massachusetts Institute of Technology recently conducted a study showing that the lack of math skills has had an increasing impact on wage dispersion in the economy. After adjusting for race, family background, experience and other possible influencers, their research revealed that in 1978 only a 5 percent difference existed between the earnings of males with high math skills versus low math skills. But by 1986, that gap had grown to 15 percent. Among women, the gap was even more substantial—from 12 percent in 1978 to 25 percent in 1986. Furthermore, the noncollege graduates in the study also exhibited a wage differential. By 1986, working high school grads with high math skills were earning $2,000 to $3,000 more than their less mathematically skilled counterparts.[18]

It is in everyone's interest to have a highly educated workforce. Certainly a large share of the blame for our problems in education rest on the shoulders of the education system itself. This topic alone has filled thousands of pages of reports detailing our predicament. But we also know that there has been a breakdown in the family unit in the United States, and many children lack the necessary support structure at home to overcome the deficiencies in our schools. As citizens there are a few things you can do to help the situation. First, you should become active in your own children's schools. But you can also contribute to the solution by demanding that educators be held accountable for their performance and by supporting education reforms in your community, your state, and the nation.

BUSINESS AND UNION LEADERS CAN MAKE A DIFFERENCE

Yet in your businesses, you face these challenges every day, and you cannot afford to wait for society to raise the skills of the nation's people. Your competitors are aggressively pursuing your customers right now, and you must respond by providing basic and technical training. To do otherwise would be foolish. Furthermore, we believe unions have potential to become powerful allies in our quest to improve the quality of our workforce. They too can add significant value by focusing their attention on the education needs of their members.

It is likely that unions would be more successful in their efforts to attract members if they were perceived by workers as offering them something of value, like better training. This would be far more beneficial to everyone than some other tactics unions have employed.

Now is a terrific time for unions to change their perspective. They are all undergoing dramatic changes in the wake of layoffs, plant closures, and reengineering of processes. For example, the United Auto Workers' long-time president Owen F. Bieber retired in June 1995 and was replaced by Stephen P. Yokich, union vice president and head of the union for General Motors. Yokich is now faced with a UAW membership decline of nearly 50 percent since its 1979 peak. The 1994 UAW count of 760,000 members appears to have stabilized as continued layoffs at GM have been offset by hiring at Ford and Chrysler. With a new leader and impending contract negotiations, the opportunity for constructive change is heightened.

However, it is incredibly difficult to lead these efforts. Politics, union traditionalists, and uncreative minds all stand in the way of progress. At GM more cuts or at least revisions of the stringent union contract must take place if GM's struggling parts operations are to compete with nonunion factories paying one-third of GM's $45-per-hour labor cost.[19] Yet in early 1996, a 17-day strike in Dayton, Ohio, set off a chain reaction of plant closures across the company and cost GM $900 million in the first quarter of 1996. Based on this and other union troubles, GM has decided to take a stand. As contract negotiations near, one GM official commented, "We've always had a line we weren't willing to cross. In the negotiation, perhaps the line has been moved a bit closer because of concerns about our competitiveness."[20]

While a cooperative tone and mentality improve the chances of finding common ground, business leaders must have the courage to make difficult and sometimes painful decisions regarding union negotiations.

In light of more tough stands by management, some unions have loosened their restrictions in hopes of keeping jobs and increasing members' skills. Companies with smaller, local unions have a better chance of negotiating such changes. Business leaders should continue to push for union concessions that will increase productivity and not simply reduce the workforce. In this way the unions and management can become allies in the struggle to remain competitive in the world market.

To work effectively with unions, business leaders must understand the political pressures facing union leaders and their constituents. Many unions are struggling with division among their own ranks. Union leaders are at risk of becoming misaligned with their own membership. They are fearful of losing their power and thus fight efforts such as empowerment and expanded job responsibility for the workers. Ironically, workers may find themselves aligned with the company management, seeing their union leaders as obstacles to progress. In the *Journal for Quality and Participation,* Edward Cohen-Rosenthal suggests that

> When some union leaders act paternalistically toward their members' wishes . . . it breeds a view of the union that distances it from its membership . . . Backroom deals that are not aligned with the interests of the members rob the union of its real base of support—its members.[21]

Evidence suggests that workers are interested in and excited about becoming more involved in their companies. Economist Richard Freeman of Harvard and law professor Joul Rogers of the University of Wisconsin at Madison conducted a study of 3,500 low- to mid-level workers in 1994 and early 1995. The Worker Representation and Participation Survey found that almost two-thirds of employees interviewed wanted to play a more participative role in the workplace. One worker said, "Why doesn't management . . . have the sense [to know that] if workers love to get up in the morning and come to work, they're gonna produce like hell?"

Yet many of the interviewees rejected the traditional concept of union activity. One of the study's focus groups in Charlotte, North Carolina, included a database analyst, sales representative, an insurance underwriter, and a bookkeeper. This group of "knowledge workers" firmly opposed unions—"bad news" said one—since they have come to be associated with strikes and self-interested union bosses. More importantly, however, these workers described the need for a flexible and collaborative support network based on elected representatives to work with management on a company-specific basis. What they described was more like a blend of Europe's work councils and Japan's company-sponsored unions. They also described a workplace with more worker involvement and gain-sharing or stock ownership rather then mandated wage increases.[22] Many firms have moved to models similar to the one described above— and without the need for an official union or contract.

Southwest Airlines, an often quoted and idolized provider of low-cost, high-reliability air transportation, is working with its unions to bring company and union interests into alignment. In November 1994, Southwest announced an unprecedented 10-year contract with its pilots' union. The contract stipulated productivity-related bonuses and stock options in lieu of wage increases during the first five years. According to Vivian Lee, Smith Barney airline analyst, the agreement is likely to put Southwest's already low operating costs out of reach of other carriers.[23] Through this agreement, management and the union found a way to create a sustainable competitive advantage that provides benefits to both parties.

Following the Southwest lead, AMR Corporation CEO Robert L. Crandall is seeking wage concessions and pay tied to productivity gains at American Airlines. After accumulating $1.3 billion in losses during the 1990s, American finally posted significant profits in 1995. Aided by an improving economy, Crandall cut over 8,000 jobs, dropped unprofitable markets, and beefed up service to core routes. In addition, he reduced costly jet service and replaced it with turboprop service to 30 small cities, all while dropping the total fleet by 49 planes. Now that the asset base is in order, Crandall is looking for labor savings of $750 million.

Northwest Airlines won $886 million in concessions in 1993 and U.S. Air has been negotiating reductions as well. But Allied Pilots Association President James Sovish defended the tough stance with American saying, "There is no near- or midterm financial distress in this corporation." Crandall, however, is not willing to wait for a crisis to take on the union. He is threatening to continue to shrink the airline portion of AMR and funnel resources into profitable areas such as the SABRE Group, which earned about half of AMR's operating income in 1994. According to other AMR board members, these tough tactics are no bargaining ploy.[24] The company has made the decision to invest only in businesses that provide adequate returns to the shareholders, and if wage concessions are not forthcoming, American Airlines will not be among this group.

In the coming months and years, we expect more business leaders to see that by aligning interests with their unions (such as mutual survival) they can find ways to increase the performance of their companies, the incomes of their employees, and the wealth of the nation. Business leaders should challenge union representatives to join them in efforts to upgrade the skills of the workforce and improve the employability of every employee and the competitiveness of the company. Yet if cooperative efforts are unsuccessful, more hardball tactics are still appropriate until unions realize the need to change and become partners in the revitalization of U.S. companies.

MOVING ON

In chapter 3 we continue our discussion of divisions in the workplace. The new generation of workers, often referred to as Generation X, presents leaders with unique challenges as they attempt to integrate and motivate this group in the workplace.

ENDNOTES

1. Warren Cohen, "What Have You Done for U.S. Lately?", *U.S. News & World Report*, November 6, 1995, p. 40.
2. Kevin Kelly, "Will the Talks at Deere Hit Bedrock?", *BusinessWeek*, October 31, 1994, p. 48.
3. E. J. Dionne, Jr., "The Wrong Fight, The Right Reasons," *Washington Post*, November 23, 1993.
4. Steven V. Roberts, "Workers Take It on the Chin," *U.S. News & World Report*, January 15, 1996, p. 44.
5. Gene Koretz, "Where Has All the Labor Gone," *Business Week*, December 12, 1994, p. 30.
6. William Rasberry, "The Choice: Train for Useful Jobs or Slip into the Underclass," *The Daily Progress*, Charlottesville, Virginia, November 19, 1993, p. A6.
7. "A Nation at Risk," The National Commission on Excellence in Education, 1983.
8. Thomas Toch, "The Case for Tough Standards," *U.S. News & World Report*, April 1, 1996, p. 53.
9. Nancy J. Perry, "How to Help America's Schools," *Fortune*, December 4, 1989, p. 139.
10. William B. Johnston, *Workforce 2000: Work and Workers for the Twenty-First Century* (Indianapolis, IN: Hudson Institute, 1987), p. xxi.
11. Ibid., p. xxii.

12. Peter F. Drucker, "The Age of Social Transformation." *The Atlantic Monthly,* November 1994, pp. 53–80.
13. Susan Dentzer, "Anti-union, but Not Anti-unity," *U.S. News & World Report,* July 17, 1995, p. 47.
14. Mary Helen Yarborough, "Unions are Targeting Pro-management States," *HR Focus,* April 1994, p. 1.
15. William Baumol, "America's Productivity Crisis," *New York Times,* February 15, 1987, p. 2.
16. Frank Swoboda, "MUST Construction Take Its Hires with Salting or Without?", *The Washington Post,* April 16, 1995, p. H5.
17. "Workers of the World Compete," *The Economist*, April 2, 1994, p. 69.
18. Gene Koretz, "One Plus One = Higher Wages," *Business Week*, June 19, 1995, p. 30.
19. "Will Yokich Breathe Fire into the UAW?", *Business Week,* December 5, 1994, p. 64.
20. Rebecca Blumenstein, "GM to Break with Peers in UAW Talks," *The Wall Street Journal,* April 26, 1996, p. A2.
21. Edward Hohen-Rosenthal, "On Arrogance and Participation," *Journal for Quality and Participation,* March 1994, p. 63.
22. Dentzer, p. 47.
23. Susan Chandler, "United: So Many Cuts, So Little Relief," *Business Week,* December 5, 1994, p. 42.
24. Wendy Zellner, "American Airlines May Be Too Healthy," *Business Week,* October 31, 1994, p. 114.

3

CHAPTER

Divisions in the Workplace: Generation X—Where Do They Fit?

While unions have been a major source of division in businesses for decades, another division is only beginning to take hold. Most people in the United States have heard the phrase "Generation X," which was coined to describe the 69 million Americans aged 18 to 34. But few have considered the implications this group will have on society and the workplace.

This generation is a far different animal than the baby boom generation that is of equal size. Over 65 percent of Generation Xers enrolled in college, more than any other U.S. generation. And this group works 3.6 percent longer each week than the national average. But where do they work? Certainly the hiring giants of the past—GM, IBM, Xerox—are not providing the jobs or luring the candidates. In fact, a University of Michigan and Marquette University study in 1993 found that entrepreneurs between the ages of 25 and 34 started 70 percent of the new businesses in the United States.[1] Many young workers have worked at a larger company, but left in frustration. As managers whose only sustainable competitive advantage is people, you should be thinking about what this means for your organization, its goals, its measurement and reward systems, and its ability to attract and keep employees. We will have more to say about this problem in chapter 9.

SKEPTICISM ABOUNDS

The perceptions around this new generation are mixed. Xers themselves are frustrated with what they perceive as the lack of opportunities (i.e., jobs), social and economic turmoil, and a generally dismal future relative to that of the post–World War II baby boomers. Growth is slow, deficits are high, and we get the sense that they seek something beyond career progression as a measure of success. Many have seen their parents laid off by their long-time employers and, therefore, distrust employers in general. *Training* magazine profiled the X Generation in April 1994. One Xer said, "The current workplace demands too much. We weren't placed on earth to work for United Glop. We work to do other things besides work. There is sometimes a happy confluence in our lives when work and play are identical, but this is comparatively rare." While many of us cannot understand this new perspective or are reminded of the 1960s youth revolution, Generation X will affect organizations substantially during the next 10 years.

Many of you may be skeptical of this new generation of workers. Our earlier statistics highlighted the skill gaps in basic math and English. One manager told *Training* magazine, "I submit what I have seen over and over in the workplace. An entry-level workforce where 1 in 5 are functional illiterates, unable to perform simple math, unable to identify a specified measurement on an illustrated ruler, or understand the processes of the very equipment they operate." Another said, "There's always a million excuses for why things didn't get done. Also, this seems to be accompanied by an inordinate amount of whining."[2] Certainly these opinions do not represent all managers or describe all Xers, but as generalizations, many of them strike a familiar chord. This raises several questions. Why does this generation feel so separated? How will I hire, train, and lead this new group? How will I manage the tension between old and new employees if they have different needs?

THE GENERATION Xer PERSPECTIVE

To address this problem, it is important to understand the situation facing the X Generation. Many of them are frustrated with the lack of good entry-level jobs. The term "McJob" was coined by Douglas Coupland in his novel, *Generation X,* which refers to the dead-end, temporary jobs in the service sector that many are forced to hold. Certainly hiring has been a low priority for many firms during the last five years. In fact, in 1993 big

American companies announced nearly 600,000 layoffs, 25 percent more than in 1992 and 10 percent more than 1991 when the country was steeped in recession.[3] However, this trend will not continue. Companies must hire new, young minds to help guide the changes that are taking place in America's organizations. Aging workers have a lot to lose through change, and the new Generation X workers can be an asset to lead, facilitate, and implement change. These competing forces can create hostility and division in the workplace and impede performance.

Many Generation Xers have found a place for themselves either as employees or as entrepreneurs, but the earnings statistics are less than exciting. According to the Census Bureau, median family incomes in households headed by a person under 30 dropped 16 percent between 1973 and 1990.[4] Faced with increasing health care, housing, and other costs, this generation is looking at a significantly lower standard of living than the previous two generations. It is no wonder that Generation Xers are quick to change jobs. Whether in search of more money, more promotion opportunities, or more job satisfaction, they have no fantasies about a "lifetime employment contract" or job security. Their thinking is "what is best for me today because I have no faith in what tomorrow may hold."

Margaret Regan, a principal with New York–based consultants Towers Perrin, works with companies trying to marshal the talents of this next generation of workers. Her experiences reinforce this notion of short-term and transient thinking. During seminars on what corporations should do, she frequently hears from Xers, "Get rid of the pension plan and give us day care or a health center instead." This trend has serious implications for business leaders as they evaluate hiring and training expenditures and reward and promotion procedures. Regan also notes that managers are frustrated with this group that has "one eye in the company and one eye outside all the time." Knowing that many new employees will leave within one to three years, how can you extract short-term value from them and how can you entice the "winners" to stay?

GENERATION X HAS UNIQUE SKILLS AND NEEDS

Some companies have found success in adapting to the different needs and skills of the Generation X worker. Wendy's, the fast food chain, has its own management development specialist, Karen Tracy, who notes that the company's training methods are specially tailored to this new worker. Researchers on the X Generation typically note a short attention span of about 15 minutes among these younger workers. Given this, all training sessions and films are held in 15-minute increments and are full of visual rather than audio learning.[5]

Regan also notes that companies can capitalize on the boredom problem by putting Generation Xers on several different teams and rotating them laterally to build new skills and increase the likelihood of job satisfaction and lower turnover. Several Generation X authors note that Xers have a significant capacity for processing large and diverse amounts of information, enabling them to work on multiple tasks concurrently. One training and development director for a *Fortune* 500 company dismisses the criticism that Xers do not want to work hard and pay their "dues." As he sees it, "The workplace is changing so fast and the economy is so chaotic that anyone who is thinking about doing any job long enough to pay dues is seriously out of touch. The markets you're working in today may be gone tomorrow and you may be doing something completely different. In this kind of environment, . . . nothing is constant except change." He thus concludes that Generations Xers are exactly the type of worker that the economy needs to take America into the future.[6]

THE CHALLENGE

The challenge for today's leaders, however, is to motivate these Xers to use their strengths productively and remain challenged. Xers despise the notion of face time and are frequently criticized for "watching the clock." Xers believe there is more to life than a job, and they place a high premium on separating their jobs from their personal lives. This compartmentalization and tendency to put personal life before work can be traced directly to their own personal development. Xers were the children of the first generation of mass divorce, single-parent households, or dual-income households. In all of these scenarios, parents had less time to spend with children. And today's young workers appear less willing to make the same sacrifices for their jobs and careers.

But Xers derived some benefits from their less supervised childhoods. Most are very comfortable working on their own, and most Generation X experts agree that Xers do not want to be managed and told how to get things done. With a clear objective, these Xers can be left alone to make decisions and get the job done. Xers are looking for support and approval the way children look to a coach or a parent for support. This highlights the importance of developing managers armed with interpersonal, motivation, and communication skills who can provide feedback to employees while giving them room to be entrepreneurial. According to Liesel Walsh, a consultant with Big Picture Marketing and an Xer herself, "Manage me by teaching me things. Manage me by showing me how to do my job. Manage me by getting me better tools. Don't manage me by sitting on me and giving me demerits because I'm five minutes late. Don't manage me by saying I can't be trusted to give the customer a 35-cent credit."[7]

Managers and "boomers" in general may be somewhat threatened by this new breed of transient worker. Not only do the two not relate, but they have different skills. And despite the less-than-impressive overall scholastic figures, millions of Xers possess knowledge of computers and technology for which companies are starving. Many boomers have gone through a period of layoffs and may feel threatened by this new breed that could easily be the "knowledge worker" that Drucker describes. Bob Filipczak of *Training* magazine put it very well:

> We've been talking for years about how we want an empowered workforce; every indication is that if you give Xers the ball, they can run with it. We want a self-directed workforce; these workers have been self-directed from a very young age. We want technoliterate workers; check. We want flexible workers; they are so flexible that job-hopping has become a way of life.

Says Regan, "I do think we got the workforce that we wanted, but we don't know what to do with it yet."[8]

TRADITIONAL BUSINESS REWARDS DON'T WORK

So what does and does not appear to motivate this worker of the future? The earlier quoted statistics on young entrepreneurs are evidence of Xers' lack of interest in traditional corporate jobs. And the corporate stereotypes of bureaucracy, hierarchy, corporate politics, face time, and meetings turn off many Xers. Generation Xers see these as time wasters that only require longer hours at work with few results. Researchers agree that Xers are more interested in solving problems, quickly moving to new challenges, and leaving time for personal life.

But what motivates these workers beyond their desire for personal time? The answer seems to be money. According to current research, Xers are worried about their economic future and that of the U.S. government. Nearly half of all Generation Xers are still living with their parents—a level unmatched since the Great Depression. Many face huge college loans and fear that they will also be saddled with higher taxes to pay off two generations of deficits. With all this perceived economic pressure, Xers are reported to be more motivated by money than previous generations.

Furthermore, Xers appear to lack the ideological drivers of some earlier generations. The implications are immense. Xers want to know how they will be measured, how they are doing, and when they will be rewarded. Robert Lukefahr, a Wharton MBA and founder of Third Millennium, a political group that represents Xers, advises businesses to reevaluate their reward systems if they want to motivate Xers. "You're not going to get [these] people to do things because they have a deep sense of mission," he says. According to managers at Wendy's, previously successful rewards such as "Employee of the Month" are less motivational than concrete, economic rewards such as money or free coupons for food or entertainment.

Lukefahr also highlights training as a motivator. While companies may be less inclined to train these nomadic employees, Xers seek opportunities to expand their skills and improve their marketability. Companies that focus on training, such as Proctor & Gamble and McKinsey & Company will continue to attract the best and brightest Xers. Furthermore, employees will be less likely to leave if they continue to learn beyond their initial training and orientation period.[9]

Overall, the dynamic of this new X Generation offers challenges to business leaders. Hiring, rewarding, and keeping a skilled and flexible workforce that can integrate well with the current boomer population is no small task. Training managers to effectively motivate in a less structured environment has been a business challenge and consultants' dream since the 1980s. Companies that do not deal with the skills and needs of Generation X will be devastated. As discussed in chapter 9, entrepreneurial behavior is a necessity in all firms, and is often found in new, young people. The declining numbers of talented young people heading for corporate America is a strong signal that most companies have not adequately responded to the changing needs of this younger generation. For the companies that *can* provide a flexible, training-oriented, and high-reward environment, the payoff is enormous. Not only will they be able to attract and select the best "knowledge workers," but they will have the infrastructure to motivate, support, and sustain a competitive advantage based on superior people.

MOVING ON

In chapter 4, we will focus our attention on the effects of our nation's affirmative action policies and the divisive problem of racial conflict. Both have contributed greatly to division in the workplace and to the destruction of the work ethic. Our affirmative action policies are in desperate need of change. Business leaders cannot avoid these issues. They affect not only the workplace but the future well-being of out nation.

ENDNOTES

1. Richard J. Newman, "A New Spin on the Economy," *U.S. News and World Report*, May 8, 1995, p. 54.
2. Bob Filipczak, "It's Just a Job," *Training*, April 1994, p. 21.
3. "Survey: The World of Multinationals—Big Is Back," *The Economist*, June 24, 1995, p. 5
4. Filipczak, p. 23.
5. Ibid., p. 24.
6. Ibid.
7. Ibid., p. 26.
8. Ibid.
9. Ibid., p. 27.

4

CHAPTER

Affirmative Action and the Workplace

A few years ago, a University of Virginia basketball player was taking a management class, and the subject was affirmative action. During discussions, he was asked the question:

> *Q:* What would happen if the University of Virginia instituted an affirmative action policy requiring the basketball coach to have on the court at any given time a mix of black and white players roughly equal to the proportion of their respective racial groups in the university's undergraduate student population? (About 11 percent of the University of Virginia's undergraduate students are black.)
>
> *A:* Do you want to win?

His answer was revealing. It demonstrated his appreciation for the team's ultimate goal, winning games, and what it takes to achieve it. It also revealed his belief that to win, teams must field the best players they can, based on their skills and performance.

To paraphrase Vince Lombardi, in college sports winning is not everything, it is the only thing. Today, if college coaches cannot win they are replaced quickly by others who can. Alumni demand winning teams, so they can have pride in their school and participate, albeit vicariously, in the thrill of victory. College administrators demand winning teams so they can raise money to support their school's other programs. (There is a strong positive correlation between the success of a university's athletic teams and the willingness of alumni to give money to the school.)

The goal in college athletics is to win games, and college coaches do everything they can to win. College administrators in all but a few select schools would never even consider imposing requirements on their coaches unilaterally that would hamper them in their quest for victory. Even with the threat of NCAA sanctions, many college administrators allow the admission of "student athletes" who are unprepared academically and then do not stand in the way of their graduation, even if the students have failed to complete their academic work.

These same university executives do not hesitate to hire faculty and administrators who, at times, are marginally qualified in order to achieve racial, ethnic, and gender "balance and diversity," as if balance and diversity are the goals of our universities. It is as if performance matters in sports, but not in academics. Businesses throughout the United States have done the same thing. While many businesses are forced to achieve specific minority hiring levels to qualify for government contracts, not all businesses are controlled by the affirmative action regulations. Yet, under pressure from the government many businesses have hired people to achieve "diversity."

In this chapter we are not attempting to debate the qualifications of any group; but we do use specific examples to support the assertion that factors such as race, sex, or religion should not be considered in hiring and reward decisions. We believe that business leaders and their companies should focus on skills and performance above all else. By taking the emphasis away from performance and placing it on "diversity," employee morale, the work ethic, and the ability of our firms to compete in rapidly changing markets are in jeopardy.

With the much documented decline of the U.S. manufacturing sector and the rise of the service sector, people have become the driver of U.S. competitiveness. People, not machines, are the primary source of productivity growth; and economists agree that productivity growth is the key to long-term economic success and improved living standards. Therefore, we must utilize our best people, regardless of their sex, race, or religion, if we hope to maximize our competitiveness.

The effects of our affirmative action policies have been far different than the originators of the concept initially intended. When affirmative action began, the impetus driving the movement was to provide blacks and other minorities with equal opportunities to pursue their education and work-related goals. But along the way, the movement got off track. What started as a program to ensure equal opportunities for all individuals has evolved into a program that seeks equal outcomes of group representation and income. Affirmative action proponents point to a barrage of evidence showing minority underrepresentation in schools, jobs, and politics as reasons to continue the preferential treatment efforts. However, this flies in the face of the premise on which America was built, that hard work and merit, not race or religion or gender or birthright, should determine who prospers and who does not.

While blacks are the most studied and discussed of all minority groups when affirmative action discussions arise, they are only a portion of the individuals who qualify for minority status. Because of immigration, in the 30 years since the origin of affirmative action, blacks have gone from more than two-thirds to less than half of America's minority population. Protected groups now make up 70 percent of the workforce, including nearly all immigrants, most religious groups, women, the elderly, homosexuals, and American-born blacks, Hispanics, Asians, and Native Americans. With heterosexual, Protestant, white men the primary unprotected group as well as a minority of the workforce, it raises the question of whether minority classifications have served their purpose and are no longer necessary to ensure a diverse workplace.

Regardless of your opinions on minority classifications overall, we believe there are detrimental side effects from affirmative action programs, and business leaders will eventually need to address them. First, affirmative action has blurred the focus and increased the costs of many organizations. In today's "take no prisoners" business environment, anything that reduces our ability to compete must be scrutinized carefully and objectively, and then corrected. Second, our affirmative action policies reduce the emphasis on individual performance and skills by sending the message that minority status is a factor that must be considered in hiring and reward decisions. Nothing has more potential to destroy the work ethic than the realization that what people actually do is less important than factors over which they have no control. Third, affirmative action has heightened the emphasis on the differences in people. This emphasis on differences has resulted in cultural divides and conflict that tear at the heart and soul of our society. As countless examples suggest, in pursuing the goal of equality we have simply gone too far.

HOW DID IT ALL BEGIN?

Affirmative action began with good intentions. It was designed to give people equal opportunity to succeed. Vice President Richard M. Nixon, as head of President Eisenhower's Committee on Contracts, was the first person to recommend "limited 'preferential' treatment for qualified blacks seeking jobs with government contractors." Later, John F. Kennedy formalized affirmative action by issuing an executive order in 1961 calling for "affirmative action as a means to promote equal opportunity for racial minorities in hiring by federal contractors."[1] President Lyndon B. Johnson only extended Kennedy's initiative.

Later as president, Nixon's Labor Department introduced the Philadelphia Plan, "a quota system that required federal contractors in Philadelphia, and later Washington, to employ a fixed number of minorities."[2] We moved from a Nixon presidency that formalized and extended affirmative action; to a Ford presidency that tried unsuccessfully to limit affirmative action; to a Carter administration that extended affirmative action by openly making appointments of federal judges with that criterion in mind; to a Reagan administration that did little to alter the course of affirmative action in the United States.[3]

President George Bush did little to deal with the mounting problems associated with our affirmative action policies. In the 1992 campaign for the presidency, President Bush and candidate Bill Clinton debated the issue. Clinton portrayed Bush as an opponent of affirmative action and as a man insensitive to the needs and wants of blacks and other minorities. Bush tried to portray Clinton as a man out of touch with the mainstream in the affirmative action debate, but in reality the two men's philosophies toward affirmative action were virtually identical—neither was willing to take action on the difficult issue. In fact, a senior adviser for President Clinton commented in 1996, "We're going to wait until it's a crisis before reacting."[4] Yet cultural crises are occurring all over the world with great suffering and cost. As Arthur M. Schlesinger Jr. wrote in his book, *The Disuniting of America:*

> On every side today ethnicity is the cause of the breaking of nations. The Soviet Union, Yugoslavia, India, South Africa are all in crisis. Ethnic tensions disturb and divide Sri Lanka, Burma, Ethiopia, Indonesia, Iraq, Lebanon, Israel, Cyprus, Somalia, Nigeria, Liberia, Angola, Sudan, Zaire, Guyana, Trinidad—you name it. Even nations as stable and civilized as Britain and France, Belgium and Spain and Czechoslovakia, face growing

ethnic and racial troubles. "The virus of tribalism," says the *Economist,* ". . . risks becoming the AIDS of international politics—lying dormant for years, then flaring up to destroy countries."[5]

The United States is not divinely protected from these same problems. As business leaders and citizens, we cannot afford to wait for crisis to come to America. We should act now to prevent these problems from damaging our system any more than they already have.

AFFIRMATIVE ACTION BLURS THE CORPORATE FOCUS

In concrete terms, the affirmative action statute, Title VII of the 1964 Civil Rights Act, prohibits employer discrimination against minorities in all businesses. In addition, Executive Order 11246, issued in 1965, requires federal contractors to develop affirmative action plans for complying with Title VII. According to Christopher Jencks, author of *Rethinking Social Policy*:

> By the late 1960s most large American firms had such plans, and at least in principle their progress was being monitored by the Office of Federal Contract Compliance (OFCC). Narrowly construed, affirmative action refers only to these plans. In everyday usage, however, it embraces all efforts to improve black job opportunities that go beyond eliminating formal discrimination, regardless of whether these efforts are mandated by federal law.[6]

However, skepticism and cynicism about our affirmative action policies have grown as the nation has come to understand what affirmative action means in practice and how it has affected the workplace. As Nathan Glazer said in a paper published in *The Public Interest*, "The expectation of color blindness that was paramount in the mid-1960s has been replaced by policies mandating numerical requirements. That is what we mean today by affirmative action."[7]

These numerical requirements have evolved to the point where they impact corporate hiring, firing, reward, and promotion decisions. Today, many organizations have diversity programs and diversity managers whose goals are to ensure that specific numbers of minorities are hired and employed. Clearly put, organizations state that diversity is a goal, yet in practice they are seeking to meet specific quotas. In seeking these "numbers" the company lets its focus and energies move away from performance to other matters. From this, it is not hard to believe that less qualified candidates are sometimes hired over more qualified applicants to "make the numbers."

Surprisingly, businesses across the country have adopted the quotas approach to remedying past discrimination without making much of a fuss. According to Theodore Payne, Xerox manager of corporate employment, "We have a process that we call 'balanced work force' in Xerox, everybody understands that, and it's measurable, it's goals . . . . Relative numbers. That's the hard business, that's what most people don't like to deal with, but we do it all the time."[8] What Payne is talking about is quotas, pure and simple, and Xerox is not an exception. Many U.S. businesses do the same thing.

While businesses not involved in government contract work are not required to implement affirmative action plans, many do. These businesses go beyond setting goals to setting quotas, so the distinction between the two is meaningless. "In practice—as defined by more than 20 years of legislation, regulation and judicial opinions—they are the same thing, and everybody knows it. A substantial majority of *Fortune* 500 companies have very clear affirmative action goals for minority hiring, and they treat those goals as quotas."[9]

Much of the reason for these quotas is to develop a defensive shield against discrimination lawsuits. But the law that applies for most businesses is the antibias law, which requires that businesses do not discriminate. It does not mandate affirmative moves or quotas for hiring minorities. In fact, one early study, by University of Chicago economist James J. Heckman, showed that during the years 1964 to 1975, the antibias law "had a greater effect than affirmative action in promoting black employment."[10]

While much is written about blacks and affirmative action, the effects of this program reach all minority groups. Tama Starr, owner of a neon sign company in New York City, wrote to the *Washington Post* to describe her experience with anti–Canadian American discrimination charges and the resulting lost time her company endured. She said the New York State Division of Human Rights ordered an intense examination of her company's payroll "by age, race, color, sex, creed/religion, marital status and disability, with special emphasis on Canadian-Americans." Starr wrote,

> Everybody in my employ is a member of a "protected minority." Every one is female, gay, foreign-born or foreign ancestry, religious or atheistic, dark-skinned or melanin-impaired, single or married, old or young. They are physically, mentally or culturally disabled . . . It is impossible to find anyone not entitled to a group entitlement.

In another example, Linda Chavez, a columnist, notes that 19 separate federal regulations benefit "economically disadvantaged" bankers. In some programs, women, blacks, Hispanics, Asians, and American Indians are "presumed to be socially and economically disadvantaged" and can win affirmative action rewards regardless of how much money they have.[11]

From their comments, it is clear that Tama Starr and Linda Chavez are frustrated and amazed by this system of preferential treatment. But businesspeople all over the country have experienced similar situations. We must speak out about the difficulties these programs place on businesses if we hope to instigate change.

Even more frustrating is the fact that many agencies of the federal government are *required* to pursue affirmative action goals. These goals say nothing about quality and competitiveness. For example, the Defense Department has a goal that 5 percent of its procurement budget ($112 billion in 1994) be awarded to firms owned by "socially and economically disadvantaged individuals, meaning women and minorities." The State Department insists that "not less than 10 percent of money appropriated for diplomatic construction shall be allocated to the extent possible to minority contractors." The Transportation Department has determined that "except to the extent that the secretary determines otherwise, not less than 10 percent of the money authorized in the $151 billion transportation act passed in 1991 will be spent on small business concerns owned and controlled by socially and economically disadvantaged individuals."[12]

Based on our affirmative action guidelines, the government is forced to achieve group representation goals rather than focusing solely on performance goals. The result is that the government has frequently been criticized for selecting higher-cost contractors to satisfy minority business requirements. This not only costs taxpayers more money, but it can result in insulating businesses that may not be as cost competitive.

Ironically, even some government contractors who embrace affirmative action report difficulty in finding qualified people to meet their minority hiring quotas. One example is Pacific Gas & Electric, a San Francisco–based utility, a longtime proponent of affirmative action. Barbara Coull Williams, PG&E's human resources vice president, complains, "We're always playing catch-up." Now this federal contractor is asking Washington for relief in the form of satisfying affirmative action requirements with a pilot program of mentoring and leadership development rather than the hard quotas it now has.[13]

Given this system of reward for minority designations, it is no surprise that many individuals and companies have found ways to game the system.

Whites and minorities alike have set up schemes of ownership to enable companies to be designated as "minority owned" and receive preferential selection from federal, state, and local governments. Ward Connerly, a member of the University of California Board of Regents, an outspoken opponent of affirmative action and 50 percent owner of a business with his wife, comments, "If I were to own, say 51 percent, we could make a very nice piece of change." White contractors would come calling, hoping to link up with a "minority owned" company to satisfy affirmative action guidelines and qualify for business with the government. According to Connerly, "They ask me to go into business with them to be their minority partner . . . Look, I was born in Louisiana. I remember drinking from 'colored only' water fountains. That was degrading. But this is almost as bad. I won't be defined as an 'affirmative action' businessman. I want to be judged by the quality of my work."[14]

While government requirements are the law, many other companies voluntarily follow these guidelines and therefore blur the focus on performance. Eventually, more performance-oriented and competitive competitors will use this strategic error as a wedge to pry away their customers. Once lost, regaining customer loyalty is difficult.

While companies are worrying about affirmative action numbers and government guidelines, they are spending valuable time that could be applied to improving their costs, customer service, quality, and so on. Business leaders have plenty to worry about—from satisfying customer needs to employee training to competition—without adding extensive government regulations and human resource mandates on top of it all. No one can estimate the cost of lost time and reduced focus on performance, but the direct cost of diversity planning is exorbitant.

AFFIRMATIVE ACTION HAS BEEN EXPENSIVE

Regardless of your opinions on the qualitative impacts of affirmative action, it is hard to refute the cost of affirmative action and other diversity programs. "The impact may easily have already depressed GNP (in 1991) by a staggering four percentage points—about as much as we spend on the entire public school system."[15] Direct costs, including money spent on fines, damages, and forms, totaled $17 to $20 billion;[16] indirect costs, the time it takes to complete paperwork, diversity training, and other activities, totaled $96 billion, $95 billion of which was paid by the private sector.[17]

AFFIRMATIVE ACTION UNDERMINES THE FOCUS ON INDIVIDUAL PERFORMANCE

While the direct and indirect costs are high and the costs of lost time and focus are impossible to estimate, we believe the affirmative action policies also run the risk of undermining the work ethic of employees. Affirmative action reduces the focus on individual performance and increases the reliance on nonperformance criteria for selection and reward. Rather than rewards based on skills and performance, affirmative action and other multiculturalism programs provide advantages based on minority status. As we said earlier, nothing is more discouraging to people and nothing has more power to destroy the work ethic than seeing people selected or rewarded based on criteria other than performance.

In his book *In Defense of Elitism,* William Henry, a man who spent most of his professional life working as an editor for *Time* magazine and who described himself as a card-carrying member of the American Civil Liberties Union to denote his liberal heritage, said,

> Talent, achievement, practice, and learning no longer command deference . . . We have foolishly embraced the unexamined notions that everyone is pretty much alike, . . . that self-fulfillment is more important than objective achievement, . . . that a good and just society should be . . . more concerned with succoring its losers than with honoring and encouraging its winners to achieve more and thereby benefit everyone . . . We have taken the legal notion that all men are created equal to its illogical extreme, seeking not just equality of justice . . . but equality of outcomes.[18]

Henry went on to say, "Multiculturalism promotes quotas over competition and allocation of resources over attainment of them."[19] And quotas immediately raise questions and suspicion. "White skepticism leads to African-American defensiveness," says Sharon Brooks Hodge, a black writer and broadcaster. "Combined, they make toxic race relations in the workplace."[20]

Frustration with our affirmative action policies is growing among white men and minorities alike. While most Americans seem to accept affirmative action as a reality in the workplace and society, increasingly, they are speaking out against it. A recent *Wall Street Journal*/NBC survey found that two out of three Americans oppose affirmative action.[21]

Affirmative action in the education system is a clear illustration of how preferential policies reward students for minority status rather than performance alone. And California is at the forefront of the debate to eliminate race-, ethnic-, and gender-based preferences altogether. Reverse discrimination in California's state-supported school system made headlines as schools turned down many students of Asian descent who were more qualified than their white or black counterparts. One admissions officer put it, "The university has a responsibility to provide access to all sectors of the people of California."[22] But Ward Connerly, a black member of the University of California Board of Regents, commented on the quotas in the state's university system: "What we're doing is inequitable to certain people. I want something in its place that is equitable and fair."[23] He continued, "If the system is fair, my only response is, 'Let the chips fall where they may.' . . . I don't give a hoot about diversity for its own sake. I want to see us better educate more kids."[24]

These students were punished because they had worked harder and done better—all the things society tells them to do. Yet the school system would not hold the other, less qualified students accountable for their own lack of performance. They were admitted because of a classification, not because of merit. While the California example is extreme, similar situations occur every year in schools across the nation. Even the most exclusive, primarily private schools failed to measure all students against the same standard.

According to the Consortium on Financing Higher Education, at 26 of the top universities in the United States (among them Harvard, Yale, Berkeley, Dartmouth, Stanford, Northwestern, Johns Hopkins, Brown, MIT, Duke, University of Virginia, Princeton, and others), black students who enrolled scored on average 180 points lower on SATs than white students. Asians, on the other hand, earned a median score 30 points higher than whites.[25] Under this system, students are being selected to meet group representation targets rather than being selected based on individual performance.

Given standardized tests and requirements, educational examples of nonperformance-based rewards are more prevalent. In the workplace, where performance evaluations and subjective assessments take the place of standardized tests, it is more difficult to measure and compare individual performance. Therefore, affirmative action programs only create further difficulty and controversy by giving employers reasons to reward that are clearly not performance related. These nonperformance-based rewards often result in frustration and antagonism among employees. Therefore, leaders must find ways to measure individuals and reward individual performance. Multiple levels of review, several quantitative measures, skills checklists, and so on are only a few examples of ways to objectively evaluate employees based on performance. Without a clear and strong link between performance and reward, strong performers will have less incentive to perform and weak performers will have less incentive to improve.

We believe that affirmative action is harmful because it undermines the focus on individual performance. In some cases such as education and government contractors, specific numeric targets are set for minority hiring. Because of these targets, many minorities face undue skepticism over their capabilities and successes. Countless minorities have voiced their desire for fairness and objective treatment. Many recognize that affirmative action is a dark cloud that raises questions about their own capabilities and successes.

According to Glenn Loury, an outspoken black opponent of affirmative action and professor at Boston University, "When blacks say we have to have affirmative action, please don't take it away from us, it's almost like saying, 'you're right, we can't compete on merit.' But I know we can compete."[26] As Loury suggests, every individual should compete on merit, and each individual's performance should be evaluated without the stigma of doubts, skepticism, and anger that go hand in hand with affirmative action. Removing these stigmas benefits all minorities who succeed and takes away the excuses of white men who fail.

To be successful, firms must be able to provide top-quality products and services at competitive prices. To do this, they need the best-qualified and best-trained people they can get in every job—no matter what their color, background, or beliefs. The only way to hire and keep good people is to reward based on performance. Business leaders owe it to their companies to take a look at their reward policies and ensure that they focus on performance. As discussed in more detail in chapter 8, anything less subverts efforts to improve performance and has the potential to destroy the work ethic of our most talented performers.

AFFIRMATIVE ACTION IS DIVIDING AMERICA

Finally, affirmative action is tearing the country apart. It has contributed to the growing resentment for and distrust of the federal government and the judicial system, and it is dividing cultural groups in America in ways the creators never imagined.

The side effects of affirmative action have appeared in many facets of life in America, including who we are allowed to vote for in congressional elections. Until it was declared unconstitutional in June 1993, redistricting with the expressed goal of creating minority legislative districts was a common practice. When lawmakers met to redistrict, they distinctly set out to divide the races. In state legislatures across the nation, white Republicans joined forces with blacks to draw redistricting maps to mutual advantage. This cross-party alliance created perhaps a dozen new black-majority congressional districts—and twice as many white ones for the GOP to target in the suburbs.[27] This behavior only further divided American society. Rather than abiding by the principles of our representative democracy, we had segmented society into racial and ethnic groups and in the process virtually guaranteed racial conflict.

The Court, in declaring racial gerrymandering unconstitutional, set a new and significant tone regarding preferential treatment. Supreme Court Justice Sandra Day O'Connor wrote in her opinion, "Racial gerrymandering, even for remedial purposes, may balkanize us into competing racial factions."[28]

According to George Will, our affirmative action policies have encouraged "identity politics—the politics of thinking that you are but a fragment of the racial or ethnic group to which you belong and you have few if any obligations beyond it. Such policies have taught this by making it admirable—and lucrative—to identify with grievance groups defined by their resentments of the larger society."[29] More than ever before in our history, we need to unite and learn to work together to compete. You cannot do this by dividing the people in your organization. We should all remind ourselves of the military tactic "divide and conquer" as a clear formula for victory over any opponent. You simply do not intentionally set out to divide your own organization—unless you want to destroy it.

We assert that affirmative action and other preferential treatment initiatives contribute to the divisions occurring in American society. These policies set the stage for continued political battles between blacks, whites, Hispanics, Asians, women, and others. Each group is trying to claim its share of the American pie. All the while, too little attention is being given to the size of the pie itself. It is not difficult to see what is happening—our nation is becoming divided every day, and too few people are willing to talk about it openly and constructively.

The only way a nation can prosper in the long term with divisive policies in place like our affirmative action policies is if the competitors are weak. Clearly, our competitors are not weak, and we are courting disaster.

AFFIRMATIVE ACTION DOES NOT WORK

According to Heather MacDonald writing for *The New Republic*, "Despite the grand rhetoric of its advocates, there is little evidence that diversity management can solve the problems it purports to address . . . where a deficit of business skills, not a proliferation of racism, is the overwhelming reason many minorities fail to advance . . . But the resources spent maintaining the fiction of equal preparedness would be better used to assist minorities lacking business skills to compete on merit alone."[30]

A recent article cited in *The Economist* provides support of MacDonald's assertion. While not pertaining to all minorities, the article evaluates black community economic patterns in America and cites several statistics that compare native-born blacks to immigrant blacks. It notes,

> In 1990, the median family income for black Americans was $21,548 compared to nearly $30,000 for African-born blacks and more still for blacks born in Jamaica. American-born black households had a higher poverty rate, 31.6 percent, than any black immigrant group except those from the Dominican Republic. Cubans, Haitians, Jamaicans, Trinidadians and black Africans all did better.

The article goes on to suggest that education and marital patterns are primary reasons for these differences. "America's 200,000 black African immigrants, who account for 15 percent of the foreign-born black population, are the most highly educated ethnic group in America. Three quarters have some college experience; one in four has an advanced degree . . . And, fewer than half of American-born black households have two or more earners; but in every other immigrant group, at least 60 percent do."

In addition, evidence suggests that black immigrants are more entrepreneurial than native born blacks. "An analysis of business registrations in Miami in the early 1990s found that Hatians, among the harder-pressed of the immigrant groups, were many times more likely to begin a small business than American-born blacks."

The Economist asserts,

> Figures like these suggest that racism does not account for all, or even most, of the difficulties encountered by native-born blacks . . . Employers, when asked, frankly say they prefer to hire immigrants over native black or Latino workers. Once on the job, strong immigrant networks mean that other immigrants tend to be hired when new openings emerge.[31]

While racism certainly exists in society today, it cannot be solely blamed for society's ills. Evidence suggests that cultural factors may play a role in the economic differences among various minority groups. Given this, we do not believe that affirmative action is an appropriate or even effective response to society's cultural problems.

While it is clear that many minorities have benefited, data over the last 30 years supports the notion that these policies have actually hurt many among the black minority they were meant to help. According to Christopher Jencks in his book, *Rethinking Social Policy*:

> The ratio of black to white employment [measured by weeks worked among men] declined fairly steadily from 1965 to 1981. These dates coincide almost exactly with the period when employers worried most about meeting federal affirmative action requirements. In the late 1980s, when affirmative action rules were less of a threat and the relative cost of hiring black B.A.'s was lower than it had been a decade earlier, their employment prospects began to improve relative to whites.[32]

This data suggests that affirmative action may have played a role in the decline in the ratio of black to white employment because it raised the cost and complexity of hiring black workers. Jencks also said,

> If a firm has to pay black workers more than in the past, and if it also has to be more cautious about disciplining them or passing them over for promotion, it is likely to ask itself whether blacks are worth what they now cost. If the answer is no, it will look for ways of reducing the number of blacks on its payroll . . . Title VII [the Affirmative Action Statute] made firms more cautious about hiring blacks because they knew black workers had more rights than their white counterparts, and firms prefer workers with as few rights as possible.[33]

Certainly many minorities have profited from affirmative action programs, especially those who are educated and working. Yet these are the very individuals who do not need the advantage of affirmative action. We believe affirmative action has hurt many lower-skilled minorities by reducing their attractiveness as employees and reinforcing the stereotype that minorities cannot compete on their own.

Neither racism nor cultural disadvantages can be overcome with reverse discrimination. They must be eroded by the sheer force of performance of individuals. Booker T. Washington shared this sentiment nearly 100 years ago. As one of America's most influential black orators, educators, and leaders, Washington warned, blacks should "not be deprived by unfair means of the franchise [but] political agitation alone will not save him. Back of the ballot, he must have property, industry, skill, economy, intelligence, and character . . . no race without these elements can permanently succeed."

Ironically, the United States is not the first nation to discover that preferential treatment policies fail because they undermine performance and protect some less qualified individuals.

During the mid-19th century in Great Britain, jobs in the British Civil Service were handed out on the basis of family connections in an affirmative action–like program for the upper class. Yet as Britain became a world leader with increased economic power and responsibility, reformers argued that these jobs should go to the most intelligent individuals based on competitive examinations.

The move toward performance-based selection was adopted and was so successful that policy makers applied the same performance expectations to universities and schools. The education system, therefore, set out and succeeded "to construct a system capable of discovering real ability wherever it occurred, and of matching that ability with the appropriate opportunities."[34]

The United States successfully developed for nearly 200 years on the basis of individual performance and reward. And in 30 short years, affirmative action has undermined the goal of equal opportunity and replaced it with the goal of equal outcome. We must reverse this pattern and set the example for our future generations that reward based on anything other than performance is unacceptable.

THE SUPREME COURT IS MOVING SLOWLY TO SOLVE THE PROBLEM

Things are changing ever so slowly. Despite efforts by the U.S. Supreme Court over the past 20 years to end race-, gender-, and ethnicity-based preferences unless they are "narrowly tailored to promote a compelling state interest,"[35] entrenched government bureaucracies at the federal and state levels have been slow to reverse preferential policies. We have a long way to go, but we are headed in the right direction. What is needed now is for business leaders to speak up and let people know how affirmative action has affected their organizations—how rewarding anything except performance hurts their organizations, their people, and ultimately the communities in which they operate.

According to Supreme Court Justice Sandra Day O'Connor, "There is no such thing as a 'benign' racial classification . . . Governmental distinctions among citizens based on race or ethnicity . . . exact costs and carry with them substantial dangers . . . To the person denied an opportunity or right based on race, the classification is hardly benign."[36]

William O. Douglas, thought by many to be the most liberal Supreme Court justice ever to have served, had this to say in 1974 about the denial of a white man's admission to law school because he was white: "The Equal Protection Clause commands the elimination of racial barriers, not their creation in order to satisfy our theory as to how society ought to be organized . . . A segregated admissions process creates suggestions of stigma and caste no less than a segregated classroom . . . One other assumption must be clearly disapproved: that blacks or browns cannot make it on their individual merit."[37]

Justice Lewis Powell was more succinct than Douglas in his analysis of the Court's historic 1978 Bakke case, which raised serious questions about reverse discrimination to remedy past inequities. He said, "Preferring members of any one group for no reason other than race or ethnic origin is discrimination for its own sake. This the Constitution forbids."[38]

As Nat Hentoff, a well-known and respected advocate for our constitutionally protected right of free speech and for a color-blind judicial system, has said, "When general racial preferences—intentionally and with government support—discriminate against individuals who are not of that race, the Constitution has been substantially diminished."[39]

The problems with our courts today have not occurred in isolation. They are part of a much larger trend that affects our businesses, our schools, and every other institution in our society. We have consistently failed to hold people accountable for their actions, and the cost of this grievous error has been incredibly high. We will have much more to say about this problem in chapter 8.

DIVERSITY CAN WORK TO EVERYONE'S ADVANTAGE IF IT IS MARKET DRIVEN

To deal with race problems in businesses, nearly 75 percent of America's 50 biggest companies have appointed "directors of diversity" or "diversity managers" whose job is to modify corporate cultures so that they suit the needs of all employees. In addition, "diversity training" is a requirement at many large companies, and the diversity consulting industry is growing by leaps and bounds, charging fees as high as $10,000 per day.[40] While the cost of diversity programs and enforcement is estimated at over $100 billion annually, companies report that the benefits are not overwhelming. A 1993 Conference Board study found that fewer than a third of the companies using diversity training considered them to be successful; half thought they made no difference at all.[41]

This is not to say that we believe diversity is bad. Quite the contrary. Diverse consumer markets are demanding that companies have a diverse employee base. We believe companies should pursue market-based diversity. Avon Products offers an example of this concept. In 1993 a district sales manager for Avon Products in Atlanta noticed an increase in the local Vietnamese and Korean population. She actively recruited both Vietnamese and Korean employees to overcome the language barrier to reach these new customers. With their cultural know-how, these new employees sold products door-to-door to this mostly first- and second-generation ethnic group. And with great success, both Avon and these new Avon ladies did well.

Was this government imposed? The result of a diversity program at Avon? An attempt to meet affirmative action quotas? The brainchild of a new "diversity manager"? Of course not. These people were hired because of a specific skill or trait that gave them an advantage in the market. It is hard to argue with hiring based on these skill-driven guidelines. And opportunities like this are abundant—and they are driven by economically sound market needs. By the year 2000, white males will represent only 45 percent of America's workforce, with one-third of this group protected by another group classification. This leaves 70 percent as minority workers.[42] These same workers are also consumers with distinct tastes. Companies that can meet the specific needs of this changing demographic construction of America will have a distinct advantage.

Consumer products and service firms were among the first to exploit this opportunity. For example, 130 of 800 Sears, Roebuck stores are located in or near Hispanic communities. To ensure effective customer service, Sears staffs these locations with bilingual or Hispanic employees. Pillsbury and Kraft General Foods believe that diversifying their management ranks has helped them quickly and effectively develop foods for black and Hispanic consumers. This trend is present not only in domestic markets but in staffing for overseas business as well. Companies are looking for American-born or -educated people with international backgrounds to move into markets from the Far East to Africa to South America.

It does not take a diversity manager or quotas to make these market-based decisions. In fact, evidence suggests that not all companies will jump on the diversity bandwagon. Christian & Timbers, an executive search firm, conducted a survey of new jobs for 1996. Vice president of diversity was among the top five "not so hot" jobs, forecasted to suffer a 25 percent decline in demand. In contrast, "knowledge" jobs are in high demand as Internet, multimedia, and technology jobs are expected to grow by nearly 100 percent.[43]

Diversity is the word that describes the American melting pot and in fact the world. Business leaders should view diversity as a competitive weapon to be used logically and strategically. Increasing the diversity among the employee base creates new challenges for everyone, but the results speak for themselves. Few can argue with market-driven diversity that rewards companies for their foresight and people for their performance. In addition to the consumer market advantages, early evidence indicates a correlation between innovativeness and diversity. The University of Michigan Business School conducted controlled experiments of both homogeneous and ethnically diverse groups where each group was assigned the same problem. Not surprisingly, the diverse groups achieved better results, most likely due to their broader spectrum of experiences.[44]

Companies who insulate themselves from the realities of the diverse market will likely find themselves outmarketed by other competitors over the long run. The bottom line is that leaders must have the courage to make decisions based on business issues and reward people based on performance. Leaders should seek to instill these basic values and let the market and results speak for themselves. In this way, leaders can avoid the charge of preferential treatment as well as the trap of excessive attention on a single issue.

WHAT MUST WE DO?

Business leaders should join in questioning the affirmative action policies America has employed for more than three decades. The financial and social costs have become too high. To be competitive, firms must focus on performance and in doing so hire the most qualified people they can, train them well, and reward those who get the job done.

On a very specific level, business leaders should read and understand the affirmative action and antibias laws. With this knowledge, they can evaluate the regulations that impact their organization. In most cases, businesses have self-imposed diversity "goals" that are not required by the law. Given this, most business leaders can move away from concerns over affirmative action and reinforce the notion that all hiring and reward decisions will be based on performance and skills.

As noted earlier, it is not easy to find totally objective performance measures. Therefore, leaders should implement regular performance reviews by multiple individuals. These reviews should establish, measure, and track multiple quantitative and qualitative measures. These measures obviously vary by company and industry; therefore, human resource experts and managers should be involved with planning and implementing these reviews.

In today's competitive global markets, we need and we must have performance from everyone. Our policies and our actions must focus our attention on this reality. If we want performance, we must reward performance. We should discourage policies that treat people differently based on their race, gender, or ethnicity. Overall, managers must find ways to evaluate individuals fairly. Anything that stands in the way of doing so should be eliminated. This includes following unmandated affirmative action guidelines. For federal contractors and others with mandated quotas to meet, leaders can follow the path of Pacific Gas & Electric and ask the government to let skills-based training and other employee development programs take the place of hard quotas.

OVERCOMING DIVISION IN THE WORKPLACE

A recent class at the Harvard Business School discussed the decline of Great Britain from its position of world leadership during the last 100 years. The class concluded with a discussion of the reasons this could or could not happen in America. The lists were quite telling. On the positive side, students noted the large free-market system, the dispersion of industries, reasonably strong work ethic, recent resurgence in U.S. performance, and others. Virtually every one of the 10 reasons was related to our nation's infrastructure and the free-market mechanisms present in America.

However, the negative forces were quite different. That list contained only three items: (1) poor education system and trends, (2) mismatch of skill base and skills needed for the future, and (3) racial division and social unrest. Each of these relates directly to our ability as a nation to allocate and utilize our most important asset—people. To date, the scorecard in this area has not been impressive. As note in the previous chapters, declining educational achievement, inadequate transfer of people from industrial to higher-skilled jobs, and friction among diverse groups have all resulted in wasted resources. This pattern must change. Companies must invest in people and turn to performance as the primary measure for reward. Business leaders must find the courage to look beyond the many challenges and to take action to pursue the opportunities that will not only improve business performance but improve the competitiveness and vitality of our society.

A FINAL NOTE

Currently, it is common for people who oppose affirmative action policies to be regarded as racist or sexist, but they are not. Who are the racists or sexists? The ones who believe that if we reward only performance we will achieve diversity, because people from diverse groups are fully capable of performing, or the ones who believe women, people of color, and people with different ethnic origins could not make it in a world where performance and rewards are closely linked? We believe diverse groups can perform, and they should be rewarded for performing. Anything else sends the wrong signal and runs the risk of reducing our competitiveness.

MOVING ON

It is extremely difficult to confront the issues that impede performance. These issues are often controversial, and they have the potential to create disharmony in organizations. Thus, they are avoided at great cost. In the next chapter, we turn our attention to the harmony obsession.

ENDNOTES

1. Sylvester Monroe, "Does Affirmative Action Help or Hurt?" *Time*, May 27, 1991, p. 23.
2. Ibid.
3. Nathan Glazer, "The Affirmative Action Stalemate," *The Public Interest*, Winter 1988, p. 100.
4. Steven Roberts, "Affirmative Action on the Edge," *U.S. News & World Report*, February 13, 1995, p. 35.
5. Arthur M. Schlesinger Jr., *The Disuniting of America*, Foreword.
6. Christopher Jencks, *Rethinking Social Policy* (Cambridge, MA: Harvard University Press, 1992), p. 49.
7. Glazer, p. 102.

8. Peter Brimelow and Leslie Spencer, "When Quotas Replace Merit, Everybody Suffers," *Forbes,* February 15, 1993, p. 81.
9. Bob Cohn and Tom Morganthau, "The Q-Word Charade," *Newsweek,* June 3, 1991, p. 17.
10. Catherine Yang, "A Race Neutral Helping Hand?", *Business Week,* February 27, 1995, p. 120.
11. John Leo, "Feel Abused? Get in Line," *U.S. News & World Report,* April 10, 1995, p. 21.
12. Kevin Merida and John R. Harris, "Sampler of Preference Programs," *Washington Post,* April 5, 1995, p. A-4.
13. Yang, p. 120.
14. Joe Klein, "The End of Affirmative Action," *Newsweek,* February 13, 1995, p. 36.
15. Brimelow and Spencer, "When Quotas Replace Merit," p. 80.
16. Ibid., p. 90.
17. Ibid., p. 82.
18. William A. Henry III, *In Defense of Elitism* (New York: Doubleday, 1994), pp. 12–14.
19. Henry, p. 65.
20. Roberts, p. 35.
21. Ibid., p. 32.
22. Albert Shanker, "No Whites Need Apply?", *New York Times,* July 10, 1996.
23. Roberts, p. 37.
24. Peter Applebome, "The Debate on Diversity at the University of California Shifts," *The New York Times,* June 4, 1995, p. 22.
25. Richard J. Herrnstein and Charles Murray, *Bell Curve* (New York: Free Press, 1994), p. 452.
26. Roberts, p. 35.
27. "The New Politics of Race," *Newsweek,* May 6, 1991, p. 25.
28. Roberts, p. 38.
29. George Will, "Circus of the Century," *Washington Post,* October 4, 1995, p. A-25.
30. Heather MacDonald, "The Diversity Industry," *The New Republic,* July 5, 1993, p. 25.
31. "Black Like Me," *The Economist,* May 11, 1996, p. 27.
32. Christopher Jencks, *Rethinking Social Policy* (Cambridge, MA: Harvard University Press, 1992), p. 55.
33. Jencks, p. 57.

34. "Bell, Book, and Scandal," *The Economist*, December 24, 1994, p. 70.

35. Nat Hentoff, "Scholarships and Race," *Washington Post*, January 20, 1996, p. A-23.

36. Joan Biskupic, "Court to Hear Pivotal Case on Racial Policy," *Washington Post*, January 17, 1995, p. A-4.

37. Nat Hentoff, "Playing the Race Card," *Washington Post*, October 8, 1994, p. A-19.

38. Ibid., p. A-19.

39. Ibid., p. A-23.

40. "A Strong Prejudice," *The Economist*, June 17, 1995, p. 69.

41. Sager, p. 4.

42. "A Strong Prejudice," p. 69.

43. Ira Sager, "The List: Go Digital, Young Man," *Business Week*, January 29, 1996, p. 4.

44. Ibid., p. 4.

5
CHAPTER

What End Harmony?

Leaders' jobs are incredibly difficult because they must keep an eye on the future needs of their organizations and on the needs of the present. Too often, individuals wilt in the face of day-to-day crises and are timid and insecure about making hard choices. Many times the desire to avoid conflict and preserve harmony in the workplace is at the root of the problem. But preserving harmony may mean sacrificing the long-run interests of firms for short-term, imaginary gains. Leaders' efforts to appease and pacify discontented individuals and groups, therefore, often reduce the ability of their firms to compete in the rapidly changing global market. Let us explain what we mean.

In chapter 2, we gave examples showing how workplace division caused by adversarial relationships between labor and management have led to enormous difficulties for firms attempting to compete in the increasingly competitive global market. In many firms, management and labor behave as though they are on different teams with entirely different goals and objectives. The result is negative for everyone involved, including managers, workers, investors, suppliers, and the communities in which the firms operate. Managers and workers must change their behavior if they want their firms to be competitive. Furthermore, as discussed in chapter 3, leaders must recognize the skills, capabilities, and weaknesses of different individuals and various groups. We addressed the problems and the opportunities associated with integrating Generation X into U.S. firms. The potential this group possesses is enormous, but it will only be wasted if leaders fail to recognize and nurture this talent.

In chapter 4, we focused on the negative effects of well-meaning, but misguided, attempts to right the wrongs of the past through affirmative action policies. Many of these actions, which were intended to solve problems, have created difficulties instead. This method of eliminating inequities in the workplace has instead cemented inequities and taken the focus away from performance-based reward. The reduced emphasis on performance has led to a reduced work ethic, mediocrity, and frustration among leaders and workers alike.

All of these three sources of division—unions, age, preferential treatment—have slowed the efforts of firms to improve their competitive positions. In the global market, there is no substitute for performance. With ever increasing pressure to produce top-quality products and services at competitive prices, these policies insulate mediocre performers and make achieving excellence (the standard firms should pursue) virtually impossible.

Although these problems are important, they will not be addressed unless our leaders have the will to confront controversial issues and make difficult choices. Too many times, they elect to play it safe and avoid controversy and the disharmony it has the potential to generate. Potentially, this obsession with harmony is more dangerous than any other problems leaders face; it threatens to drive out creative activity and the dedication and persistence of the true change makers on whom we are so dependent for our future success. Leaders must guarantee that their firms encourage questioning, constructive dissension, and deep thinking. While some degree of harmony is necessary, excessive devotion to harmony can destroy an organization.

CONFLICT IS A NECESSITY

Because the world in which we live is changing so rapidly, firms must change constantly and improve continuously if they hope to prosper and grow. Therefore, leaders must ensure that continuous improvement is a way of life for everyone in the organization. Since change, conflict, and temporary disharmony are inextricably linked with continuous improvement, attempting to avoid them has the effect of thwarting progress.

In his book *Mastering Change,* Leon Martel says that many firms have committed three common errors and failed: "Believing that yesterday's solutions will solve today's problems, assuming that present trends will continue, and neglecting the opportunities of future changes."[1] Failing to adapt to changes within the environment and adhering to the "business as usual" philosophy is a very dangerous habit for any organization. As Martel says, "The more companies rely on past experiences, the greater the margin of error is."[2]

Why do managers become oblivious to the changes in the environment that threaten their organizations? Why do they not understand that change is as important to corporate prosperity as breathing is to the human being? A recent study found that in 57 large-scale bankruptcies between 1972 and 1982, the characteristics were incredibly similar. "Few failures were sudden: most experienced a prolonged 10-year decline in accounting performance, suggesting that, as managers, we are typically much slower to change than the environment our firms inhabit."[3]

Martel points out that the United States steel industry has only itself to blame for its hard times. The firms in the industry failed to adapt to obvious changes taking place in other parts of the world and "caused the American steel industry to overproduce iron ore, underrate technological change, overestimate demand, and largely ignore the growth of foreign competitors."[4] This failure caused many problems as U.S. steelmakers in the 1980s produced far more iron ore than they could use, ignored their obsolete, and often inefficient, equipment, and paid too little attention to foreign competitors who could deliver slab steel at prices far lower than they could match. Had it not been for tariff protection provided by the U.S. government, firms in the steel industry probably would have responded effectively to the changes in their industry and would not have experienced many of the problems they did. In effect, steel companies sought harmony through protectionism and lulled themselves into a false sense of security.

AT&T before its breakup in 1984 is another good example of this phenomenon at work. According to Charles Fombrun, "AT&T was an inertial system, lumbering into the future with an antiquated mission, a meaningless competitive strategy, and a complacent, bureaucratic culture."[5] This culture, and the bureaucracy that protected it, caused many of AT&T's problems. The company's employees failed to see beyond their day-to-day activities. Thus, they were unprepared for the rapid changes taking place that would forever change their company and the world in which we live.

In addition, the company had an "implementation-oriented culture that discouraged risk-taking, innovation, and change."[6] We owe a debt of gratitude to the U.S. government for forcing AT&T to sell off the operating Bell companies and compelling it to compete for business without monopoly protection. The telecommunications industry is now progressing at a pace that would have been inconceivable prior to the AT&T breakup, and firms like MCI, Sprint, and Motorola are competing with AT&T and providing us with top-quality products and services at competitive prices. As we will see in chapter 8, even AT&T is regaining its lost competitive momentum.

Businesspeople who want to prosper in the future should pay attention and learn from these examples. The problems that afflicted AT&T and firms in the steel industry can destroy any organization. As we have said before, there is nothing wrong with harmony. But when the obsession with harmony takes control, the ability to compete and the very survival of an organization are threatened.

BUREAUCRACIES AND THE HARMONY OBSESSION

Bureaucracies, which exist in every organization, tend to resist change, and they prefer the "tried-and-true" approaches that worked in the past. Let us be clear about this point: Bureaucratic momentum and inertia in organizations can be overwhelming. They exert tremendous influence on the way people behave and cause them to spend their time and energy protecting the status quo and pressuring others to conform to the conventional way of doing business. Left unchecked, bureaucracies can stifle creativity, destroy an organization's ability to compete effectively, make achieving excellence an impossibility, and ultimately cause an organization to fail. We will have more to say about this in chapter 9.

Ironically, success is a breeding ground for bureaucratic growth. The more prosperous a firm is, the more resources it can use to hire people to do the work at hand. Too often people are added, and levels of management to supervise them, without carefully considering the value added of each additional job. As this process continues, bureaucratic momentum starts to build, and as we have said before, bureaucracies tend to resist change.

Arnold Toynbee did a great job of explaining why success often leads to the failure to respond appropriately to change and why it can have devastating effects on an organization:

In evolution, [the saying] 'nothing fails like success' is probably always right. A creature which has become perfectly adapted to its environment ... has nothing left over with which to respond to any radical change. It becomes more perfectly economical in the way its entire resources meet exactly its current and customary opportunities. It can, therefore, beat all the competitors in the special field; but, equally, should the field change, it must become extinct.[7]

Meg Greenfield, editorial page editor of the *Washington Post,* talked about the same problem from another perspective. She said, "Yes, we have to address problems. But the worst way would be by resistance of the kind that has given us, in the past, nonproductive featherbedding in various industries and rigor mortis arrangements in places like the U.S. Congress. ... Companies, professions, institutions that insist on clinging to obsolete techniques and habits look attractively stable/traditional for a while— tweed and pipes and solid oak desks, that sort of thing; then they look charming; then quaint; then ridiculous; then dead."[8]

Pressure to conform and to stay on the "proven" path are ever present dangers in organizations with well-entrenched bureaucracies. Employees in these organizations place a premium on efficiency, and deviating from standard operating procedures is viewed as wasteful and risky. But in reality, this approach "limits, rather than mobilizes the development of human capacities, molding human beings to fit the requirements of a mechanical organization, rather than building the organization around their strengths and potentials."[9]

When bureaucracies become too powerful, the employees and the organization lose. The "employees lose opportunities for personal growth, and organizations lose the creative and intelligent contributions that employees are capable of making given the right opportunities."[10] Confronting and subduing bureaucracies are critical roles leaders must perform. If they fail to perform these roles, the very survival of their organizations will be threatened.

What is harmony? The Random House dictionary says that *harmony* is an "agreement; accord; a consistent, orderly, or *pleasing* arrangement of parts."[11] When we think about harmony, we think about organizations that emphasize the importance of agreement and finding and preserving consensus. In organizations where very few people disagree, who instigates change? How does the organization prosper and grow in the fast-paced world in which we live? Our obsession with harmony led Richard Pascale in his book *Managing on the Edge* to call organizations "the ultimate conservatives"[12] as they tend to do again and again only what they already know how to do.

We live in a world that takes great pride in innovation and creativity, yet we often forget that creativity and innovation are incubated in organizations that encourage questioning and dissent. Typically, major breakthroughs come about as the result of the efforts of individuals who break the rules and practically force their ideas on the organization, or they come from small groups of people who are not content with the way things are. Leaders must learn to protect these people and to deal with those who would attempt to suppress them as they do their vital work. Without them and their efforts, businesses will not prosper.

As we said earlier, successful organizations learn not just to accept change but to champion it. In his book *Mastering Change,* Leon Martel says, "We live in a world of change, yet we act on the basis of continuity. Change is unfamiliar; it disturbs us. We ignore it, we avoid it; often we try to resist it . . . As a result, we experience unnecessary losses and miss unseen opportunities."[13]

Leaders must resist the temptation to stay with the tried-and-true approach. Although the status quo philosophy can destroy an organization in the long run, in the short run it is probably the most efficient way to do business. Business students learn this early on in business schools. When they graduate, it is reinforced by investors, governments, unions, and boards of directors who apply tremendous pressure for short-term results. Keeping these groups reasonably happy is important, but long-term success demands investing regularly in new and better ways of doing business and in new product and service ideas.

Another reason managers prefer the status quo orientation to give-and-take in the workplace is that give-and-take creates conflict, and dealing with conflict and differences of opinion is time-consuming and frustrating. It is much faster and easier for them simply to make decisions on their own without consulting others. Since most managers are promoted and rewarded for short-term performance and they know that deviating from the status quo has short-term costs, most of them simply avoid it. The result is that a manager's performance is measured increasingly by how well he uses the traditional approach.

There is too little incentive for managers to look for innovative alternatives that address problems in fundamentally different ways, even though the new approaches might produce better results. The objective most firms pursue is to avoid disasters by operating on safe ground.[14] This approach to doing business must change.

Leaders must learn to successfully manage conflict and use it to help the company, since "there is no real growth or development in the organizations or in the individuals within it if they do not confront and deal directly with their problems."[15] Conflict is essential for success, for the "seeds of the future are always enfolded in the oppositions shaping the present."[16] Every organization needs a leader who has the will to act as a catalyst, one whose goal is to "mobilize rather than dictate, to inspire rather than repress, to lead rather than control."[17] As Gordon Lippitt states, "Millions of good productive ideas have been lost in organizations where the climate does not allow for honest differences of opinions. Many times pertinent points of view are 'filtered out' before they get to top management."[18]

From his detailed studies of successful and unsuccessful organizations, Richard Pascale learned that "the subtle but distinct quality of the survivors is that their organizations became engines of inquiry."[19] The harmony obsession is found most often in organizations run by domineering people who seize power and make all the important decisions. Pascale points out that the effect of these "elite" people is to "drive an organization toward excess, and narrow the frame in which learning occurs."[20]

An obsession with harmony causes a multitude of problems. According to Gareth Morgan, an expert on management issues, "It can create organizational forms that have great difficulty adapting to changing circumstances; it can result in mindless and unquestioning bureaucracy; . . . and it can have dehumanizing effects upon employees, especially those at lower levels of the hierarchy."[21]

Excessive devotion to harmony stifles independence and individualism. Additionally, it causes a high degree of conformity and lack of creativity. Under these circumstances, people become risk averse, and their organizations become stagnate and inflexible. When employees become accustomed to this type of environment, it is very difficult, even frightening, for them to give up the temporary comfort that harmony provides and to subject themselves to the rigors of competition.

THE CONSENSUS BUILDING FRAUD

According to Dr. Amanda Sinclair from Melbourne University's Graduate School of Management, consensus building is often the result of "unilateral decisions imposed by powerful leaders" rather than the result of a mutual solution arrived at by the group as a whole.[22] This type of management hurts the organization, because in each decision, "The competitive

edge is dulled and the contribution of the higher achievers and more original thinkers is lost."[23] As Warren Bennis states, "The individual who sees
things differently is the company's vital link to change and adaptation."[24]
We must not discourage individuals from sharing their ideas.

Consensus building, as it is practiced in most organizations, exacts a
high price. Rather than inspiring commitment, loyalty, and dedication, it
results in mere acceptance of ideas on the part of employees and more cen-
tralized control by managers. Provocative, innovative, and revolutionary
ideas are lost, and organizations move toward finding the "lowest common
denominator" that will irritate and disturb the smallest number of people.
As a result, many potentially good ideas never surface, and organizations
settle for mediocre performance. In the increasingly competitive global
market, mediocre performance is simply not good enough. Furthermore,
rather than stimulating challenging objectives that are rewarding both personally and professionally, a preoccupation with consensus building
causes most companies to pursue goals that inspire no one. Thus, they drift
along, and drifting along is a formula for disaster in a world that is changing at breakneck speed.

GENERAL MOTORS

General Motors is a good example of a company with a history of avoid-
ing conflict. These characteristics played an important part in reducing the
competitiveness of the automobile giant. As we pointed out before, the
1980s marked a turning point for GM. Until that time, GM was recognized
as the leader in the global automobile industry, but during the 1980s, the
company's problems, which had been festering since the end of World War
II, started to become evident. Richard Pascale's interviews with General
Motors' employees in the late eighties made clear that "GM suppresses
conflict, giving contention little avenue for expression."[25]

Very little changed at GM in the early 1990s. According to Pascale,
"At GM we see a company that, despite a strong market position, able
executives and engineers, and vast financial resources, is largely paralyzed
. . . Its elites are out of balance, constructive tension is lacking, and many
of the norms that prevail there dampen debate and initiative."[26]

GM's Saturn project has been touted as an attempt to break the mold
and create a new and better GM, but it has not worked out that way. Rather
than blazing a new trail, the Saturn project has focused its resources and
the energy of its employees on copying the successes of Honda. According

to Tom Peters, the Saturn project is just an imitation Honda's work in 1985. As GM struggled to catch up with Honda by copying, Honda went about its business improving its cars even more. The lesson should be clear to business leaders. You cannot get ahead of your competitors by copying what they did almost a decade earlier. As Peters says, "For the biggest company in the U.S. to have that much of a failure of imagination is terrible."[27]

Ironically, Honda successfully implemented a contention management strategy. In the 1980s, the company "dedicated itself to explicitly surfacing and managing contention in a constructive way, by holding seminars in which subordinates can openly question bosses and challenge the status quo."[28] This environment facilitated open discussions and encouraged employees to share their ideas and question those of others.

Pascale's comparison of General Motors and Honda further illustrates the value of dissent in an organization. Pascale attributes the success of Honda (versus GM's lack of success) to the following critical factors that were present at Honda but not at GM:

- A deeply ingrained habit of self-questioning.
- Obsessive attention to external measures.
- A drive to do things better than the best in the industry.
- A well-tuned system for managing the contention that these three factors generated.[29]

FORD MOTOR COMPANY

Ford Motor Company (the subject of chapter 12) also encountered difficulty with bureaucracy and lack of open communication prior to developing a successful way of managing contention. As Pascale learned from his interviews with Ford executives, the reason that the company is successful today is because it revamped the way the organization worked. Pascale found that, like most organizations, Ford suffered from excess control. Ford executives would solve problems by creating additional rules, which really did not solve the problems. Ford employees described the environment as one without dialogue. "It was bureaucratic gridlock. The edicts had to come from on high. You had to be nuts to argue anything."[30]

One example of the way successful contention management can turn a company around is the difference in the Ford Motor Company before and after Don Peterson took charge. Before Peterson, Ford suffered from a lack of creativity, overbearing bureaucratic leaders, and an ineffective decision-making process, among other things. After Peterson took charge, however, major changes were made in the way Ford managed its business.

Today Ford's Executive Development Centers are safe havens where employees can dispute each other and discuss key issues that the chairman and president are currently dealing with. Experts are brought in, and the employees challenge each other with questions and problems. Ford's Executive Development Centers are an important part of the organization as they reinforce the concept of teamwork and encourage the employees to think about the goals of the company. At these sessions, all points of view are represented and each employee gets a chance to argue his or her point.

Everyone benefits from looking at the problem situation from a larger perspective. Because of the Executive Development Centers, employees are able to learn from each other's expertise and then make rational decisions based on the information obtained, all of which help Ford.[31]

One of the most vivid examples of the value of dissent is the competitive relationship that existed between Don Peterson, the product man, and Red Poling, the finance man. Disagreements between these two individuals helped Ford in the long run, because their disagreements facilitated changes in the organization. Rather than destroying the company, Peterson and Poling seemed as if they were constantly attempting to outdo each other in promoting change. As Pascale states, "When one discovered a process that worked, it was reverse-engineered by his rival."[32]

By learning how to successfully deal with conflict and use it to their advantage, Ford executives, under the leadership of Peterson, were able to turn the company around. Peterson understood the role of dissent in promoting organizational change, and through his leadership, Ford "harnessed creative tension to foster adaptation and continuous learning."[33] Peterson realized that a strong, overbearing leader discouraged dissent, and thus he strove to diminish the centralization of power within the company.

According to Peterson, "Lasting transformation requires employees to accept responsibility for, and contribute wholeheartedly to the change that is sought." Peterson saw the executive not as the sole decision maker, but as a "prodder, facilitator, and catalyst."[34] Without this new outlook, Ford never would have developed the Taurus, which was unlike any of the cars the company had made before.

These examples demonstrate the value of dissent in bringing about organizational change. No matter how uncomfortable a confrontation may be, "Openness, candor, and frank feedback should not be equated with hostility or obstructionism." In fact, it is "those who shut off the ideas and contributions of their subordinates who are really the obstructionists."[35] Conflict makes organizations come alive, as it "counters tendencies towards lethargy, staleness, apathetic compliance, and similar organizational pathologies." Conflict creates a "'keep on your toes' atmosphere where it is dangerous to take things for granted."[36]

Ford's strategy for change was to develop leaders who understood the importance of dissent and would be able to facilitate change within the organization. Ford's contention management system has been successful because it allows employees to surface concerns, making it "safe" to disagree and challenge the ideas of others. Ford has continued to emphasize the importance of innovation, and one of Ford's objectives is to be "25 percent faster in creating new products"[37] than its competitors. Ford's belief that contention management fosters change has enabled the company to become a leader in new product development.

GENERAL ELECTRIC

Perhaps the best example of the value of dissent is GE's chairman and CEO Jack Welch and his undying commitment to organizational change. (We will deal with Welch and the changes he instituted at GE in detail in chapter 11.) Welch's philosophy toward change inspired him to implement a program called Work-Out, which is responsible to a large extent for GE's becoming a successful, adaptive, and flexible organization. This company-wide program consists of monthly, multiday sessions in which employees meet and exchange views on the vision of the company. After exchanging views, the employees then work together to eliminate the factors that are keeping the vision from being realized.

Welch explains the philosophy behind the program:

> We're not going to succeed if people end up doing the same work they've always done, if they don't feel any psychic or financial impact from the way the organization is changing. The ultimate objective of Work-Out is to have 300,000 people with different career objectives, different family aspirations, different financial goals, to share directly in this company's vision, the information, the decision-making process, and the rewards. We want to build a more stimulating environment, a freer work atmosphere, with incentives tied directly to what people do.[38]

Encouraging dissent not only gets other ideas and opinions "on the table," but it lets the leader know where others are coming from and helps employees understand changes occurring within the organization. The goal of Work-Out is to establish an environment "where every man and woman in the company can see and feel a connection between what he or she does all day . . . and winning in the marketplace . . . the ultimate job security."[39] Having employees involved in the decision-making process is vital to the organization's success, because it is only through their support that smooth, effective transitions can be made. Welch's attitude toward employee involvement helped him turn GE around, and his success "depended not only on his ability to ram change throughout GE, but on his ability to provide support for people to work through organizational transitions."[40]

To encourage employees to challenge each other's views, leaders need to cut back on bureaucracies within their companies relentlessly and to avoid the tendency for decisions to be made only by the higher-ups. Welch understood the importance of decentralized power, and worked to redefine the relationship between boss and subordinate. Ideally, Welch wanted to get people accustomed to "challenging their boss *every day*."[41] He wanted workers to be continually pushing upward on top management, forcing them to make changes. Welch insisted that communication was the company's link to success, and he encouraged confrontation with goals such as "getting different people with different views together in a room and making them 'thrash it out.'"[42]

In Jack Welch, we see an emerging leadership model and a man with the will to lead. He stresses communication, involvement, and commitment to change, ingredients that can drive an organization and enable it to succeed. GE began the 1980s as a company with almost $23 billion in annual revenues and $1.4 billion in net earnings. Under Welch's leadership, the company ended the decade with almost $50 billion in annual revenues and close to $4 billion in earnings.[43] By 1989, GE was the "sixth most profitable firm in the world."[44]

CREATING CONSTRUCTIVE TENSION TO ENHANCE PERFORMANCE

The first step in creating constructive tension in an organization is to move away from the preoccupation with stability and to focus on developing resilient organizations. As Richard Pascale put it, we need to avoid the tendency to seek refuge in a "fail-safe" world and focus on thriving in a "safe to fail" world.[45] Without failure, there is no learning and there can be no growth. A "safe to fail" world is one in which people are challenging themselves to extend beyond their present capabilities. Organizations need leaders who encourage employees to push themselves to their limits and beyond. Successful leaders are "committed to problem-finding, not just problem-solving. They embrace error, even failure, because they know it will teach them more than success."[46]

FINDING BALANCE BETWEEN STABILITY AND CHANGE

While we have illustrated the detrimental effects of an excessive devotion to harmony within an organization, we must note that too much conflict can cause many organizational problems as well. The key to maximizing performance in organizations is to find a balance between the forces of stability and the forces of change. As Tichy and Devanna note, "Organizations that cling too tightly to tradition present us with dramas of eventual decline, while organizations that fail to regain their equilibrium after embarking on a change spin out of control and eventually destroy themselves."[47]

Once a wide range of ideas have been considered, leaders must focus attention on the best ideas and use them as a foundation for developing a shared vision. Ultimately unity, focus, and consistency in vision and goals enable firms to compete in today's global markets. But to be successful in the long term, they must also be willing to change anything that might improve performance, including their vision and goals. Too often, the fear of change prevents this from happening. We turn our attention to this issue in the next chapter.

ENDNOTES

1. Leon Martel, *Mastering Change* (New York: Simon and Schuster, 1986), pp. 16–23.
2. Ibid., p. 257.
3. Charles Fombrun, *Turning Points* (New York: McGraw-Hill, Inc., 1992), p. 56.
4. Martel, pp. 257–258.
5. Fombrun, p. 51.
6. Ibid., p. 52.
7. Richard Tanner Pascale, *Managing on the Edge* (New York: Simon and Schuster, 1990), p. 15.
8. Meg Greenfield, "The Laptop Revolution," *Washington Post,* February 20, 1995, p. A 29.

9. Gareth Morgan, *Images of Organization* (Newbury Park, California: SAGE Publications, 1986), p. 38.

10. Morgan, p. 38.

11. Jeff Stein, *The Random House College Dictionary* (New York: Random House, 1980).

12. Pascale, p. 11.

13. Martel, p. 11.

14. James R. Emshoff, *Managerial Breakthroughs* (New York: AMACOM, 1980), p. 39.

15. Gordon L. Lippitt, Leslie E. This, and Robert G. Bidwell Jr., *Optimizing Human Resources* (Reading, Massachusetts: Addison-Wesley, 1971), p. 191.

16. Morgan, p. 265.

17. Fombrun, p. 163.

18. Lippitt, This, and Bidwell, p. 35.

19. Pascale, p. 29.

20. Ibid., p. 237.

21. Morgan, p. 35.

22. Linda English, "The Tyranny of Teamness," *Australian Accountant,* November, 1988, p. 14.

23. Ibid., p. 16.

24. Warren Bennis, "Creative Leadership," *Executive Excellence,* August 1991, p. 6.

25. Pascale, p. 240.

26. Ibid., p. 261.

27. Tom Peters, "Total Quality Leadership: Let's Get It Right," *Journal for Quality and Participation,* March 1991, pp. 10–15.

28. Pascale, p. 26.

29. Ibid., p. 259.

30. Ibid., p. 153.

31. Ibid., p. 163.

32. Ibid., p. 124.

33. Ibid., p. 142.

34. Ibid., p. 66.

35. Lippitt, This, and Bidwell, p. 35.

36. Morgan, p. 190.

37. Jerry Flint, "Follow that Ford," *Forbes,* April 27, 1992, pp. 44–45.

38. Pascale, p. 209.

39. John F. Welch Jr., "Speed, Simplicity, and Self-Confidence: Keys to Leadership in the 90s," *Executive Speeches,* July 1989, p. 22.

40. Noel M. Tichy and Mary Anne Devanna, *The Transformational Leader* (New York: John Wiley & Sons, 1986), p. 157.

41. Ibid., p. 210.

42. Ibid., p. 210.

43. Welch, pp. 19–23.

44. Pascale, p. 175.

45. Ibid., p. 108.

46. Warren Bennis, "On the Leading Edge of Change," *Executive Excellence,* April, 1992, p. 6.

47. Tichy, Noel, and Devanna, pp. 27–28.

6

CHAPTER

Bringing About Strategic Change and Incremental Change

"It must be considered that there is nothing more difficult to carry out, nor more doubtful of success, nor more dangerous to handle, than to initiate a new order of things."[1]

—Machiavelli, *The Prince*

The topic of change in the business environment has likely received more press than any other topic in recent years. And for good reason. While change has occurred throughout the history of the world, recent decades have seen the rate of change increase exponentially. Both organizations and people within organizations have been struggling with and resisting this change—it is part of human nature. But change is inevitable; it is critical to success and survival; and it can be painful. While both planned and unplanned change can be painful, the implications of fighting change are far more disastrous.

History is laden with examples of companies and economies that refused to change, resulting in continued decline and often dissolution. Much of Great Britain's fall from world leadership in the 20th century is the direct result of its resistance to changes in technology in its once global cotton industry. America has already lost most of the television, VCR, textiles, and steel industries. The list goes on and on. And companies like

General Motors, Ford, Chrysler, and Xerox had to be driven to crisis by Japanese competitors before they acknowledged the need for change.

The 1980s served as a splash of cold water for many U.S. companies and workers. For the first time in history, others were doing things better, making things cheaper, and creating products faster. And the once loyal American consumer made the decision to buy imports over domestic goods. The industries listed above were the first to face this new threat, and in most cases the reactions were too little too late. However, some companies were able to pull themselves together and make monumental changes in the way they run their businesses. In chapter 12, we discuss Ford at some length, detailing their confrontation with failure and how they transformed themselves into a winning organization.

CHANGE IS AN ALLY

Our objective in this chapter is to paint change as a friend and the ability to change as a competitive weapon. Change has long been viewed as inconvenient, unnecessary, and painful. But we assert that it does not have to be that way. Throughout the book, we will look at some amazing success stories—none of these firms succeeded without pain and casualties. However, there are several kinds of change. Companies that successfully compete in the global market will be masters of two kinds of change— continuous incremental change and occasional strategic leaps.

Some companies are very good at one, but do not have the skills or approach to master the other. Some theorists argue that they are mutually exclusive. However, we believe that organizations need both. For example, a focus on continuous improvement is the logical strategy for a company in a leadership position. It is in the company's interest to keep the rules of the game the same. Yet, when a competitor or new entrant leapfrogs the leader in product, service, quality, and so on, continuous improvement falls short. What is needed is a strategic leap to regain the leadership position.

The Harvard Business School teaches its students this lesson in terms of customer buying factors. Students evaluate a company's products, services, market position, and so on and define each as either a "winner" or a "qualifier." Qualifiers are the requirements that any competitor must have to be considered by a potential customer. Winners, however, are the one or two items that are most important to the customer and usually drive the buying decision. Companies that excel on the winners and meet all the necessary qualifiers are often those that follow a strategy of continuous improvement. They know the rules of the game and have built organizations that play well within those rules. Less competitive companies, however, have no interest in maintaining these rules and will look to change the game to one in which they can excel and win.

The U.S. automobile industry provides a recent example. Up until the 1970s, U.S. automakers were the leaders in making large, comfortable cars. The car buyers wanted size—in fact, during the 1950s and 1960s bragging rights often revolved around who had the longest car! Yet in the 1970s, Japanese automakers, with the help of the oil crisis, sought to change the car-buying game and establish a new set of "winners." The Japanese offered inexpensive, small, basic cars and found that a market did exist. They took this low-end market and used it as a training ground.

The large U.S. automakers were uninterested in this low-volume, low-margin business and ignored this seemingly minor change in the game. Yet during the next several years the Japanese focused on reliability and quality; soon Honda and Toyota offered cars that were cheaper and more reliable than anything in the U.S. market. Customers had never been given the option to discriminate on quality and reliability, but the Japanese changed the game and took enormous share and profits from the Big Three.

Even more interesting is the current trend in car buying. As U.S. companies spent most of the 1980s trying to catch up on quality, the Japanese were working on changing the game again. They are experimenting with complete customization to the buyer's request. Certainly this has been done in the past, but at the cost of several months' wait. The Japanese are now saying, "You can have it any way you like, and we can deliver it within a month." Not only are they dedicated to continuous improvement in the "qualifiers," but they are constantly looking for and developing the "winners" of the future.

So why wait until the leadership position is lost? The winners of the future are already preparing themselves by developing the skills to make strategic leaps and incremental gains concurrently. And the only way to achieve this is through focus. The frontline employees must be given more responsibility and accountability for continuous improvements in current operations. With an empowered and effective frontline organization, the leaders have more time and energy to focus on strategic direction and planning. Without this division of duties, leaders will continue to find themselves fighting today's problems with no time to prepare for the future.

So how common is it that a leading company can actually implement both of these initiatives effectively and at the right time? Not common enough. The Japanese have had a virtual monopoly on these skills for a decade. Big U.S. companies struggled throughout the 1980s to meet the new competitive standards and many have only recently regained profitability. The 1970s and 1980s were times of fierce competition in many industries, and companies were forced to make dramatic changes. We believe this period of turmoil, and in some cases crisis, has provided leaders, managers, and workers with an appreciation of the need for change and a better ability to turn change from a foe to a friend. Companies who can effectively and continuously change will have the most important competitive weapon for the future.

Yet we do not advocate change for the sake of change. Many leaders fall prey to the latest initiatives and consulting fads. At one point, one of the Big Three U.S. automakers had over 30 "top-priority" corporate initiatives that all involved some sort of change. With this proliferation of priorities no one knows where to focus, resulting in little progress. Furthermore, this "program-of-the-month" approach leads to cynicism among middle managers and employees as they begin to doubt the competence of their leaders.

Asking people and organizations to change is extremely difficult, and actually implementing changes takes significant time. Thousands of companies have tried "reengineering" in recent years and fully 70 percent of those have failed to meet their initial objectives. On large-scale projects, leaders must evaluate the situation facing them and make logical decisions on why to change, what to change, and how to change. They must communicate their intentions and provide the leadership and resources to make the effort a success.

This process is fraught with challenges and setbacks. But if selected, high-impact changes are successful, employees and managers become more comfortable with the notion of small changes in their day-to-day activities. The combination of these countless small changes yields extraordinary improvements as well as a more flexible organization. Tom Peters is one of the earliest proponents of change. In his book *Thriving on Chaos* he asserts,

> Change must become the norm, not cause for alarm. The bottom line: if you can't point to something specific that's being done differently from the way it was done when you came to work this morning, you have not "lived," for all intents and purposes: you surely have not earned your paycheck by any stretch of the imagination. Furthermore, the incremental changes of today must almost unfailingly be in support of non-incremental change— that is, a bold goal to be achieved in record time.[2]

In this passage, Peters discusses the concept of incremental change as different from strategic leap changes and proposes that they should work in conjunction. In fact, we believe that these two types of change compound each other, enabling a company to make all changes faster and with less pain than companies who excel at only one.

RESISTANCE STIFLES MOST CHANGE EFFORTS

Before talking about the types of change, it is vital to discuss one of the most significant barriers to change—fear. Fear comes from many sources, but in nearly all cases it manifests itself in the form of resistance. Fear of change is nothing new, from a young child changing schools to the first day at a new job—we all know this feeling. The feeling itself is not nearly as damaging as the behavior it provokes. Burke wrote in 1756, "No passion so effectively robs the mind of all its powers of acting and reasoning as fear." This can be seen over and over as usually pragmatic people turn to inaction, negative thinking, and even sabotage in an effort to block change.

Often leaders think of line employees as the eventual "buyers" of a change and the ones most likely to have fear and mobilize resistance. John Kotter and Leonard Schlesinger of the Harvard Business School outlined several reasons for resistance in their well-known article, "Choosing Strategies for Change." They propose four categorical reasons for resistance: (1) a desire not to lose something of value, (2) a misunderstanding of the change and lack of trust, (3) a belief that the change is not good for the organization, and (4) a low tolerance for change.

Certainly all of these are reasonable, and all can be overcome. Reasons three and four require strong communications and review of the change itself. However, as competition increases and threatens the livelihood of firms and employees, these reasons are becoming less important. Reasons one and two, however, are fundamentally leadership problems. They are the most frequent and most difficult to solve because they are symptoms of the lack of trust between employees and managers. Today many companies tout "people" as their greatest resource, but they fail to develop the trust and stability that encourages people to stretch their capabilities and take risks. Forging new territory without a safety net is like expecting a baby to take its first steps without a pair of outstretched arms ready to help. This leap of faith is exactly what leaders ask their people to take every time they initiate a change; yet many leaders underestimate people's need for support and reassurances that preliminary failures will not lead to punishment.

Two more less talked about but equally powerful sources of fear are the result of the increased team interaction and quantitative requirements in the workplace. Leaders must recognize that empowerment, self-directed teams, and problem-solving task forces require people to speak out in group settings and utilize various analytical skills. While these may not seem like significant problems to managers comfortable with giving presentations and tracking costs, consider the trepidation for line workers who may have limited public-speaking experience or who have done little math since high school. A psychological change often occurs when conversation moves from casual conversation in the cafeteria to a team room; this factor alone can stifle the individual's ability to contribute and thereby weaken the team. In fact, consultants who work with shop floor change efforts note this challenge to engage some individuals in the process. These two particular causes of fear cannot be ignored and should be a part of all change-related training programs.

Fear is not only an issue with lower-level employees. Many leaders would actually argue that middle managers, union bosses, and other power holders see change as threatening to them personally. As we discussed in chapter 2, union leaders have proven far more resistant to change than their constituencies. Companies are trying to push responsibility and control down to the frontline workers. While this trend may empower the union members, it bypasses union leaders and their roles as decision makers, controllers, and representatives. And not only union leaders feel this loss of power. Middle managers everywhere have seen their role change from one of power and direction over employees to one of feedback and support for employees. Many have even seen their jobs simply disappear. Given the pattern of layoffs during the late 1980s and early 1990s, it is no surprise that middle managers are often unwilling participants in major change efforts.

Before moving into the types of changes, we must share one of the single greatest and most devastating tales of resistance in recent history. It is a story not often cited in business texts; it is about a nation, a once great nation, that has nearly destroyed itself by resisting the changes happening around it. Great Britain was once the most powerful nation in the world. Through its many colonies, it dominated world trade during the 1700s and 1800s. Wage levels and living standards were the highest in the world.

Much of this domination resulted from sourcing raw materials overseas and manufacturing intermediate or finished goods in Great Britain. The single most important product for Britain in the late 1800s was cotton cloth. In 1890, the cotton industry represented 26 percent of the nation's exports and was the largest manufacturing employer in the country. At the heart of this boom were machines. Britain had traditionally been responsible for most industrial inventions that would eventually make their way overseas. But during the last two decades of the 19th century, cotton industry inventions were shunned and technological progress came to a screeching halt.

Why did this happen? For over 100 years, the dominant process in British cotton was mule spinning. In fact, this skill was quite respected. Mule spinners became known as the "Aristocrats of the Cotton Trade." The British became so well known for this technology and trade that countries around the world clamored for the business. While the United States, Japan, India, and others were trying to take a share and develop newer, faster technologies, Great Britain became entrenched in the spinning technology which had brought it success.

During the late 1880s, however, American inventors developed a new spinning technology and began using it. By 1913, 87 percent of U.S. spinners had been upgraded. But in Great Britain, only 19 percent had been upgraded, despite the fact that British firms were actually manufacturing this new equipment and exporting it around the world. By 1914, weaving had a similar story. Only 1 to 2 percent of all looms in Britain were automatic while the United Sates boasted nearly 40 percent. Britain's cotton industry was simply unwilling to change, despite the growing competitive pressure. In this year one cotton mill owner in Great Britain is noted to have said, "Let us hear no more childish twaddle about foreign competition." Sound familiar?

You can probably guess the outcome. By early 1929, British cotton exports were barely 50 percent of the 1913 level. Quality and cost were completely uncompetitive in the world market. Yet change still did not occur. By 1954, over half of British spinning still used the mule spinning process and only 12 percent of British looms were automatic. Most firms supplied only domestic needs, aided by high import tariffs. The external trade was nearly extinct. Not until the 1960s did anyone respond. Several corporations tried to consolidate and integrate the industry, but with little success. Between 1979 and 1980, British output of cotton and other fibers fell by 44 percent and cloth by 33 percent. They have never recovered.

Britain was plagued by resistance to change for nearly 100 years. Certainly this is longer than any firm can sustain losses, but the example illustrates just how powerful resistance can be. Britain faced resistance from the "skilled trades" who viewed new technology as not only threatening but dehumanizing. Their voice was so loud that it gave rise to the British

Labour party, which continued to demand wage increases. Firm owners were extremely fragmented and primarily small. Many owned fully depreciated mills dating back to the 1800s. They had no incentive to stop production if they could make even a small amount of money. And the government helped them do so by erecting trade barriers.

Excuses were easy to find—World War I, the Depression, World War II—because no one wanted to admit that Britain's power was faltering. Industries come and go in developed societies, but Britain held on to its ailing cotton industry so long that the nation wasted valuable resources that could have been applied elsewhere. And the impact was clear; Great Britain lagged the rest of Western Europe by over 2 percentage points of GDP growth from 1953 to 1973. [3] They could not change to become competitive, and they could not force reallocation from cotton into another sector. Britain's people, both leaders and workers, were stifled by fear—the fear of admitting failure, and the fear of change.

Other industries in Great Britain suffered as well. While GDP growth lagged behind all other industrialized nations, social programs took on a larger portion of Britain's economy. All these factors contributed to a decline in manufacturing competitiveness that continued until the 1980s. Beginning in the 1980s, however, Margaret Thatcher's tough medicine broke many of the entrenched organizations and gave Great Britain its first hope of a turnaround in nearly 100 years.

FEAR CAN BE OVERCOME

While Great Britain is an extreme example, the pattern is familiar. Fear can stifle even the best organizations and people. It is the responsibility of national leaders and business leaders to recognize this fear and address it. Successful leaders handle this in a variety of ways. Some create fear and a sense of urgency by warning that staying the course is certain death and change represents a chance for survival. While often used, this strategy is difficult to implement unless the underlying data supports the notion of crisis.

John Kotter, noted Harvard Business School professor and expert on change, frequently tells stories of CEOs' attempts to create this organizational "panic." He asserts that nearly 50 percent of organizational change efforts fail because they are unable to create enough urgency to "drive people out of their comfort zones."[4] One drastic example he cites is to use acceptable accounting measures to understate earnings and create the perception of trouble. The U.S. Big Three automakers had real losses in the late 1980s and tried to use this to bargain with unions and suppliers. However, as soon as car sales recovered in the early 1990s, profits returned and the urgency diminished. Regardless of the method, creating a sense of urgency is critical to generate the initial momentum for change.

While creating a sense of urgency is critical to change, no leader can rely on repeated crises to instigate change. Strong leaders take a longer-term approach. They may use crisis to get the ball rolling, but they use incremental change soon thereafter. To motivate change, leaders must reward risk-taking and accept failure as a natural part of this strategy. Longtime CEO of Johnson and Johnson James Burke is widely known as a leader who recognized failures and sought to learn from them. He frequently tells the story of his first encounter with professional failure. At the time he was product manager for Johnson & Johnson, and his product market failed to materialize. When the CEO called Burke into his office, he was certain he was being fired. The CEO asked him what had been his error and if he had learned anything. After his reply the CEO reached out and shook his hand, thanking him for taking chances and learning from his mistakes. He promptly told Burke to keep on taking chances and even making some mistakes—as long as they were new mistakes, not repeats. This exchange had a major impact on Burke's own personal actions as well as his approach to leading others. He, too, has been known to relay this message to his employees, praising not punishing them for taking risks.

Taking risks is often associated with crisis and the necessity for drastic change. However, successful companies take risks when business is best. President John F. Kennedy said, "The time to repair the roof is when the sun is shining." New Ford Motor Company chairman Alex Trotman appears to agree with these words. The Ford that nearly fell by the wayside is back with a vengeance. In 1994, Ford reported record earnings of $5.3 billion, up 110 percent, on record revenues of $128 billion, up 18 percent. Ford's U.S. market share is over 25 percent, held back only by its current capacity to produce its hot Taurus, Mustang, and Explorer models.[5]

Yet in the midst of its 1980s turnaround and resulting 1990s financial success, Trotman is driving Ford to change. He believes his vision to tear apart Ford's regional structure and combine operations into one single, global company will result in a Ford that is more nimble and efficient, bringing cars to market faster and cheaper than competitors. Trotman is not only trying to change Ford's operations, but he hopes to change the mind-set of this 91-year-old company to one that embraces change.

You can read lengthy articles about teams, training, involvement, and so forth, but we believe this is wasted effort if the leaders of the organization fail to "walk the talk." We all know good examples of companies that have program after program to "train" employees, yet it only takes a short time talking to employees to know that trust and acceptance of failure are often lacking. No top-down changes will occur unless the leaders first set the example. This is exactly what occurred at Diamond Offshore, one of the world's largest oil and gas drilling contractors.

Following its acquisition of Odeco Drilling in the early 1990s, the drilling company faced a highly competitive market with excess capacity and low oil and gas prices. Lackluster performance hindered the company from achieving price premiums and full utilization. Yet CEO Robert Rose was determined to turn the company around. He commissioned a customer satisfaction study by consultants A. T. Kearney, Inc. to identify the company's performance relative to competitors and to prioritize customer issues. The resulting below average ratings sent Rose and his management team into action.

Within one month of the study, Rose had written personal letters to every customer and had begun a several-month effort to visit customers. In addition, he made multiple presentations to his employees, both onshore and offshore, to inform them of the company's position and the need to improve. His messages and his action plan were clear and consistent— Diamond Offshore should be the world's best drilling contractor—and Diamond Offshore could be the world's best drilling contractor with the effort and involvement of every employee.

Within one year the results were dramatic. In a follow-up study by A. T. Kearney, the same customers who had rated Diamond Offshore poorly rated them the best in the world. Finally in 1995 an unrelated industry study by Wertheim Schroder also rated Diamond Offshore the best drilling contractor in the industry. While the changes were carried out by employees across the world, the turnaround was championed and fueled by the energies of CEO Rose. Not only did he demand change of his people and organization, but he led the effort through his own actions and example.

Turnaround situations, like those involving Great Britain, Ford, and Diamond Offshore, require fast, decisive, and sometimes painful action. They require leaders with courage who are not afraid to remove resistors and who can stand up against criticism without wavering. Turnarounds are not pleasant, but often successful turnaround leaders thrive on the chaos that they create. This creates the challenge; moving out of crisis mode and back into a strong, continuously improving business is difficult for both leaders and employees. Often this phase requires a different leader. Few people have the skills to successfully move from the crisis leader to empowerer. But the evolution must occur.

STRATEGIC LEAPS PROVIDE MOMENTUM

Strategic leaps do not include the near death experience of turnarounds. Strategic leaps are generated by taking fairly infrequent but significant actions that have a strong impact on the competitiveness of the business. Some examples include new leaders, major product redesigns, new technologies, entry into new markets, facility overhauls, strategic alliances, and so forth. These types of actions often require a short learning period during which performance may actually decline. Once the organization has mastered the tools needed for the new approach, a surge in productivity and overall competitiveness occurs. If the leap is successful, companies often begin looking for another hurdle or challenge for the future. In the meantime, improvements stagnate, yielding the stairstep pattern of change shown in Exhibit 1.

Weyerhaeuser, a paper and forest-products company, has recently taken several strategic leaps to improve its bottom-of-the-industry performance. Since becoming the company's first nonfamily CEO in 1991, John W. Creighton Jr., a low-key man lacking industry background, has led Weyerhaeuser to become one of the industry's most profitable companies. He forced change in several areas. Within his first year, he divested many of the noncore businesses. In addition, he pushed the company through an 18-month reengineering effort to redesign the way each mill and tree farm operated. He spent over $1 billion to modernize three paper plants. Each of these served as a strategic surge, which together added $700 million to

EXHIBIT 1

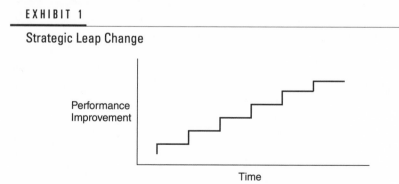

Strategic Leap Change

Performance Improvement

Time

operating earnings by 1995. Over $100 million was cut from corporate overhead, but the rest came through cost reductions and improved output. Some plants have increased output per log by 15 percent and are producing 45 percent more lumber per hour than in 1990.[6] While the entire industry has benefited from higher paper prices, Weyerhaeuser has rocketed past many of its competitors in both earnings and stock price appreciation. Through these strategic leaps, the company has regained its competitiveness—the challenge will now involve finding additional strategic improvements while learning how to make incremental gains.

The strategic leap approach had its roots in the 1960s with the onset of formal strategic planning as the guiding force of the business. Strategic planning revolved around an overall corporate goal, or goals—usually financial—such as ROI, earnings growth, or sales targets. The company then used its strategic planning department to figure out how to achieve the objective. The assumption was "we need to find an action that will get us there." This approach led U.S. companies down a path of major endeavors to yield huge jumps in competitiveness.

This approach grew rapidly in the 1960s and 1970s. Nearly every *Fortune* 1000 company developed a large and powerful strategic planning group to lead the company down the "right path." Lots of money was involved in each decision; therefore, strategic leaps required a high level of expertise and intellect in senior and planning positions. It also understated the role of workers and supervisors. In hindsight it is easy to see the attraction of strategic planning and performance leaps versus incremental, continuous improvements. During the 1960s, the number of MBAs, consultants, lawyers, and investment bankers grew and provided the necessary set of skills to plan these huge business moves. This group was new, flashy, and easier to manage than traditional employees. In addition, unions were extremely powerful and becoming increasingly rigid in their dealings with management. Strategic leaps not only reduced the reliance on union interaction but also the need for highly trained, process-knowledgeable, long-term employees.

Furthermore, the strategic planning process placed most of its emphasis on structural and market changes. Very few, if any, planning groups focused on manufacturing and operating capabilities to leapfrog the competition. The emphasis fell on new products, new markets, and new ventures that required strong top-down management.

While this may sound like a complete bashing of strategic planning, it is not meant to be. Planning filled an important void in American management. It focused on thinking about the future and measuring quantitative performance indexes. It leveraged the people and skills that were becoming available. In moderation, each of these has a positive influence on the business. However, the early success of strategic planning yielded excessive growth in its power and influence that overshadowed the other people, capabilities, and needs of the organization.

Just look at some of the largest companies in the United States today. Which ones always seem to have manufacturing problems, union problems, an inability to make incremental improvements? Which ones are so embraced in an old strategy or planning process that they cannot make a change? Likely you will find a large strategic planning group or at least the remains of one replaced by a horde of strategy consultants. With it you will also find a frontline organization that lacks training, responsibility, and accountability—all the result of years of heavy supervisory direction and lack of employee involvement in operations decision making.

So does this mean we should scrap our strategic planning departments and use of consultants altogether? Of course not. But it does mean that companies must learn how to use them without strangling the rest of their capabilities. Certainly the Japanese are known for their ability to make short-term incremental gains that eventually accumulate into major competitive advantages. They have also learned how to make significant leaps in markets, products, and processes to keep the competition struggling to catch up. We are proposing that U.S. companies must learn to succeed at both strategic leaps and incremental gains. And this is not easy.

Strategic leaps often require large amounts of money and planning. Most companies can manage that. But it is often overlooked that companies must have the capabilities to understand the change at all levels of the organization—this is the key to successful implementation—and this is where most strategic change efforts fail. Many companies were involved in mergers and acquisitions during the 1980s in hopes of finding strategic advantages. However, these strategic mergers typically fail to provide real returns. According to an October 1995 *Business Week* article and Mercer Management Consulting, 50 percent of the 150 largest deals since 1990 eroded shareholder value; another 33 percent provided only marginal returns, leaving only 17 percent of these deals with substantial returns.[7] And one of the primary reasons for these failures is the underemphasized and underdeveloped capabilities of the organization and its employees to fully understand the operations and, therefore, to turn the plans and strategies into successfully implemented actions that enhance performance.

Despite the failures of many recent strategic moves, the importance of developing a series of strategic leaps is clear. Competitive advantages do not last forever. In fact, evidence shows that new processes that improve production are short-lived at best. Recent studies reveal that 60 percent to 90 percent of all "learning" diffuses to competitors. In addition, unionized workers typically pocket two-thirds of any productivity gains in manufacturing. The sustainability of new product innovation is not much better. Competitors reportedly secure detailed information on 70 percent of new products within a year after their development. Furthermore, imitation is nearly a third cheaper and a third faster than developing the product from scratch.[8] And competitive pressures are only increasing as the rate of product, process, and technology change rises dramatically.

Today's strategic leap improvements are often the means for companies to improve from a substandard position and generate momentum among the employees to pursue incremental gains. Many companies in the 1980s and 1990s used this approach of strategic change as a springboard to continuous improvement. Allied Signal CEO Lawrence Bossidy has now become an example of a leader who can make change happen. He took over the helm of Allied Signal in 1991 after a long and successful career with General Electric. He is a proponent of what he calls the "burning platform" theory of change. In an address to McDonnell Douglas in 1993, he described his theory this way:

> When the roustabouts are standing on the offshore oil rig and the foreman yells, "Jump into the water," not only will they not jump, but they will look at the foreman with less than benevolent regard. Only when they see the flames shooting up from the platform will they jump. There may or may not be sharks in the water, but to stay on the burning platform means certain death, so they jump and swim for their lives. Chrysler's platform was burning; they changed. IBM's platform was not visibly burning; they did not. GE's platform was not visibly burning, and they did.[9]

He warns that the platform is burning out there for every company, whether you can see the flames or not. At Allied Signal, Bossidy made a strategic leap by refocusing on the people in the organization. He assessed the position of the company through talking with customers and employees, evaluating the competitive positions of each business, and assessing the financial realities. Based on these efforts he and others at Allied Signal recognized that "we were less than world class, and less than world class was unacceptable."[10] More specifically, they discovered several organizational problems.

- The company was hemorrhaging cash.
- The company's 43 businesses were guarding their own turf.
- There was duplication of administrative functions in accounting, human resources, computers services, and other areas.
- There were 200 purchasing locations.
- The company was inner directed with little focus on the customer.
- Top-down decision making with little training and teamwork was the norm.

For each of these issues, Allied Signal planned and executed a change. Sharing of information and consolidation of purchasing and support services provided immediate cost reductions and improved productivity firmwide. The company implemented a mandatory four-day, intensive team training program to prepare the company for a strategic change. By 1993, after only two years at Allied, every one of Allied's 88,000 employees from Bossidy to the janitors had attended the training, and each person had worked on at least one project using the team approach. And the results speak for themselves. By 1992, Allied teams developed and implemented some 870 separate projects that contributed to a 5.6 percent productivity improvement during flat sales and an additional $400 million in operating income.[11]

So what did Bossidy as the leader do to make these changes happen? Many leaders face the same challenges yet fail. Bossidy went on a traveling campaign to speak to the employees and share his tough, straight talk as well as his vision. Within 60 days he had spoken to over 5,000 employees in sessions of no more than 500 people. He sought to create an environment in which people could and would speak out. The sessions were often lengthy as employees asked tough questions about layoffs and plant closures. But Bossidy was committed to answering every question—and with honesty. He told them that given the declines in defense expenditures and aerospace, layoffs were inevitable. He remained clear in his message and in his reliance on people to make it happen.

Bossidy likens himself to a coach. "I think you don't change a culture. I think you coach people to win. Basically people want to be successful. They want to go home at night and feel that they've made a contribution." So Bossidy gave them the skills and opportunity to make a difference, and the employees did. Bossidy started this journey with a strategic leap to focus on people at this once top-down company. But it is likely he saw no other way. According to an interview he gave to the *Harvard Business Review* in 1995, "Companies don't change incrementally. They change in quantum jumps. If you shoot for anything less, you don't get any change. You may fall short, but still you've made a big difference."[12]

STRATEGIC LEAPS ALONE ARE NOT ENOUGH

Once a strategic leap is made and the benefits achieved, the organization must refocus a portion of its energies on incremental improvements. Successful strategic leaps do not occur at regular increments; they occur when the opportunity or threat arises. Therefore, to maximize the value of the major change efforts, all organizations need the capability to learn, understand, and fine-tune their operations to achieve continuous, smaller gains. Exhibit 2 shows this effect graphically.

INCREMENTAL CHANGES MAXIMIZE STRATEGIC ADVANTAGES

Incremental change requires an entirely different set of organizational skills. While strategic leaps can rely on top-down management, strategic planning, and consultants, incremental change requires expertise and participation at all levels. To achieve both of these requirements, a company must have committed, long-term employees who have a sense of ownership and pride in their work and are willing and able to take risks and experiment. While incremental changes do not typically require significant financial outlays, they do require an empowered culture that rewards risk-taking and occasionally failure. 3M embraces this culture of experimentation. Jim Collins, coauthor of the best-seller *Built to Last: Successful Habits of Visionary Companies*, describes the 3M approach.

> If you add enough branches to a tree and intelligently prune away the deadwood, you'll likely evolve into a collection of healthy branches well positioned to prosper in an ever-changing environment . . . For every successful Post-it in 3M's history, there are tens of unsuccessful experiments that never saw the light of day.[13]

Given the inherent uncertainty of this approach, it is easy to see why many leaders and managers have a harder time implementing change through incremental steps. As mentioned earlier, fear stands as a barrier. People, such as foremen and managers, are reluctant to transfer power to the front line, fearing they will have no control but remain accountable for

EXHIBIT 2

Continuous Improvement Change

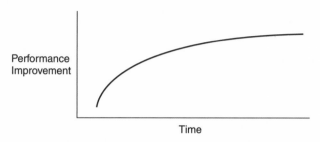

results. Senior leadership is the only means to reduce the fear and free the creativity needed for employee-driven change.

To achieve major progress through incremental change requires many changes in the management approach used by most U.S. companies. In Japan, people are well-educated, cross-trained, given cross-functional assignments and are members of teams. American companies are still struggling with each of these areas. Chapter 2 cites a series of unimpressive statistics on education; training and education funds have fallen as a percent of nondefense spending; unions still stand in the way of many cross-training efforts; and many companies have yet to make the transition from "talking committees" to "working teams."

While many companies try reengineering to achieve strategic leap changes, others have taken less drastic approaches to reengineering to teach their organizations how to learn and achieve incremental gains. Corning, a technology company headquartered in a small Appalachian town, is best known for its ill-fated joint venture with Dow Chemical to produce silicone breast implants. Less talked about is their successful and relatively painless experience with reengineering. After hearing about the attempts by nearly two-thirds of large American companies and the resulting 70 percent failure rate, Corning vowed to avoid the drastic layoffs and "corporate anorexia" in its change effort. In January 1994, the company asked numerous key employees to leave their traditional jobs and redesign the company's operations. They were allocated space, access to senior management, and freedom with which they organized into process teams.

Throughout the effort, the teams held "town meetings" to inform all employees and provided two-way communication for employees to voice concerns. The teams also searched the company's 24 plants to find best practices and leverage purchasing from outside suppliers. While none of these changes were revolutionary, they have produced results. From CEO to shop floor, the levels of managers have fallen from seven to five, forcing managers to focus on broad strategy rather than operational detail. So far, Corning estimates that their incremental efforts will produce $50 to $60 million in savings over three years on annual income of $280 million—and all without massive layoffs.[14] Furthermore, the employees are learning how to change without excessive fear—a key component of all successful continuous improvement efforts.

Other companies have gained incremental improvements by reengineering one process at a time rather than the entire organization at once. Ford Motor Company achieved a 75 percent productivity improvement through its changes in the accounts payable process. Milliken & Company achieved an 89 percent improvement in filling customer orders. Citicorp achieved a 67 percent gain in processing mortgage applications. Toyota earned a 40 percent improvement in product development.[15] Each of these companies achieved results by focusing on a specific process for improvement. Gains do not have to be revolutionary, but companies typically find hundreds of small changes that together have a major impact.

The incremental approach alone, however, is not the means to prosperity. Companies must marshal their skills and resources to deliver occasional strategic leaps as well as continuous improvements. Without strategic leaps, other companies will leapfrog you, or you will eventually find diminishing returns as you focus more energy and resources and derive smaller benefits. This phenomenon, among others, is plaguing the Japanese economy today. As a society, Japan has invested over 30 percent of its GDP, but GDP growth has waned to less than 2 percent from 1990 to 1995. Without new industries and products (i.e., strategic leaps) to spur growth, Japan is only wasting money by continuing with such high investment levels.

WINNERS EXCEL AT BOTH STRATEGIC AND INCREMENTAL CHANGE

A few American companies are leading the way in integrating both types of change in their organizations. They share two common traits—strong leadership at the helm and a strong frontline organization making it happen every day. Allied Signal took major strategic actions—cost cutting, consolidations, and so forth—to drastically change its position. Now, under CEO Lawrence Bossidy, they are also planting the seeds for implementing continuous improvement. They are focusing on people—training,

EXHIBIT 3

Combination Strategic Leaps and Incremental Improvement

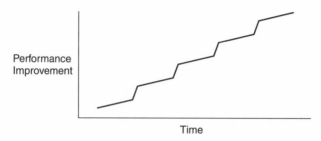

Performance Improvement

Time

team projects, rotations—all in an effort to improve competitiveness by improving the skills of the frontline organization. Without the necessary skills, employees cannot be expected to take responsibility for continuous improvement. According to Bossidy:

> At the end of the day, all the things that make a company a winner—superior technology, leading-edge products, innovative services—all of these are the products of the minds of your employees. The corporate leaders who find a way to activate people's minds and harness their natural desire to succeed will be the leaders of tomorrow's great companies.[16]

And once these minds are activated, countless examples of companies show that people will take the responsibility and deliver results far beyond management's expectations. Not only are the employees more enthusiastic and fulfilled with their jobs, but leaders' time is freed to focus on the external environment and the needs of the future.

With the ability to change both strategically and incrementally, an organization can maximize its improvements. Exhibit 3 illustrates how the potential improvement pattern of the combined approaches yields a greater slope than either strategic or continuous change could achieve alone.

Milliken & Company, winner of the Malcolm Baldrige National Quality Award and longtime proponent of U.S. manufacturing excellence, excels in both strategic and continuous change. Milliken spends significant management time and money studying new markets, new products, and new equipment. The company relies on a variety of high-quality and innovative products to keep it ahead of import competition. Yet Milliken is also known for its exceptional ability to find incremental improvements in cost, quality, process, and service. While the skills required to be successful at strategic thinking and continuous improvement are different, their development goes hand in hand.

At Milliken, management seeks both strong planning and excellent implementation, but they have a strong bias toward implementation. Needless to say, Milliken was not a champion of strategic planning like General Motors, General Electric, and AT&T. Milliken follows the path of strategic thinking without extensive planning infrastructures. Milliken management is wary of sophisticated strategic planning systems because of the negative side effect of eradicating the entrepreneurial spirit among the line organization. So how does Milliken maintain a balance between the need for strategic leaps in technology and products with those of a learning organization that can make continuous improvements? Its organizational leaders focus on both—in writing, in talking, in management time and attention.

Milliken has not achieved success by chance. The company is known for staying ahead of the competition through both strategic advantages and superior execution. The company invests heavily in R&D and new equipment to provide the occasional strategic leaps. In addition, Milliken develops many of its own processes and machines to stay ahead of competitors with proprietary competitive advantages. The company's management also spends significant time visiting leading companies in other industries to force new thinking at the top. Early students of Tom Peters, the Milliken management team promotes strategic thinking and change without a formal strategic planning group.

But Milliken is most lauded for its ability to execute well. From customer response time to production productivity to energy costs, the company rigorously pursues incremental gains. To achieve these gains Milliken relies on its employees. They are cross-trained and rotated across various jobs. The company believes that putting new eyes and ears in different environments will reveal opportunities that others have missed. Process improvement teams are located in every plant to support the line operators and guide continuous improvement efforts. And Milliken recognizes every idea contributed by its people. Yet the expectations are high. Absences or late arrival results in below maximum wages per hour relative to "perfect attendees." Sharing rallies provide a forum for employees to present their ideas and answer questions. Furthermore, Roger Milliken, chairman and CEO, attends these rallies and personally congratulates the initiators of every implemented change effort.

All of this interaction helps build an atmosphere of teamwork and trust. A recent disaster tested the limits of both the employees and management. In January 1995, Milliken's carpet-finishing complex in LaGrange, Georgia, burned to the ground. The company's response was rapid, coordinated, and dramatic. Rather than mourn the loss and make excuses, Milliken took the fire as an opportunity to show customers just how good a supplier it could be. The management team took immediate action and planned the company's response. And the employees, both in production and sales/service, were prepared to implement that response. Within four days, salespeople called nearly 2,000 affected customers and offered reassurances that critical needs would be met. By 3:00 A.M. the next day, over 30 employee teams were addressing every possible concern, from personnel to reconstruction. Each team produced a report of its findings and action plans to Chief Operating Officer Dr. Tom Malone by noon. And what about the employees displaced by the fire? Many companies would have taken the opportunity to force layoffs—but not at Milliken. Within two weeks, 600 of the 720 employees had new positions in Milliken facilities—some as far away as Great Britain and Japan.[17] Here again, the leadership team set the strategy and relied on the flexible frontline organization to carry out the actions.

Dedication and rapid response like that at Milliken cannot occur overnight. But the benefits of such an atmosphere are clear. Not only does Milliken excel during normal operations, but the implementation orientation of its culture was critical during its time of crisis. The leaders at Milliken exert significant effort to foster this atmosphere of employee-led continuous improvement; and by doing this successfully, the leaders have more time to focus on the critical, yet more sporadic strategic leaps to carry Milliken into the future.

LEADERSHIP IS THE KEY

The Allied Signal and Milliken examples both illustrate the importance of people at all levels of the organization in making these changes work for a company. And successful change implementors like these companies all have strong leadership. Strong does not mean top-down or controlling. It does mean setting the standard with actions and words that allow employees to develop trust and courage to take risks and have accountability for incremental improvement. By giving the frontline decision-making power to the frontline employees, management does much more than improve morale and job satisfaction. Management frees time for itself to focus on the future and in doing so unleashes the creative powers of the entire organization. With creativity comes change and with change comes a competitive weapon that is hard to replicate or overcome.

The lesson, therefore, is clear. To remain a long-term leader in any market, the organization must have the capabilities to make not only strategic changes but incremental improvements as well. And to develop each of these skills, leadership must empower its people to make continuous change and focus its own efforts on the strategic leaps to carry the organization into the future.

MOVING ON

We now turn our attention to team building.

ENDNOTES

1. Niccolo Machiavelli, *The Prince.*
2. Tom Peters, *Thriving on Chaos* (New York: Alfred Knopf, 1988), p. 464.
3. William E. Lazonick, "The Decline of the British Cotton Industry," Harvard Business School Case - 9-391-253, p. 1–20, 1984.
4. John P. Kotter, "Leading Change: Why Transformation Efforts Fail," *Harvard Business Review*, March–April 1995, p. 60.
5. James B. Treece and Kathleen Kerwin, "Ford: Alex Trotman's Daring Global Strategy," *Business Week*, April 3, 1995, p. 95.
6. Dori Jones Yang, "The New Growth at Weyerhaeuser," *Business Week*, June 19, 1995, p. 63.
7. Phillip Zweig, "The Case against Mergers," *Business Week*, October 30, 1995, p. 125.
8. Pankaj Ghemawat, "Sustainable Advantage," *Harvard Business Review*, September–October 1986, p. 53.
9. Lawrence A. Bossidy, Chairman and CEO Allied-Signal Inc., address to McDonnell Douglas Masters Program, Long Beach, California, July 1, 1993.
10. Ibid.
11. Ibid.
12. Noel Tichy and Ram Charan, "The CEO As Coach: An Interview with Allied Signal's Lawrence Bossidy," *Harvard Business Review*, March–April 1995, p. 78.
13. Tom Brown, "Greatness That Endures," *Industry Week*, September 5, 1994, p. 14.
14. "Reengineering with Love," *The Economist*, September 9, 1995, p. 70.

15. "Making Reengineering Work," a White Paper prepared by Development Dimensions International for the PEPI Conference Reengineering Forum, October 1994, p. 3.

16. Lawrence A. Bossidy, Chairman and CEO Allied-Signal Inc., address to McDonnell Douglas Masters Program, Long Beach, California, July 1, 1993.

17. David Greising, "A Company That Knows How to Put Out a Fire," *Business Week*, February 27, 1995, p. 50.

7
CHAPTER

Teamwork: Leadership from the Top

Teams are one of the most powerful managerial concepts in the history of business. And much has been written about teams from the perspective of the individual—empowerment, decision making, training/knowledge, accountability. Already, more than 80 percent of leading U.S. companies use teams in one form or another. Yet 80 percent of U.S. companies are not leaders in the marketplace. Therefore, something sets apart organizations that derive great value from their teams. We believe that "something" is leadership—leadership from the top as well as leadership within the teams.

Yet some companies, like Shelby Die Casting Company, have taken a radical team approach that appears to require no leaders. The Shelby, Mississippi, metal-casing manufacturer was desperate to save its plant from closure. Management renamed the plant's line workers "associates," assigned them to teams, and provided group problem-solving training. Yet racial problems between mostly minority line workers and mostly white supervisors stymied progress. Supervisors failed to listen and workers failed to offer opinions. Finally, the company chairman, G. Rives Neblett, took a drastic step. He eliminated the supervisors' jobs, saving $250,000, and let the workers run their own teams. Productivity rose by 50 percent, and profits doubled within two years.

It sounds like a dream come true. And all without leaders? Not really. The supervisors were removed because they were *not* providing leadership. But leadership was provided by Chairman Neblett. He removed the divisions among the workforce. According to Neblett, "People at the plant are not allowed to think about race anymore. It is not an issue."[1] He also reinforced the sense of urgency with the threat of plant closure and held the workers directly accountable for the plant's survival. He encouraged the workers to use their minds and provided them with an opportunity to make a difference. All in all, he provided leadership.

There is no substitute for leadership. Organizations need it. Individuals need it. And even empowered teams need it. This chapter addresses the critical role of leaders in making teams successful. Organizations that effectively utilize teams have not only strong team leaders within the team but strong leadership at the top of the organization. Both of these roles are critical. While many organizations have one or the other, few have marshaled the resources and developed the attitudes that generate both the effective application *and* day-to-day progress of teams.

Organizations that achieve outstanding performance through teams have one other necessary component—consistency within the shared responsibilities of organizational leaders and team leaders. Jim Collins and Jerry Porras, coauthors of the best-seller *Built to Last: Successful Habits of Visionary Companies,* emphasize the need for consistency. According to their research, visionary companies

> Put in place pieces that reinforce each other, clustered together to deliver a powerful combined punch. They search for synergy and linkages. A key concept that came out of our work is the notion of "alignment"—all the pieces of the organization aligned to work in concert to send a consistent set of reinforcing signals. If the signals sent are consistent with each other, you tend to get much more organized and effective behavior. If they are inconsistent, who knows what you'll get?[2]

DEFINING ROLES

Today's competitive workplace is forcing both managers and frontline workers alike to reevaluate their roles in the organization. Given the rate of change and the size and complexity of operations, few if any leaders have the skills or knowledge to direct all organizational activities. As discussed in chapter 6, leaders must view their role as one of strategic thinking for the future and support of day-to-day operations. Employees must be given the responsibility and accountability for actually carrying out the day-to-day activities and decision making. Robert Reich, U.S. Secretary of Labor under President Bill Clinton, describes this new contract in the workplace. "As a manager, I will do everything I can to make my employees increasingly valuable. As a worker, I will do everything I can to make my company profitable."[3]

Making employees increasingly valuable is what teams are all about. Top management must not only recognize the need for this change in contract, but lead the effort through words, actions, and examples. Senior-level leaders play the pivotal role of deciding when and where teams are appropriate in their organizations. In addition, these leaders are responsible for understanding the types of teams available and which type to apply to each specific situation. Teams are particularly effective in two instances—problem-solving groups and self-managed groups who make or do things. Each type can be very powerful; but each type must be applied and supported differently. The effective application of teams is the direct responsibility of senior-level leaders.

The team leader's role is quite different. The team leader's primary function is to guide the team's approach, methods, and interaction. Regardless of what type of team is enacted, the team leader oversees the day-to-day progress of the group toward its objective. Jon Katzenbach and Douglas Smith, coauthors of *The Wisdom of Teams*, describe the role and challenges facing team leaders as those who

> Act to clarify purpose and goals, build commitment and self-confidence, strengthen the team's collective skills and approach, remove externally imposed obstacles, and create opportunities for others. Most important, like all members of the team, *team leaders do real work themselves*. Yet, in each of these aspects, team leaders know or discover when their own action can hinder the team, and how their patience can energize it. Put differently, team performance almost always depends on how well team leaders strike a critical balance between doing things themselves and letting other people do them.[4]

Finally, both senior-level leaders and team leaders share the responsibility for support and well-being of the team. This support involves ongoing commitment to the objective, honesty and communication, clear accountability for results, and a fair reward system. Overall, these shared roles require both leaders to maintain a clear, consistent, and strong focus on performance—not effort, not behavior, not team makeup—only results. No team can succeed without it.

LEADERS AT THE TOP - TEAMS ARE A TOOL

Teams are just like any other tool. They can be very powerful if used correctly, and they can be complete time wasters if used inappropriately. There is no doubt that teams have the potential to drastically improve performance. The success of team proponents such as Ford, GE, Allied Signal, Motorola, and Johnsonville Foods cannot be disputed. Yet teams alone are not enough. Strong management and a competitive strategy must guide the use of teams.

To effectively guide the use of teams, management must understand what teams are and when teams are appropriate. First, a team is *not* any group of people who work together. *Nor* is it the entire workforce of a division or company. A team *is* a discrete group of individuals with a common, specific goal who hold themselves accountable for performance as both individuals and as a group.

Because of this shared accountability, teams are most appropriate when coordination of various steps, skills, or individuals is necessary. Tasks that do not require coordination are better left to individuals. Highly specialized analytics or simple tasks are better performed by an individual who can quickly and accurately complete the task. William Tracey, team-building expert and author of several books including *Critical Skills,* warns, "Teams should never be assigned to tasks or functions that can be better performed by a single manager; they should be used only when they can be more effective than a single individual."[5]

As leaders, we encourage you to look closely at your organization, processes, and tasks. Oftentimes the potential benefits of a team are not readily apparent. Flocks of geese provide an unusual but very appropriate example of how a team can achieve the same objectives as an individual, but with better efficiency and safety. Every aspect of the flock organization remains focused on the achievement of a common goal. Egos, titles, divisions, or excuses are not permitted to deter the group from its objective. People can learn some valuable lessons from these seemingly simple creatures.

A Flock of Geese

- Each member is responsible for getting itself to wherever the flock is going: Each member looks to itself—not the leader—to determine what to do.
- Every member knows the direction of the flock. Sharing the common direction makes assuming the leadership role easier.

- Every member is willing to assume leadership when the flock needs it. When the lead goose gets tired, a fresher goose from back in the pack assumes the leadership position. The flock then maintains the fastest pace.
- Followers encourage the leaders. Members honk from the rear to encourage the leaders to maintain the fastest pace.
- Members look after each other, helping all members achieve the goal. If a wounded goose goes down, two geese follow it and protect and feed it until it either recovers or dies. They then resume flight, either finding their original flock or joining another.
- When the nature of the work changes, the geese reorganize themselves for the best results. They fly in a "V," land in waves, and feed in fours.
- Cooperation and teamwork result in exceptional performance. The uplift from the members in front provides additional range and speed for the entire flock.

Geese illustrate several simple but effective lessons about the benefits of teams over individuals. Group encouragement spurs additional effort, leaders are necessary but interchangeable, organization of work depends on the task, accountability for individual and group performance is paramount, and seemingly small adjustments can yield amazing results.

Before launching into organizationwide team efforts to seek dramatic performance increases, leaders must also understand that teams are an expensive and time-consuming proposition. Given the new set of skills required for conflict management, decision making, problem solving, and so on, companies often spend an additional 10 to 15 percent of an employee's annual salary/wages for the necessary training. Furthermore, time consumed in training averages four to six hours per week, or 10 to 15 percent of the workweek. Given these costs, companies must expect in excess of 15 percent productivity gains to offset the initial costs of lost time alone.[6]

While successful team efforts far surpass the 15 percent productivity gains, they typically do not happen overnight. Many managers underestimate the difficulty associated with becoming a team driven organization. Peter Drucker, management guru and proponent of the "learning organization," warns leaders, "You can't rush teams. It takes five years just to learn to build a team and decide what kind you want." While these estimates may seem long, research on teams consistently shows that most companies take more than a decade to make a full transition to self-managed teams.

One senior human resources vice president of a *Fortune* 500 company described his company's lengthy but worthwhile implementation of teams.

> We used to have 780 people; now we're down to 400. The structure used to be eight managers and a raft of supervisors, about 25 . . . We've been able to do this at the same time that our work has doubled. These teams are self-directed. They do their own appraisals and manage their compensation.

Yet the vice president continued, "We started this in 1985, and it took us eight years to train people for team building . . . We took it one piece at a time . . . It's a very powerful thing to have these teams doing this type of work without any input from management."[7]

Because leaders often fail to realize the long learning curve for achieving high-performance teams, many leaders lose focus and withdraw the necessary commitment and resources. Teams are not a quick fix. They are a long-term investment in people and in the future. But the returns are well worth the investment.

Certainly empowered teams like this are the envy of most organizations. Yet getting started does not require full organizational rollout. Most companies experiment with teams in a few pilot areas, learn as they go, and convert their organizations as necessary. The "as necessary" depends on the need for and urgency of change. In *The Wisdom of Teams*, Katzenbach and Smith provide four pointed questions to evaluate the magnitude of and readiness for change within an organization.

- Does the organization have to get very good at one or more basic things it is not very good at now (e.g., new skills and values)?
- Do large numbers of people throughout the entire organization have to change specific behaviors (i.e., do things differently)?
- Does the organization have a track record of success in changes of this type?
- Do people throughout the organization understand the implications of the change for their own behaviors and urgently believe that the time to act is now?[8]

If the answers to the first two questions are "yes" and the second two are "no," then a major change is necessary. The urgency of the change is dependent on the financial situation and competitive environment of the company. Just as at Shelby Die Casting Company and Allied Signal, the situations were urgent and the preparation was low. However, both had courageous leaders who took drastic steps. Among these steps were rapid and widespread team implementation.

In less critical situations, leaders have more time to prepare themselves and their organizations for the move toward teams. Both problem-solving teams and self-directed work teams can be explored. Yet leaders must be wary of growing complacent. Leaders and teams must feel the pressure and need for change whether they see the "burning platform" or not.

PROBLEM-SOLVING TEAMS FOR FAST RESULTS

Problem-solving teams are the most widely used and easily implemented of all team formats. *Training* magazine reported in 1994 that 100 percent of the *Fortune* 1000 had used these project specific teams.[9] These teams can provide fast results, but senior leaders must understand their capabilities and limitations.

Much of the ease in implementation is due to the design and purpose of problem-solving teams. They are typically a part of some type of corporate program or agenda—quality circles, project teams, task teams, continuous improvement teams, et cetera. The objective of problem-solving teams is to evaluate and provide recommendations on how to solve a specific problem. Problem-solving teams are not meant to make or do things; their charter is to recommend and when appropriate to implement. These teams often comprise volunteers who take on the responsibility in addition to their regular jobs. While the teams typically meet for a few hours per week, the length and frequency of meetings is driven by the team and its objective. Once recommendations are made to senior management, however, the team is disbanded or given a new assignment.

Senior-level support for problem-solving teams is critical from the outset. Senior leaders must provide a clear and specific problem, meant to be solved in a relatively short time frame. Because of the short, focused effort of the team, selection of individuals with the appropriate skills and information to tackle the problem is critical. By aligning the proper skill sets, extensive training is not required to find a solution. Many teams go through interpersonal training courses, yet the focused and short-term nature of the assignments typically overcome significant personality conflicts. These teams stick to solving a specific problem and avoid the more managerial issues faced by self-directed work teams, such as hiring, firing, compensation, reward, and so forth.

While problem-solving teams are more easily initiated and supported, they have one great challenge to overcome—implementation. Typically the team presents recommendations to senior management and then disbands. Management decides whether to proceed and then designates a person or group to implement the recommendations. More often than not, this group is not the problem-solving team. This creates several problems. First, the team typically does not see its recommendations through to implementation. As owners of the recommendations, the team members have personal stakes in seeing their ideas reach fruition. Yet these energies and egos are wasted by removing them from the process.

Second, if recommendations are not followed or implementation falls through, team members may have negative feelings toward their team experience and communicate them to their co-workers. Negative perceptions of team experiences will only impede future team efforts within the organization.

Third, the people being impacted by the recommendations often do not understand the logic behind the proposed changes. Without the problem-solving group to explain the rationale, the implementation group may be skeptical and unnecessarily resist the change for lack of communication. Fourth, top leaders often fail to hold the problem-solving team accountable for timely and thoughtful recommendations. All of these problems are a direct result of the lack of commitment by senior leaders. Voluntary team members work in good faith that leaders will respond to their recommendations; therefore, leaders must remain committed or risk losing the respect of the team members and ultimately the organization.

Lack of commitment by senior leaders was to blame in the implementation failure of a problem-solving team at Burlington Northern. A team of 14 people at Burlington Northern was given 45 days to achieve the weighty task of recommending the best organizational approach to marketing. To do the majority of the work, the team leader chose an experienced core group who had skills, knew the company, and had no political baggage. Within 45 days they delivered a set of recommendations that drastically challenged the current approach to marketing. The team had a thought-provoking and rewarding discussion with top management and then disbanded.

However, neither the problem-solving team nor senior management thought to involve the marketing organization in their process. Top management passed the recommendations on to marketing, but marketing was neither asked to, nor did they, spend time trying to understand the changes.

Resistance was high as many of the recommendations required major changes and risks within the marketing group. Without either a "believer" in the marketing group to spearhead the effort or pressure from the top, the marketing people did nothing. Top management failed to hold them accountable for implementation, and nothing changed.[10]

To make problem-solving teams as effective as possible and overcome the potential pitfalls, organizational leaders should follow several guidelines:

- Define a problem and specify a clear goal of solving it in a given time period.
- Spend time thinking about the skills needed to solve the problem and assign individuals with these skills to the team.
- Keep eyes and ears open for possible obstacles to the team's progress (i.e., political, personal, skill sets), and work vigorously to remove them.
- Initiate only a few, high-profile teams and commit time and energy to them.
- Involve team members in the management decision-making process or at least the decision rationale to ensure that team members do not feel their time was wasted.
- Involve team members in implementation as communicators, facilitators, leaders and/or workers. Encourage early involvement of potential "changees" through interviews, information sessions, and so forth.
- Recognize and thank team members for their time and effort, regardless of the outcome. Ensure that performance appraisals include the extra effort and accomplishment.

Early on, leaders should initiate only a few, high-impact problem-solving teams to which they can devote time and energy. After leaders learn how to utilize these teams, they can be spread throughout all areas of the organization. Milliken and Company, discussed in chapter 6 as a leader in continuous improvement, has earned its reputation in large part from its effective use of problem-solving teams. While problem-solving team members generally have other full-time jobs, Milliken sometimes assigns people to problem-solving efforts full-time.

During the recession of the early 1980s, Milliken needed to curtail some of its operations, but was opposed to initiating painful layoffs. To solve the dilemma, Milliken pulled the excess people from the operation and assigned them to a variety of problem-solving teams. The projects were all of a short-term nature, but as problems were solved, individuals were assigned to other problems. In less than a year, the problem-solving teams had identified and achieved savings well in excess of the cost of the members' compensation. Through attrition, many of these "full-time problem solvers" eventually made their way back into full-time jobs and were instrumental in leading future problem-solving teams.

Countless examples exist to demonstrate successful and failed problem-solving team efforts. It is within the power of the organization's leaders to improve the odds that their own organization will be among the winners.

SELF-MANAGED TEAMS—LEADERS SHOULDN'T JUST LET GO

Self-managed teams are by definition more dependent on the employees themselves, and therefore have been more difficult for leaders to implement. Despite widespread praise, only 50 percent of *Fortune* 500 companies report using self-directed work teams as a part of their organizational structure as of 1994.[11] Yet while the leader's role is less defined, senior leadership remains critical to the team's success. The senior-level leader's role in these empowered teams lies in defining the performance expectations, setting up the structural and support systems, and maintaining focused attention on the progress and results of the team.

Self-directed teams, otherwise known as self-managing teams, autonomous work groups, high-commitment teams, or empowered employees, represent an entire change in organizational design. The traditional hierarchy of managers, supervisors, and workers is replaced by a working team entirely responsible for its own operations. The team members are individually and jointly accountable for performance and results. To build this accountability, team membership is full-time, mandatory, and part of the job itself. These teams improve their performance by continually identifying and solving problems—everything from minor housekeeping issues to process redesign. They control everything from scheduling, production, and quality, to selecting and often rotating leadership, to evaluating each other, to hiring, disciplining, and firing members.

In this "supervisor-free," more personally rewarding environment, employees are exposed to all of the team's operations and skills. This exposure not only forces learning on the job but constantly challenges members to evaluate more productive ways to work.

All of this freedom and exposure is precisely what frightens many managers and organizational leaders. Many leaders do not realize that they now possess an even more critical and highly leveraged position in the organization. No longer can leaders earn their keep by solving day-to-day problems—they must take on the vital role of establishing a vision, a thoughtful strategy, and an executable plan. Self-managed teams can be a very powerful weapon in executing the plan. Therefore, leaders must be sure they are moving in the right direction, applied in the right areas, and adequately supported. Katzenbach and Smith, coauthors of *The Wisdom of Teams,* counsel top management to concentrate on the performance challenge at what they call the company's "critical delivery points"—that is, places in the organization where the cost and value of the company's products and services are most directly determined. Such critical delivery points might include where accounts get managed, customer service performed, products designed, and productivity determined.

These experts also agree that teams do not always produce better performance at these "critical delivery points." They counsel:

> If performance at the critical delivery points depends on combining multiple skills, perspectives, and judgments in real time, the team option makes sense. If, on the other hand, an arrangement based on individual roles and accountabilities is the best way to deliver the value customers require at the right cost, teams may be unnecessary and possibly disruptive.[12]

It is up to the organization's leaders to make these decisions. And they should be made carefully. As discussed earlier, the personal and financial costs of implementing widespread self-directed work teams can be extremely high. And the rewards can be both slow and uncertain in materializing. Leaders should be wary of overextending the organization's resources unless crisis dictates radical action. Senior-level leaders often underestimate the extensive training, room for experimentation and failure, and employee reallocation that are required before teams can be successful. Furthermore, teams of all kinds can quickly be perceived as the "flavor of the month" by employees if leaders do not communicate their rationale for and commitment to this new organizational structure.

Employees are quick to notice if leaders take the "empowerment thing" too far and paralyze the organization with teams. One unionized manufacturing company became so overly enamored with the team concept that union members complained.

> Hell, we always ran this place. But when we had a problem we could go to the boss . . . We can't get anybody in management to talk to us without

getting in a team. And we're considered bad people if we can't solve all our own problems. There's a supervisor over there who's been here for 30 years and has the answer, but we get shamed out of asking him. It goes against the team rules.[13]

Clearly leaders face a difficult challenge of yielding control to workers while providing the necessary support structures and guidance to achieve success. There is no single recipe to achieve this balance, but one thing is clear. Self-directed teams require strong leadership from the top—both in planning and supporting the effort.

Several guidelines are useful for leaders as they consider the implementation of self-directed teams.

- Evaluate the organization, talk to customers, and compare against competitors to determine the "critical delivery points."
- Determine the company's performance in these critical areas relative to customer needs and competitor capabilities.
- Prioritize the critical areas by importance to the customer, the performance gap, and potential for successful change.
- Evaluate the coordination requirements for each critical point to establish its potential for organization into a team.
- Determine the organization's team support capabilities (training, financial resources, time, etc.) and select the top few critical areas where teams are appropriate; establish teams based on work groups, processes, or other logical breakdowns; identify potential team leaders.
- Set high performance expectations for the team and communicate them repeatedly and consistently to the team and the organization.
- Allow for failures, but press for learning, measure progress, and communicate "small wins."
- Hold the team and individuals accountable for performance and establish a reward system based on performance of the team as well as each individual's contribution.
- Remain committed to *performance*. Period.

In addition to the guidelines above, senior-level leaders share several additional responsibilities with the internal team leaders. These responsibilities will be discussed later in the chapter.

INTERNAL TEAM LEADERS—THE OIL THAT STOPS THE SQUEAKING

Organizational leaders set the stage for strong team performance, but the team leaders make it happen. Not only is the team leader responsible for the progress and results of the team, but he or she must guide without overpowering the team as it struggles to set norms, resolve conflict, change members, solve problems, and make mistakes. Most importantly, though, the team leader must keep the team focused on performance.

By focusing on performance, the team can minimize the many problems inherent in having large groups of people working together. Lofty performance goals focus people's energies on the goal rather than each other. Lofty performance goals also imply that no individual can achieve the goal alone. Only the team can make it happen. Therefore, individuals find it easier to set aside egos, titles, and personality conflicts in pursuit of team performance. The Outward Bound program enhances team building by setting one challenging team objective and holding each individual accountable for the team's results. The team fails if all members do not complete the challenge—climbing a wall, finishing a course, crossing a river, and so forth. Specific team objectives have a leveling effect that nullifies the titles, perks, and politics of the workplace. By removing these barriers, the team leader can keep the group focused on the specific objective and encourage them to evaluate how each team member can individually contribute to achieving the team's performance objective.

Once the team is established and has a clear objective, the team leader must work to get the team off to a good start. Meetings are the typical arena for initial team interaction; therefore, they must be effective. The leader must set the tone with his or her own behavior. Ego can lead to the rapid downfall of the team leader if he or she becomes distracted by self-importance. Leaders who are late, dominate meetings, leave for phone calls, or otherwise violate the "rules" will never achieve the commitment, discipline, and communications required to make the team successful. These dynamics can only be achieved by setting some team behavioral norms. According to Katzenbach and Smith, coauthors of *The Wisdom of Teams*,

> The most critical initial rules pertain to attendance (for example, "no interruptions to take phone calls"), discussion ("no sacred cows"), confidentiality ("the only things to leave this room are what we agree on"), analytical approach ("facts are friendly"), end-product orientation ("everyone gets assignments and does them"), constructive confirmation ("no finger

pointing"), and, often the most important, contributions ("everyone does real work").[14]

It is not the leader's role to define these behaviors, but to initiate discussions and let the team develop its own norms. But it is the leader's role to follow them.

Resolving conflicts is one of the team leader's most difficult yet most important roles. The leader walks a fine line between forcing early resolution of conflicts and letting the team solve them naturally. The problem with natural team resolution is that it often takes a long time, allowing problems to fester and worsen. While uncomfortable, team leaders must force discussion over conflicts as early as possible. Whether personalities, processes, skills, or behaviors are at issue, the team cannot develop itself and remain focused on the performance objective if underlying problems exist. On occasion, resolution may require changing the makeup of the team. Just as sports teams often stumble if a player is removed due to injury, penalty, or discipline, business teams face disruption when members are lost. If an individual has to be removed and replaced, though, it is in the team's interest to make these changes early. The team leader must remain alert to all of these potential conflicts and respond quickly.

Problematic conflict, however, is not the same as healthy disagreement on ideas. Team leaders must foster an atmosphere of open discussion and challenging debate. This requires the leader to actively engage all members of the team, not just the most vocal individuals. Low participators often have very good ideas but are reluctant to contribute because they are often interrupted or squeezed out by dominant individuals. Considerable research shows that the most frequently stated and discussed ideas tend to be adopted by the group, regardless of their quality. Norman Maier, the author of the *Psychological Review* article "Assets and Liabilities in Group Problem Solving," calls this the "valence effect" and identifies it as a major reason that teams make poor decisions.[15] When great disparity exists among the contributions of various team members, leaders should take it as a clue that the process is not effective and must be adjusted.

Some teams suffer from a lack of conflict and challenge among the members. This phenomenon, often referred to as "groupthink," typically affects teams of friends, longtime co-workers, and teams with powerful social pressures to conform. These teams become impotent when concurrence seeking becomes so dominant in a cohesive group that it overrides the realistic evaluation of various alternatives. This problem was discussed in detail in chapter 5.

Some very famous decision-making teams have exercised poor judgment due to groupthink. President John F. Kennedy asked his advisers the question, "How could we have been so stupid?" during the Bay of Pigs debacle. Indeed, how could one of the most intellectually talented sets of advisers, including Dean Rusk, Robert McNamara, Robert Kennedy, Arthur Schlesinger Jr., Allen Dulles, and others, have failed to ask questions, raise doubts and concerns, or make contingency plans for such a dangerous invasion? Irving Janis, author of "Groupthink," spent two years studying decision-making teams that made ill-fated decisions—he blames groupthink.

According to Janis, groupthink brings with it a sense of invulnerability and selected listening. President Kennedy's advisers relied on surprise to ensure that the invasion would succeed. Yet they ignored warnings that plans for the invasion had been leaked. Furthermore, they underestimated the capabilities and response of Premier Fidel Castro. None of Kennedy's advisers ever publicly questioned the CIA's assumptions about Castro's military might or willingness to use it. Only one member raised doubts at all. Arthur Schlesinger Jr. expressed his strong objections in a private memorandum to President Kennedy and Secretary of State Rusk, but he was unwilling to speak out publicly within the team.

Based on his research, Janis believes President Kennedy raised more questions than others over the Bay of Pigs plans, yet he

> encouraged the group's docile, uncritical acceptance of defective arguments in favor of the CIA's plans. At every meeting, he allowed the CIA representative to dominate the discussion . . . And at the most crucial meeting, when he was calling on each member to give his vote for or against the plan, he did not call on Arthur Schlesinger, the one man there who was known by the President to have serious misgivings.[16]

Not only did President Kennedy, as the team leader, fail to encourage discussion and healthy conflict, he discouraged the openness and dialogue that is critical for effective team decision making. In this situation President Kennedy, like many team members, appeared to favor the perception of unanimity over performance. Janis warns that high-level, intelligent individuals must be especially wary of the problem of groupthink, because they have tremendous influence over people who are either too insecure or too politically motivated to challenge their views.

Schlesinger's own writings provide evidence of their groupthink. "Our meetings took place in a curious atmosphere of assumed consensus"—even though postmortem research clearly reveals that the consensus was an illusion.[17]

Team leaders must suspect and challenge unanimity, pushing team members to think critically and share their ideas. In some cases, the team leader may even have to probe members individually. To avoid potential groupthink problems, a healthy pattern of discussion and debate should be developed early. The team leader can appoint "devil's advocates" and set an example by offering a mediocre idea and letting the team dismiss it. Even outsiders or visitors can be used occasionally to provoke discussions. Regardless of the means, critical thinking must occur—and the team leader must encourage it.

The final role of a team leader is holding the team accountable for performance. Accountability is so important to performance, whether team or individual, that chapter 8 is entirely dedicated to this topic. Team leaders have the additional challenge, however, of cultivating the accountability not only for the team's performance but for each member to the others. A team leader will never succeed if he or she is solely responsible for holding people accountable. The leader must inspire a sense of mutual dependence. Successful teams become so reliant on each other that an individual will go to great lengths to avoid letting the team down. Yet poor behavior such as absence, tardiness, missed deadlines, and so on must all be disciplined. Many teams use psychological discipline, but more successful teams use schemes that are more inventive. Examples of financial punishment are abundant and effective. From senior executive teams to plant floor teams, members contribute "penance" money which is later used for team parties or charities. As discussed earlier, however, more drastic steps are sometimes required to enforce accountability. Team leaders must have the courage to discipline and even remove members who hold up the team process.

Without these five pillars—performance focus, team norms, conflict resolution, critical thinking, and accountability—team leaders will face extreme difficulty in developing productive teams.

SHARED ROLES ENSURE A CONSISTENT MESSAGE

The shared roles of organizational leaders and team leaders provide the consistency that is imperative in team efforts. Both levels of team leadership require commitment to performance, support of team needs, emphasis on accountability, and consistency of reward philosophies. Commitment, support, and accountability, however, require distinctly different actions from the organizational leaders versus the team leader as discussed earlier in the chapter. Only reward stands out as a shared role with identical responsibilities.

And reward is an area that most employees, from CEO to housekeeping staff, hold close to the heart. With over 50 percent of U.S. employees expected to participate in teams in 1995, the question of team compensation and reward has been repeatedly asked by workers. "How will I be measured? How will I be rewarded?" Organizational leaders must answer these questions with a philosophy and policies that yield consistent and fair results *and* motivate exceptional performance.

Many companies are experimenting with team pay in which each individual's compensation is tied to the team's performance. Hallmark Cards, Ameritech, American Express, and Trigon Blue Cross/Blue Shield are only a few companies experimenting with team pay. Yet team pay often leaves individuals feeling wronged. More specifically, team pay in its purest form rewards the high performers and the low performers on a team equally—based on team performance. This pattern provides no incentive for individuals to go the extra mile—nor does it hold low performers accountable for their output or encourage them to improve. In addition, teams also have roles for high-value providers as well as lower-value providers. Both roles are important and both individuals may excel in their roles. But is it logical to pay them equally?

Consider a professional basketball team. Does it make any sense at all to consider paying the Chicago Bulls' Michael Jordan the same as the other four starters if he provides 40 percent of the points and 90 percent of the hype? And how much should a star athlete be punished if his or her performance is exceptional, but the team loses? Clearly, consistently low performance by the team will inhibit the total team reward available, but the issue is allocation. Stars should be rewarded as stars—both in sports and in business. This is what accountability is all about.

Leaders, both of organizations and teams must have the courage to reward people for their individual contributions. Teams are used to enhance individual's capabilities, not hide them. The theory behind teams is that they can perform at levels beyond what individuals alone can do. In doing so, they create more value for the group, which should then be allocated based on performance. In this perfect world, everyone is better off financially. The problem intensifies when teams do not perform. Leaders of the organization must realize the value of high performers and continue to reward them as such, regardless of lackluster team performance. High performers set the performance standard to which others aspire; leaders must do everything in their power to urge individuals to excel—to move from junior varsity to varsity. By having more capable varsity players, the team benefits and performance improves. Leaders have the power to recognize, promote, and compensate—and leaders should use it to reward top performers.

Here it is important to note that some high performers may not be appropriate for teams. We firmly believe that each individual brings a special set of skills to an organization. It is a leader's challenge to understand those skills and apply them effectively in the workplace. Leaders must allocate people to areas where they can create the most value, not where current management philosophies would place them.

Leaders typically get the results that they expect and reward. Do you expect everyone to perform equally and therefore reward them as such? Or do you appreciate the different skills and capabilities that individuals possess, and therefore set different expectations and reward patterns based on them? Teams are simply individuals who work together toward a common goal with both shared and individual accountabilities. Both senior leaders and team leaders must recognize that people should be rewarded for their individual contributions.

Without senior-level commitment, support, and accountability, organizations often find themselves mired in countless unnecessary and ineffective teams. Only a few will add value, primarily those with an exceptional leader who provides the necessary commitment, support, and sense of accountability on a daily basis. Yet organizations with strong senior-level leadership must also cultivate effective team leaders. Organizational leaders may effectively use and support teams, but the team leader steers the group through the daily issues and keeps them on course.

Without consistent commitment, support, accountability, and reward philosophies from both organizational leaders and team leaders, team initiatives will continue to waste resources, frustrate workers, and deliver subpar performance. There is no substitute for leadership.

MOVING ON

We now turn to a topic that is as controversial as the topics discussed in chapter 4—holding people accountable for performance. You might think leaders would accept this view without hesitation, but they simply do not. Thus, countless organizations continue to suffer.

ENDNOTES

1. Aimee L. Stern, "Managing by Team Is Not Always as Easy as it Looks," *New York Times*, July 18, 1993, p. 3, 5:1.

2. Tom Brown, "Greatness That Endures," *Industry Week*, September 5, 1994, p. 22.

3. Robert Reich, "Leadership of the High Performance Organization," *Journal for Quality and Participation*, March 1994, p. 6.

4. Jon R. Katzenbach and Douglas K. Smith, *The Wisdom of Teams* (Harvard Business School Press, 1993), p. 131.

5. Donald McNerney, "The 'Facts of Life' for Team building," *HRFOCUS*, December 1994, p. 13.

6. Lawrence Holpp, "Applied Empowerment," *Training*, February 1994, p. 40.

7. McNerney, p. 12.

8. Katzenbach and Smith, p. 196.

9. Jack Zigon, "Making Performance Appraisal Work For Teams," *Training*, June 1994, p. 58.

10. Katzenbach and Smith, p. 245.

11. Zigon, p. 58.

12. Katzenbach and Smith, p. 247.

13. Jack Gordon, "The Team Trouble That Won't Go Away," *Training*, August 1994, p. 29.

14. Jon R. Katzenbach and Douglas K. Smith, "The Discipline of Teams," *Harvard Business Review*, March–April 1993, p. 118.

15. Norman R. F. Maier, "Assets and Liabilities in Group Problem Solving: The Need for an Integrative Function," *Psychological Review* 74, no. 4 (July 1967), pp. 239–48.

16. Irving L. Janis, "Groupthink," *Psychology Today*, November 1971, p. 74.

17. Ibid., p. 74.

8

CHAPTER

Making Everyone Accountable

Over the past 45 years, we have seen a rapid decline in individual accountability, both in society and in the workplace. Much of this decline is the direct result of changes in expectations of behavior. Society, schools, and many businesses have lowered their expectations of people, and people are now meeting these lower expectations.

Businesses have also suffered from reduced individual accountability for output quality and quantity. Legal and governmental regulations cloud the issue and take away employers' abilities to make firing and reward decisions to enforce accountability. But as worldwide competition rises, businesses cannot afford to continue to insulate people from the realities of the competitive world.

The problem is aggravated by many of the trends discussed earlier in the book. Divisions in the workplace draw unnecessary lines between people. These divisions enable people to reap rewards based on membership in a group (i.e., unions, minorities) rather than on their own performance and value-added contributions to the company. The decline in the work ethic has also hurt businesses as people expect more pay, benefits, and flexibility but are less willing to work and earn them through real productivity gains and performance-based measures. While some companies have introduced pay-for-performance programs, many organizations find them hard to enact and even harder to maintain when performance wanes. Finally the rate of change occurring in society and in the workplace is placing increased importance on individual abilities. As discussed in chapter 6, companies must look to employees to take responsibility for day-to-day operations. This responsibility includes accountability for problem solving, decision making, and results.

The paradox is clear. Just as the need for individual accountability is increasing, many of the dynamics in society and the workplace are working against individual accountability. Only since 1993 have serious national discussions focused light on these problems. Progress is slow, but as individuals, employers, and citizens, Americans must raise expectations and hold each other accountable for our actions.

Margaret Thatcher, prime minister of Great Britain from 1979 to 1990, shared her thoughts on individuals' roles and responsibilities in a democracy in an address to Hillsdale College in 1994:

> Your role in democracy does not end when you cast your vote in an election. It applies daily; the standards and values that are the moral foundation of society are also the foundation of your lives . . . It would be a grave mistake to think that freedom requires nothing of us. Each of us has to earn freedom anew in order to possess it. We do so not just for our own sake, but for the sake of our children, so that they may build a better future that will sustain over the wider world the responsibilities and blessings of freedom.[1]

Prime Minister Thatcher's message is powerful and accurate. Thatcher warns that individuals must "earn" the right of freedom and the benefits that it entails. Democracies cannot survive unless every member of society has some level of responsibility to the whole and some degree of accountability for themselves. Business is no different. And businesses cannot hope to achieve accountability in the workplace if societal norms fail to demand it in homes, schools, and society in general. For this reason, we believe that business leaders cannot wear blinders to the trends in society. They are significant and serious and must be addressed by our nation's business and political leaders.

WHERE HAS ACCOUNTABILITY GONE?

Accountability began falling by the wayside during the cultural revolution of the 1960s. Societal standards and government policies changed and the responsibilities of individuals changed with them. Professor Bruce Scott of the Harvard Business School compares the change to a pendulum swinging back and forth from rights to responsibilities. The 1960s marked a time when the pendulum swung exclusively and drastically in the direction of rights with no emphasis on individual responsibilities. In fact, the Great Society of President Lyndon B. Johnson had the negative side effect of decreasing individual responsibility because the government began providing economic support for the poor, despite the cause of their economic plight. The court system also swung in favor of "rights" with over two decades of rulings that focused on individual rights over majority well-being. For example, Philip Howard, author of *The Death of Common Sense,* documents dozens of examples of poor judgment caused by out-of-sync court rulings and governmental policies. Children suing parents, individuals suing for government protection, and customers suing over spilled coffee are only a few examples of the swing toward rights with no related responsibilities.

With the focus on rights over responsibilities as widespread as it is, business has not been able to insulate itself from the resulting problems. Congress has succeeded in "protecting" over 70 percent of the U.S. workforce in one way or another.[2] Employee discipline and termination are so cumbersome that many employers hesitate to hire new workers and will wait until they are overloaded with work to add people. This dynamic helps no one. Individuals find it harder to get a job, and businesses resort to hiring temporary workers rather than part-time or full-time people to manage demand swings.

As competition becomes increasingly intense and economic survival more difficult, more and more businesses have begun to fight back. The tide appears to be turning back in the direction of responsibilities. Some individuals have finally begun to speak out and demand more of themselves, their neighbors, their communities, and their governments. Serious discussions are beginning to take place on the issues of social accountability—welfare, illegitimacy, crime, "family values" are all receiving national attention. But the changes are not occurring fast enough.

For example, by 1992, nearly 30 percent of all children in the United States were born out of wedlock.[3] Given the current illegitimacy trends, the growth rate implies that by the early 21st century, one out of every two American children will be born out of wedlock. While interesting as a statistic, the implications for society and the workplace are serious and should raise concerns. Charles Murray, author of many societal books, including *Losing Ground* and *The Bell Curve*, warns that "illegitimacy is the single most important social problem of our time—more important than crime, drugs, poverty, illiteracy, welfare, or homelessness, because it drives everything else."[4]

His assertion is not without support. Studies repeatedly show that on average children of single-parent families exhibit lower academic performance and more behavioral problems than children in two-parent households. And as discussed in chapter 2, education and skill development have become critical success factors in the changing job market. This implies an inherent disadvantage for illegitimate children as they struggle to grow, learn, and prosper in today's and tomorrow's society.

For business leaders in particular, these patterns do not bode well for the future workforce. During the rest of the 1990s, the number of young people entering the workforce will be the lowest since World War II. Two-fifths of these individuals will be minorities, mostly blacks and Hispanics. In 1990, 45 *Fortune* 500 chief executives and university presidents, known as the Business-Higher Education Forum, published a report warning that the country can no longer ignore the isolation of inner-city minorities. The author, Steven Mason, president of the Mead Corporation, and Clifton Wharton, chairman of TIAA-CREF, the nation's largest pension fund, wrote,

> The population as a whole is aging, the growth of the workforce is slowing, and the twin burdens of greater productivity and supporting the aging population will fall mostly on younger workers . . . Our society cannot afford to lose a single one of its young people.[5]

While some will argue that these social patterns are out of the business arena, we disagree. Without accountability at a very personal level such as for oneself or one's child, it is hard to imagine making progress on accountability in the workplace.

Expectations of ourselves and others must increase before any real changes can occur. Many local communities are already experimenting with ways to help local citizens find their way off the government support system. Businesses have joined forces to train and employ previously unskilled and unemployable individuals. Schools and churches are developing additional child care services for working parents. And these efforts are not from the federal government. They are from individuals who have joined together to not only help the less fortunate but to demand that they *grab their bootstraps and pull!* At the heart of all these efforts is the objective of raising individual accountability.

Businesses should be very interested in these new and growing efforts. Not only do they result in more potentially employable individuals, but they send a message to society as a whole. By increasing individual accountability, businesses will be able to pursue more advanced and beneficial employee empowerment programs that are critical for mastering the ability to change. In addition, as accountability swings back to the individual, businesses will bear less of the burden for the behavior of customers and will have more resources to invest in new and improved products and services. Placing accountability for actions squarely on the individual benefits everyone. Individuals with strong performance are rewarded, and those with below-average results receive honest feedback and the incentive to improve. Without these two interacting dynamics, it is nearly impossible to motivate the kind of behavior that develops long-term winners, either in individuals or organizations.

ACCOUNTABILITY IN THE WORKPLACE

Businesses have suffered from the decline in accountability of both employees and customers. The threat of lawsuits from employees and customers has forced businesses to apply additional resources to nonproductive areas such as insurance, legal, and inspection. Not only do these nonproductive areas add costs, but they often reduce the responsiveness of organizations to solve problems and make logical decisions.

The city of Chicago learned just how great the costs of low accountability could be in April 1992 when the Chicago River broke through a leak in the underground rail system and flooded the basements of downtown office buildings, knocking out boilers, short-circuiting electric switches, and ruining computers, countless files, and equipment. The "leak" resulted in total losses of over $1 billion. And it could all have been avoided. Several weeks earlier, the leak had come to the attention of Chicago's transportation commissioner, and he ordered city engineers to shore up the potentially dangerous leak. However, rather than moving ahead quickly and using the reputable contractor who quoted $75,000 for repairs, he decided to put the work up for the lengthy competitive bidding process.

Only two weeks later, before the formal bidding process had even begun, the leak burst.[6] It is not clear exactly why the transportation commissioner decided to delay the critical repair. It is easy to speculate, however, that he had previously been disciplined for taking matters into his own hands and told to follow the bureaucratic procedures.

For whatever reason, an individual failed to exercise judgment and take responsibility for critical operations. It is unfortunate for everyone that so much emphasis is being placed on how things get done and whether everyone's rights are maintained as opposed to what gets done and who is responsible. It is the responsibility of business leaders to break this pattern within their own organizations and begin focusing on individual performance.

YOU GET WHAT YOU ASK FOR—AND PAY FOR

The first step toward breaking this pattern is to raise expectations. While some may argue that workers have already been pushed to the limit, evidence suggests otherwise. In fact employees themselves admit that they could perform better. In a recent study by Yankelovich Partners Inc. for William M. Mercer Inc., 70 percent of the 1,200 workers interviewed reported that they were happy in their current job. And, 86 percent believed they could boost their own productivity by over an average of 25 percent if given the right incentives and conditions. Among the barriers mentioned by workers were inadequate supervision, low employee involvement in decision making, and insufficient opportunity for advancement and rewards.[7] Most people accomplish what is expected of them; therefore, if leaders have the courage to raise expectations, hold people accountable, and reward them, the results can be surprising.

Holding people accountable and rewarding them requires objective treatment. Traditional compensations structures are under pressure because of the lack of apparent fairness. An analysis of a cross section of personnel records of U.S. manufacturing workers shows that workers with tenure of 10 years or more are paid roughly 30 percent more than recent hires. However, these higher-paid individuals rarely get higher performance evaluations than their younger counterparts.[8]

When the seniority system was developed, U.S. companies were growing rapidly and annual wage increases were the norm. Today, however, companies cannot afford to provide annual wage increases unless productivity rises as well. Leaders and workers alike must face the fact that the days of automatic prosperity are over. Here again, performance and accountability are critical. Strong performers are invaluable to organizations, and to keep them leaders must find ways to measure, track, and reward their performance.

Evidence suggests that many companies are realizing the need to tie pay with performance. Since 1988, the number of U.S. companies offering variable pay, typically bonuses to salaried employees, has risen from 47 percent to 68 percent in 1993.[9] In search of better performance, many companies are pushing the risk of ownership onto employees through performance-based rewards. Not only does this allow companies to control employee costs, but it creates an entrepreneurial attitude among workers as their incentives become aligned with the company.

And many companies and employees alike are finding pay for performance attractive. Nucor, the Charlotte, North Carolina–based steel producer, utilizes a variable pay plan based on the company's performance, business unit performance, and individual performance. Plant managers earn 25 percent less than their peers at competitors in base salary, but if the company achieves its 10 percent return-on-equity target, the managers receive huge bonuses. In 1992, Nucor needed to earn $80 million to reach the target. In fact, the company achieved $110 million, resulting in a bonus pool of $1.5 million to be divided among 14 plant managers and four top executives. On average, the plant managers doubled their salaries and exceeded the pay of their industry peers. John Doherty, plant manager of Nucor's Norfolk, Nebraska, plant, commented, "These bonuses aren't entitlements. We're running our own businesses, and we'd better perform."[10]

Yet there are risks in holding people accountable with pay-for-performance programs. In 1989, DuPont's Fibers Division signed up some 20,000 managers and workers to accept only 2 percent annual wage increases in exchange for up to 18 percent bonuses based on earnings. However, when the recession of the early 1990s hit, employees received no bonuses and became disgruntled with the program. Under pressure, DuPont abandoned the plan and raised salaries 4 percent to make up for lost raises. According to Robert McNutt, a DuPont compensation manager, "Employees just weren't ready to share risks with the company. Today, as they realize that a job doesn't mean lifetime employment and guaranteed raises, they're likely to be more receptive."[11]

Workers are not the only ones under the spotlight for improved performance and more accountability. Pay for performance is necessary at the executive level as well. Shareholders and boards of directors are cutting off the automatic multimillion-dollar salaries for CEOs who fail to deliver. Graef Crystal, professor at the University of California at Berkeley, conducted an analysis of CEO pay in 1993. He found that 48.5 percent of annual compensation could be explained by shareholder returns, company size, and sensitivity of CEO's package to stock price and dividends.[12] For example, the chairman of Salomon Brothers Inc., Deryck Maughan, was dealt a hefty drop in pay of 87 percent to $1 million after his investment banking firm posted pretax losses of nearly $1 billion in 1994. Yet Louis Gerstner, turnaround CEO of IBM, had a 34 percent compensation increase to match a 30 percent stock price improvement by IBM.

While these are only two examples, they illustrate a trend in corporate America. From top to bottom, pay for performance is holding individuals accountable for their contributions. For CEOs much of the pay volatility comes from cash bonuses. In the recent past, most companies set bonus targets of 50 percent to 60 percent of base salary. According to Geoff A. Wiegman, head of the compensation practice at Buck Consultants Inc., companies are now offering bonuses that are often 200 percent or more of salary.[13]

While the salaries alone remain high, many companies are forcing CEOs to take a stake in the company and put their own wealth at risk. Kodak has introduced a new executive pay plan that requires executives to own stock and gives the board discretion to pay some or all bonuses with awards of company stock. Programs like this can make a difference to the pocketbook. Some CEOs, such as Wal-Mart's David Glass and The Limited's Leslie Wexner, essentially worked for nothing in 1993 because the declines in their stock holding were greater than their compensation packages. And they were not alone. Professor Graef Crystal's study also found that of 105 companies whose stock fell in 1993, 58 of their CEOs actually lost money as the value of their holdings fell by more than their compensation.[14] By forcing CEOs and other executives to take a stake in the company, their personal interests are in line with the company and their accountability increases.

Board members should be held to similar standards as CEOs and executives. U.S. companies need active boards who are willing to disagree with management on critical issues. Oftentimes the board of directors is a handpicked, inside group, favorable to the CEO and unwilling to raise questions to management. While change is slow, chapter 9 discusses the role of the board in corporate America and challenges companies to evaluate and demand performance from their own board members. And indeed shareholders and market mechanisms are forcing board members to take accountability for both their action and inaction.

A recent Louis Harris poll of 500 outside directors found that more than 40 percent have been targets of a lawsuit.[15] While bringing a lawsuit is drastic, it is one of the few ways shareholders have found to hold executives and directors accountable for their decisions.

Increasing accountability through stock is not only for boards and executives. Other employees are now getting their chance for ownership through pay for performance tied to stock prices. In 1995, Bristol-Meyers Squibb Co. gave employees a one-time chance to buy 200 shares at a set price. And pilots at Southwest Airlines recently agreed to take stock in lieu of pay hikes. Yet Philip Morris has launched one of the most innovative employee stock plans to date—making stock part of workers' take-home pay. In March 1995, 7,800 union workers ratified the labor pact that gives them stock in place of wage hikes for the next two years.

Nine unions have signed off on the plan, which gives 94 shares and a 2 percent pay raise in 1997 to each union worker. Employees can choose to take the stock after 12 to 24 months, but they are not allowed to sell or vote them within this time. The union is hoping the stock will rise 5 percent to 7 percent annually, but they understand the downside. This is a giant step in bringing workers', executives', and shareholders' interests into alignment. According to Tom Preston, an electrician at the Richmond, Virginia, plant, "I think it's worth [the risk] . . . If the stock takes a real downturn, then I'll have more problems than just my raise."[16]

Attitudes and statements like this are prodding many companies like Philip Morris to give ownership to their employees, both in stock and in their daily jobs. These efforts together increase each employee's sense of ownership, involvement, impact, and accountability for results. Without managerial action, it is impossible to build the trust that is required to empower people and then hold them accountable.

BRINGING ACCOUNTABILITY TO THE WORKPLACE

Aside from financial incentives such as stock and pay for performance, leaders must change the nature of the workplace to one that values ownership and accountability for results. Making this change from the traditional top-down style takes significant time, effort, and consistency. Expectations must increase, education must prepare people, experimentation must engage people, and evaluation must inform and reward people. These four phases—expectations, education, experimentation and evaluation—must take place whether the work environment uses teams or individuals.

Setting Expectations—a Tricky Step

The first step is to break Frederick W. Taylor's traditional model of the workplace. As the "father of scientific management," Taylor is credited with imposing managerial control in the workplace through detailed work specifications and output targets. While Taylor's teaching improved productivity initially, workers fell into a role of doing rather than thinking. The challenge now is to reverse these practices and change the expectations of individuals in the workplace. Workers need to take on more day-to-day responsibility and decision making as well as to accept accountability for results. Executives must focus on the competitive environment and the future strategic direction of the company. Middle managers, long the controlling mechanism in the organization, must become supporters and information providers, both up and down the chain. And the performance expectations of each group must rise.

Already workers and competitors are overturning Taylor's model faster than managers can adjust. Harvard Business School Professor Richard E. Walton addressed the pressures to change in his *Harvard Business Review* article "From Control to Commitment in the Workplace." A model that assumes low employee commitment and that is designed to produce reliable if not outstanding performance simply cannot match the standards of excellence set by world-class competitors. Especially in a high-wage country like the United States, market success depends on a superior level of commitment, not merely the obedience—if you could obtain it—of workers. And as painful experience shows, this commitment cannot flourish in a workplace dominated by the familiar model of control.[17]

Driven by increased competition, many companies chose the path of employee empowerment and changing expectations. Those companies that found success are held up as heroes—primarily because so many failed. The missing ingredient in many of the failures was the lack of changes in accountability. While many companies set high performance expectations meant to "stretch" the organization, organized teams to share information, and reduced layers to improve information flow, very few successfully handed accountability over to the workers.

But accountability cannot be handed over blindly. Many companies have had serious problems when stretch targets and personal accountability were not constrained by the corporate culture of behavior and ethics. Kidder, Peabody & Company lost $350 million when a trader allegedly booked fictitious profits to make targets; Sears, Roebuck & Company took a $60 million charge against earnings after admitting it recommended unnecessary repairs to customers in its automobile service business; Barings Bank declared bankruptcy after a single trader lost over $ 1.2 billion on currency trading. Each of these failures was due to individuals making poor and/or unethical business decisions during efforts to avoid failure and achieve performance targets. These people had responsibility, but lost perspective on the issue of personal and corporate accountability.

Bausch & Lomb provides a recent example of how high expectations can result in perverse and destructive actions throughout an organization if the counterforces of ethics and culture are not strong. Driven by successful CEO Daniel Gill's fierce insistence on achieving double-digit annual profit growth, company managers began resorting to ineffective and sometimes unethical practices to meet targets. Customers were given unusually long payment terms, goods were funneled into the gray markets, distributors were threatened and forced to take unwanted products, and false sales were booked. Not until headquarters noticed growing receivables and lower sales in the star-performing Southeast Asian group were the schemes uncovered. Auditors investigated and found significant financial irregularities as well as half a million pairs of sunglasses, shipped but unsold and stored in a warehouse. While attention was initially focused on Hong Kong, several other discoveries of unwanted behavior were eventually found in other product divisions and geographic areas.

All the evidence pointed to a culture gone awry in its pursuit of profits. In environments where failure is harshly punished and reliance on the numbers is high, the focus moves away from good business practices. According to John P. Kotter, a Harvard Business School professor, "People spend their time trying to figure out what kind of game to play to make the numbers, not how to satisfy the customer or save money."[18]

The Bausch & Lomb system collapsed under the pressure of numbers because it failed to balance the strong emphasis on performance expectations with that of ethical accountability. Former executives say that division heads might get only a paltry bonus if they fell even 10 percent short of the aggressive earnings targets. Yet by meeting them, significant rewards were the norm. While many companies manage the earnings focus with accountability for assets such as inventories and receivables, one former B&L executive said, "You could miss your asset objectives by a mile and still get a big payday." Division leaders suggest that CEO Gill rarely discussed specific actions to meet the targets and was well known for his statement, "Make the numbers, but don't do anything stupid."[19]

Apparently "stupid" was a highly interpreted word at B&L. The organization was so overwhelmed by the focus on numbers that even customers began to play the game at B&L's expense. According to insiders, panic-stricken account managers would offer terrific deals at the end of each month, encouraging customers to wait for the deals. All of this wreaked havoc on B&L's distribution operations as 70 percent of the month's goods were shipped during the last three days of the month, requiring excessive overtime and temporary workers.[20] From a corporate perspective, these games only hurt profitability. But because individuals were so driven by their own numbers, many achieved their own targets at the expense of the whole.

While the Bausch & Lomb's story is extreme, it is not unusual. Leaders must set higher performance targets and reward those who meet them. However, leaders must also reward individuals who promote change by identifying problems, experimenting with solutions, and occasionally failing. As discussed earlier, change is critical to all organizations, and it requires a culture of empowerment—of knowledge, trust, and experimentation. While B&L's problems occurred primarily in the management levels, consider the implications of an entire organization of "empowered" people playing the same destructive numbers games. Before companies can implement these new management systems, individuals must know their role in the organization and how it fits both financially and operationally. This is the only way to ensure that people make decisions that benefit the organization.

Expectations must be high, clear, and measurable. But they must also be "right" for the organization as a whole. *What* leaders encourage and *how* leaders encourage play a pivotal role in shaping the behavior of individuals and ultimately the culture.

Education Provides the Tools

Successfully transferring accountability and ensuring effective business practices requires education. Leaders must be wary of setting people up for failure by handing over a barrage of problems with little training and skill augmentation to help them. Workers must clearly know what is expected of them, and they must be given the tools and learning to meet these expectations. By understanding operations outside their traditional roles, employees can also seek solutions that maximize the whole rather than any single part. As mentioned in earlier chapters, training is a critical tool in achieving successful change. Allied Signal, Milliken, McKinsey & Company, and Motorola are only a few examples of companies that view education as part of the job. While some companies view training as money that can too easily walk out the door, these leading organizations view it as a way to increase loyalty as well as enhance the performance of individuals.

Education must occur for both individuals and teams and on qualitative and quantitative topics. Increased employee involvement requires much higher analytical and problem-solving skills from basic algebra and geometry to reading SPC charts and technical diagrams. It also requires a move toward creative thinking, brainstorming, and logical thinking to organize and prioritize information. Finally, education should include sessions on teamwork, group interaction, and evaluations and feedback. While the raw skills and capabilities are necessary, the ability to interact and operate efficiently is what differentiates winning organizations.

Finally it is important to draw the distinction between training and learning. Training is done to or for people and typically teaches some new skill or tool. It requires little critical thinking. Learning, on the other hand, requires critical thinking about why something works the way it does. The difference, therefore, is in the understanding. This distinction is very powerful. Only people who understand something can evaluate it and improve it. Training, therefore, should be viewed as a tool to enhance employees' abilities to learn, not as the goal itself.

Certainly each organization has its own skill sets, challenges, and training needs. The purpose of this chapter is not to define these needs but to highlight the importance of education to prepare people to meet their changing expectations in the workplace. And education does not have an overnight payback. It often takes a year or more for training to be *absorbed and understood* before benefits can materialize. Therefore, training has to be a priority for leaders—and one that is not dropped when performance wanes.

Experimentation—Finding the Right System

No secret recipe exists for setting up a system that breeds accountability. What works for one organization often fails miserably at another. Developing management systems that work is driven by the corporate culture, the business environment, and the quality of the workforce and management team. This is the phase where *companies must learn how to learn,* taking the resources and incentives and making them work. This book provides examples from various companies meant to trigger creativity, but it is up to the organization as a whole, both managers and workers, to develop a system that works effectively.

Ultimately, responsibility is gained by and accountability given to people who want it. The simple question of whether workers are interested in being more involved is one that must be answered. Polls repeatedly highlight workers' desires to become active in decision making, yet it is not unusual for individuals to back away when responsibility arrives. Many companies have addressed this concern by initiating empowerment efforts in small, pilot areas and asking for volunteers. Once a successful system is working and accountability is viewed as a benefit rather than a burden, the system can be spread throughout the organization.

The second critical factor is the organization's willingness to accept failure. No individual accomplishes great things without failure. Organizations are no different. Organizations may have more resources and people to evaluate options, but failures still occur. Without them it is quite possible that the organization is unable to change, invent, or stretch its capabilities. Just as James Burke, former CEO of Johnson & Johnson, learned, failures are opportunities for learning—as long as they are not repeated. Obviously successful organizations do not string together a series of major failures. However, in every successful new product design, trial and error is natural. It is no different in other business settings. As long as the trials are small, frequent, and communicated, learning can be gained.

In addition to learning, encouraging trial and error builds trust. Trust is critical in any competitive organization as it pushes the envelope for new products, services, and processes. Trust does not mean that poor performers will not be disciplined; it means that individuals who think, stretch, and fail will not be punished; and it also means that individuals who think, stretch, and succeed will be rewarded. With trust also comes the ability to take more chances and think creatively. Creative thinking generates ideas and progress for organizations. Furthermore, individuals are much more willing to accept accountability for initiatives they develop over those handed down from the top.

Johnsonville Foods is a company whose employees take accountability to the extreme. Two scenes from the Sheboygan, Wisconsin, sausage factory are representative of the ownership and responsibility of workers at Johnsonville Foods.

Two men stand peering inside a packaging machine. The machine is designed to overwrap trays that are at least eight inches long. They want to reconfigure the machine so that it will wrap two-and-a-half-inch and five-inch trays. The engineers from the machine's manufacturer said it couldn't be done, but these two are determined to find a way. If the machine cannot be used, it will mean spending $35,000 to buy a new one. They make one more little change and—it works! They have accomplished the impossible.

Neither of these men are engineers. They are production-line workers who have *learned* the process and the machines.

Upstairs a woman is working at a personal computer. She is developing product performance specifications. She is struggling to write precise definitions of how the product should look, how to determine exact proportions for each component, and how to measure whether the product meets these specifications. She realized the specifications she and her teammates were using were not precise enough, so she stayed after her shift to rewrite them. She will take them back to the team for revisions and consensus on using them.

This woman is a production-line worker with a high school degree.[21] Sound impossible? Today stories like these abound at Johnsonville Foods, but this was not always the case.

During the 1980s, Johnsonville Foods changed its management style to involve workers in the decisions relating to their own jobs. The company leaders took a new approach to running the business. Rather than using people to build a great business, they decided to use the business to build great people. The managers relinquished their monopoly on decision making and transferred it to the workers. The training department broadened its role to general personal development and allocated funds to each individual for their own use in personal development. In addition, workshops examine individuals' skills. Each individual leaves the workshop with an assignment—to focus on improving one skill and write an objective statement and plan for achieving it. Other initiatives include job rotations, special assignments, and a profit-sharing program.

The general theme at Johnsonville Foods is *ask the workers what they think should be done*. And the results are astonishing. During the first eight years of the change, return on assets doubled, sales grew 800 percent, rejects fell from 5 percent to 0.5 percent, and the ratio of complaint to compliment letters went from 5 to 1 to 1 to 2.8. Profits and productivity rose while absenteeism and turnover fell.[22]

At Johnsonville Foods, the employees enjoy their jobs because they are involved and accountable. Individuals and teams alike are rewarded by recognition, profit sharing, and general job satisfaction. This company took the risk of changing, set new expectations of workers and managers, provided education and support, and let the people experiment with their own minds. And it worked.

While successes like Johnsonville Foods provide evidence that turning it over to the workers is the only answer, some cautionary words are necessary. Empowering people and giving them accountability for results is a powerful motivator of potentially good and bad behavior. Just as extensive pressure for results can lead to unwanted and unethical behavior, unlimited responsibility and decision making can be disastrous. It is management's responsibility to set the boundaries within which employees can roam. In other words, leaders must stop telling employees what to do and begin telling them what not to do. In other words, leaders must set behavioral boundaries.

Professor Robert Simons of the Harvard Business School draws the analogy of high-performing companies to racing cars. "Boundary systems are an organization's brakes. And, like racing cars, the fastest companies need the best brakes." He cites McKinsey & Company, a leading strategic consulting firm, as a successful example. McKinsey consults to CEOs and evaluates highly proprietary strategic data and plans. Therefore, maintaining confidentiality is critical to maintaining its reputation. The firm sets strict boundaries that forbid consultants to reveal any information—even company names—to people outside the firm. Furthermore, the company sets limits of personal conduct and states that consultants cannot misrepresent themselves to gather competitive information on behalf of clients.[23] The boundaries are clear and employees are held strictly accountable for following them. Yet within these guidelines, creativity, problem solving, and experimentation are unconstrained.

Evaluating Results—Holding People Accountable

The final critical step in moving towards an accountable organization is evaluating the performance of individuals, teams, and the organization. Dozens of texts and thousands of seminars and training programs exist to teach people how to give and take performance feedback. We believe no single method is appropriate for everyone. Individuals respond differently to criticism and praise, raising a challenge for managers to discern the best approach. However, some lessons can be learned.

Evaluations, whether from the boss, peers, or subordinates, are extremely powerful. And combining two or more reviews reinforces the existence of any problem areas. Peer and subordinate reviews are becoming more widespread and delivering results. AT&T's Chairman and CEO Robert E. Allen started asking his direct reports for feedback. He found that his "lieutenants didn't like the passive way he ran the management executive committee." So he tried to change. Allen now says he "spends more time drafting the agenda, airs his opinions freely during meetings and pushes the group harder to make clear-cut decisions." According to Allen, "Nobody likes to be told they are not performing at the maximum level."[24]

So by drawing attention to problem areas and setting higher expectations, individuals can move closer to achieving their maximum performance.

Evaluating performance is not just an annual process but should become a daily activity. Accountable organizations rely on informal feedback, primarily from peers. These are not formal review sessions, but words of praise or warning by co-workers for behavior that effects the organization. Leaders can encourage this type of behavior by following it themselves. Public words from executives and managers for small achievements as well as problems will encourage communication at all levels and show that feedback is useful and expected. Once people begin to have control over and accountability for an operation, they become more open to feedback on how to improve it. Formal evaluations should also be regular and focused on the performance against specific expectations. Without the earlier step of setting new expectations, progress cannot be monitored and evaluations can quickly become counterproductive. Without both formal and informal evaluations it is impossible to hold people accountable and reward performance.

Leaders must have the courage to hold people accountable for their actions. There is no substitute for leadership in the absence of performance. On any team, no one is more frustrated about the individual who fails to pull his weight than the other team members. For this reason, it is the responsibility of leaders and managers to correct lagging behavior or remove it. Removal of individuals is a difficult issue both personally and legally, but it must be done to benefit the team and organization as a whole. As discussed earlier, companies cannot afford to support and maintain lackluster performers.

Oftentimes, individuals are simply unprepared or in the wrong position. Athletics provides an analogy. Coaches do not let poor performers remain on the field and ruin the chances for the rest of the team. But poor performers clearly see the level to which they must aspire, and those who are driven work hard to make it. Freshmen athletes go through this cycle every year. They see the expectations, practice and receive training, experiment with different skills, and are then evaluated. Some make it—others do not. But the coach is responsible for the performance of the team; therefore, he must hold each individual accountable for his or her performance. It should be no different in business.

Business leaders have the option of whether or not to take a stand on accountability. They can choose to demand more, evaluate more, and reward and punish more. Or, they can make excuses and let lackluster performers remain a part of the team.

The choice should be clear. And it is becoming more clear not only in business but in society as a whole. Individuals must take accountability for themselves, and it is up to the nation's leaders, in politics, business, churches, and communities, to spread this message that individual performance is paramount.

MOVING ON

Ultimately, businesses need an army of entrepreneurs to overcome the ever increasing obstacles and achieve world-class performance. Developing them is a critical role leaders must play. We turn our attention to this issue in the next chapter.

ENDNOTES

1. Kim Shippey, "News and Commentary," *Christian Science Sentinel*, July 3, 1995, p. 28.
2. Philip Howard, "The Death of Common Sense," *U.S. News & World Report*, January 30, 1995, p. 57.
3. "Home Sweet Home," *The Economist*, September 9, 1995, p. 26.
4. Ibid., p. 53.
5. "America's Blacks: A World Apart," *The Economist*, March 30, 1991, p. 17.
6. Howard, p. 59.
7. Gene Koretz, "Sweet Carrots, Big Gains," *Business Week*, July 10, 1995, p. 24.
8. James Medoff, "Why Business Is Axing Older Workers," *U.S. News & World Report*, October 31, 1994, p. 78.
9. Shawn Tully, "Your Paycheck Gets Exciting," *Fortune,* November 1, 1993, p. 83.

10. Ibid., p. 88.
11. Ibid., p. 84.
12. John Byrne, "Deliver or Else," *Business Week*, March 27, 1995, p. 36.
13. Ibid., p. 37.
14. Ibid., p. 38.
15. Larry Light, "Why Outside Directors Have Nightmares," *Business Week*, October 23, 1995, p. 6.
16. Aaron Bernstein, "At Philip Morris, Blue Chips for Blue Collars," *Business Week*, March 27, 1995, p. 38.
17. Richard E. Walton, "From Control to Commitment in the Workplace," *Harvard Business Review*, March–April 1985, p. 79.
18. Mark Maremont, "Blind Ambition," *Business Week*, October 23, 1995, p. 80.
19. Ibid., p. 81.
20. Ibid., p. 82.
21. Linda Honold, "The Power of Learning at Johnsonville Foods," *Training*, April 1991, p. 55.
22. Ibid., p. 56.
23. Robert Simons, "Control in an Age of Empowerment," *Harvard Business Review*, March–April 1995, p. 84.
24. "Turning the Tables: Underlings Evaluate Bosses," *The Wall Street Journal*, October 4, 1994, p. A-1.

9

CHAPTER

Creating a Risk-Taking Environment

A 1985 article in *U.S. News & World Report* warned that "Corporate America is stagnating because its best and brightest are leaving to start their own enterprises."[1] Looking back, it appears the writers of this article were prophetic, and more than a decade later it still looks like this prophecy is valid. Older, more established firms are finding it very difficult to keep the entrepreneurs on whom they depend for their long-term prosperity. If they do not change and learn to accommodate and integrate these creative and innovative people, they will suffer, and many of them will not survive. They simply cannot afford to lose them.

As we have said repeatedly throughout this book, we are in the midst of the most rapid change period the world has ever seen, and the pace of change should accelerate in the future. Consider what is happening in the computer, semiconductor, and software industries. In the span of a single year (1995), Intel introduces the Pentium chip, which was heralded as a major breakthrough that will change the way we think about computing because it is so fast. IBM, Hewlett-Packard, Compaq, and Apple scramble to get on the crest of the wave that is building as new computer chips open up new uses and new markets for their products.

With enormous fanfare and excitement, Microsoft introduces Windows 95, an operating system that opens the door for the company to enter a vast array of new and rapidly growing markets. Netscape Communications hits the stock market for the first time and is wildly successful primarily because of its Netscape Navigator program that allows consumers to browse the Internet, and because of the talented people the company has brought together to develop new and exciting products.

Within a few short months, Sun Microsystems unveils Java, a new computer language that many experts believe will revolutionize the computer industry because it "offers software developers a way to create relatively small, self-contained programs that introduce 'interactivity'— change, motion, responsiveness—to the information shared on networks, including the graphics-rich portion of the Internet called the World Wide Web."[2] Java, and similar languages currently under development, are also expected to reduce the cost of expensive computer systems because "there is no need for an additional complex program, such as a word processor."[3] Microsoft chairman and founder Bill Gates acknowledges the impact Java and languages like it will have on the industry and announces that his company is working to develop a Java-type language of its own.

On their own, any one of these new products would be enough to revolutionize the way we do business. But they are not on their own. They are being introduced in rapid-fire succession at a time when every industry is experiencing quantum change. The opportunities these and other products create for the development of other new and exciting products in industries as diverse as automobiles, pharmaceuticals, retailing, and mass communication is breathtaking.

Businesses need entrepreneurs today more than they ever have before. To grow and prosper during these turbulent times, they must develop entrepreneurial talent and learn to innovate, adapt, and respond quickly to changes that arise at such a frenzied pace that most people will have to run hard just to keep up. As Tom Peters said, increasingly the difference between successful and unsuccessful businesses will be "an amazingly high level of entrepreneurship."[4] Simply put, leaders must teach their people to think and act like entrepreneurs.

As we said at the beginning of this chapter, the large-firm experience in attracting and retaining outstanding talent is not good. "In a recent study of career preferences conducted by Opinion Research Corp., just 1 percent of the 1,000 adult respondents said they would freely choose to be corporate managers. Careers that carry a high degree of independence, such as medicine or the law, were far more popular . . . As recently as 1990, a quarter of Columbia University's new MBAs joined large manufacturers; last year just 13 percent did so. At Stanford nearly 70 percent of the business school's class of '89 joined big companies, defined as those with more than 1,000 employees. In 1994 only about half did so."[5]

This problem must be solved, because large firms cannot survive for long if they fail to appeal to today's young, talented people who are becoming increasingly skeptical of the large-firm, bureaucratic model. Without these people, the best they can hope to achieve is mediocre performance. Thus, they will eventually cease to be competitive. You can count on this fact. Mediocre performers do not, and will not, fare well in head-to-head competition with the best firms in the world.

Firms like Microsoft are anomalies. Although they are large, they attract very talented people because the company offers them both opportunity and independence. IBM has been more typical of large firms, though. They have had difficulty attracting and keeping creative people, despite IBM Chairman Lou Gerstner's courting entrepreneurial talent and their strides to create a more dynamic company. In October 1995, Jim Manzi, chief executive of Lotus Development Corporation, resigned just three months after the company was acquired by IBM for $3.5 billion. Said Manzi, "I don't think I am exactly the right person to be leading a division inside a much larger organization . . . What was exciting to me as an independent company, the challenges we were facing, are not exactly the same. In fact, they are very, very different for Lotus inside IBM."[6]

According to Jeffrey Tarter, the editor of Boston-based Soft Letter, "Manzi was never cut out to be a faceless IBM executive, because he is too smart, too independent, too headstrong—all wonderful qualities if you are running a small company but not if you are part of an enormous corporation."[7] A few days later, another top executive at Lotus quit, and rumors suggesting that other Lotus executives were considering leaving started to fly.[8] These defections raised doubts about IBM management's ability to successfully integrate entrepreneurs. Although the qualities required to lead small, entrepreneurial companies are precisely the qualities required to lead entrepreneurs in large firms, it is extremely difficult for the typical large-company executive to accept this reality. As a result, these qualities are sorely lacking in most large firms.

Smaller firms are more appealing to talented entrepreneurs than larger firms because they offer them the opportunity to assume real responsibility early in their careers. Furthermore, they encourage them to develop their ideas, and by so doing they expand their businesses. For these reasons, many small firms are growing rapidly and are beginning to put real pressure on larger firms like IBM, AT&T, and others. As they grow, however, entrepreneurial firms can, and often do, fall into the trap of allowing their bureaucracies to dominate. When they do, they become less attractive to people on whom they are so fundamentally dependent for their success.

LEADERS MUST BE ENTREPRENEURIAL

Later in this chapter, we will talk about how to create and energize an entrepreneurial organization. To begin, though, we need to make an important point. A leader who is not entrepreneurial has about as much chance of producing the kind of results that lead to sustained high performance in rapidly changing global markets as a novice musician has of successfully conducting a symphony orchestra.

Entrepreneurship is a trial-and-error process. As Tom Peters has said, it is about trying new ideas, fixing them, and then trying them again. As a result, entrepreneurship is not neat and pretty. It moves in fits and starts, and it fluctuates as conditions vary. Therefore, it is extremely difficult for people who believe organizational processes can be defined clearly and absolutely to lead an entrepreneurial firm. First of all, they are very uncomfortable in an entrepreneurial environment. Secondly, entrepreneurs have very little confidence in them, and confidence is as important in entrepreneurship as it is in any competitive sport.

Additionally, leaders who are not entrepreneurial themselves have difficulty dealing with entrepreneurs, because entrepreneurs tend to have strong egos. They begin to develop their talent at a very young age. They question the status quo and challenge accepted practices from the time they are children. It is likely they were viewed as troublemakers and malcontents. Their teachers in school tried to squash their spirit and make them act like the other kids, only they were not like the other kids. They did not always fit neatly into groups the way other kids their age did, and they may have been viewed as socially immature. In fact, however, many of these kids were just very creative, determined, and persistent—admirable qualities in entrepreneurs that are not always regarded highly.

At home, they encountered similar problems. Their parents often had difficulty understanding them, and they tried to teach them how to "fit in." When they started working, most of their colleagues told them how important it is to keep their noses clean and not to rock the boat. In other words, if they were truly entrepreneurs they had to develop very strong egos simply to survive in the "go-along-get-along" world in which we live.

As we know from basic biology, the strongest in every species have a chance to survive and prosper, but the ones who are weak struggle and eventually disappear. This principle is true for entrepreneurs as well. The deck is stacked against anyone who is out of step with the society in which they live. For every successful entrepreneur like Bill Gates, founder of Microsoft, or Ted Turner, the subject of chapter 10, there are thousands of others with good ideas who were too weak to overcome the obstacles in their paths. Thus, most people who could be entrepreneurial do not survive, at least with their entrepreneurial spirit intact. They learn to deal with the pressure by adapting and accepting the status quo. In most organizations that means accepting mediocre performance as the norm and not pushing too hard for what they believe in.

Reigniting the entrepreneurial spark in these people is not an easy task, but it is the most important job leaders have. Because, as Harvard professor Michael Porter said, "You almost have to be a true believer to be competitive . . . Of the hundreds and hundreds of world-class companies from around the world that I studied, an enormous proportion were . . . run by some maniac who had spent at least 20 years of his life on a crusade to produce the best product."[9]

LEAD, FOLLOW, OR GET OUT OF THE WAY

Ted Turner has a sign on the wall behind his desk that says, "Lead, Follow, or Get Out of the Way." That should be the slogan of every company. To prosper, businesses must have an army of leaders, or entrepreneurs, who are willing to take risks on ideas that have the potential to produce long-term success. Not everyone is a leader, though, and there is plenty of room for people who are willing to follow leaders into battle. There is also room for people who question the actions of leaders and offer alternatives for consideration. However, there is no room in any organization for people who simply interfere with progress and offer virtually no help to those who are getting the job done.

Managers in most organizations are the most difficult obstacles entrepreneurs have to overcome as they do their work. Their "discontinuous and wavering support" is not good for entrepreneurs or for business.[10] Typically, they focus most of their attention on exploiting old ideas that have worked in the past because they are safer bets for short-term success.

However, ideas that interest entrepreneurs often produce only costs in the short run, but they have potential for producing healthy long-term gains.

From the myopic view of many managers, staying on a proven path without deviation may make sense. However, in the long run it is a formula for disaster. Improving a company's competitive position and profits requires constant improvement and the development of new and better products, services, and processes. Coming up with them is where entrepreneurs excel. Smaller firms are demonstrating every day that they are more entrepreneurial and better at developing new products and services than larger firms. Many of them have grown large and have taken their place alongside corporate giants. Intel, Microsoft, and MCI are just three examples of firms that have become household names as they have grown and prospered. Many others will become large firms as their product and service ideas gain acceptance. As a result, NASDAQ, the stock exchange preferred by smaller companies, boasts in its television commercials that it is the "stock market for the next hundred years." A quick look at the business section of any newspaper will demonstrate that many of our country's most aggressive and exciting firms, including the three mentioned above, are traded on the NASDAQ exchange.

Their commercials may be exaggerating slightly. The stock of firms like Ford Motor Company (the subject of chapter 12) and Motorola is traded on the New York Stock Exchange, and clearly they are two of the most creative, innovative, and profitable firms in the world. Still, it is becoming clear that younger, upstart firms are routinely doing things that older, more established firms find difficult to accomplish. This problem must be solved, because while small firms may be more innovative, "It takes a large firm to exploit new ideas on a global basis. Innovation must become an on-line activity in large firms, an ongoing process."[11]

To overcome this deficiency, many large firms have aggressively pursued smaller, more innovative firms as takeover targets (i.e., IBM's acquisition of Lotus). This strategy may bring people with innovative ideas into larger firms, but it is not likely to solve the problem in the long run unless leaders create climates within their firms that are supportive for entrepreneurs. Unless they revitalize their organizations, the best entrepreneurs will leave, just as they have in the past.

PROSPERITY BREEDS COMPLACENCY

Long before IBM posted its first ever operating loss in the fourth quarter of 1992, the company's problems were evident. The mammoth size of IBM and its powerful bureaucracy made it very difficult for the company to adjust to the rapidly changing markets in which it operated. IBM's CEO and board of directors simply did not comprehend the magnitude of the problems they faced.[12] They had become complacent. "Instead of adapting, IBM tried to protect its past successes,"[13] and as a result the company lost its dominant position. Ironically, the very people who could have, and should have, faced IBM's problems (its executives and board of directors) became the company's chief liabilities by failing to recognize the need for immediate, radical change.

IBM's board of directors was particularly responsible for what happened to the company. It was ill prepared to do its job. The board did not have the courage to take action before the company experienced losses,[14] and massive corporate upheaval was the product of their delay. The problems with IBM's board were deeply rooted. Its members did not understand the latest technology or its customers' demands.[15] Losing touch with their customers,[16] IBM was constantly several steps behind its competitors. Although the people serving on IBM's board were talented individuals, they sat on many boards and did not have time to give IBM the attention it so desperately needed.[17]

General Motors is another company whose executives and board of directors prevented it from facing reality and dealing with its problems. As we said before, the oil embargos in 1973 and 1979 stimulated demand for small, fuel-efficient cars, and GM was slow to adjust to the changing competitive environment. But Japanese car manufacturers were ready, and they took a big bite out of GM's market share. "As the 1980s wore on, General Motors increasingly lost touch with its customers. The company focused on flashy high-tech acquisitions and internal reorganizations rather than on building stylish and reliable cars."[18] As a result, GM's market share dropped from 52 percent in the early 1960s to about 35 percent in the early 1990s.

GM experienced problems with its board of directors that were almost identical to the problems IBM encountered. The one difference between the two boards was Ross Perot. Perot joined GM's board after the automobile giant acquired EDS, the company he founded. Perot encouraged GM to face up to its problems and to streamline its bureaucracy, but GM executives would not listen. In fact, they decided to silence him by buying his stock in GM, valued at about $350 million, for about $700 million in return for his resignation from the board. Although Perot's style as a GM board member may have been obnoxious and brutish, his assessment of the company's problems was correct, and they should have listened to him.

Archer Daniels Midland Company, ADM, is another firm experiencing serious problems with its board of directors. In the summer of 1995, the U.S. Justice Department announced that it was investigating allegations of illegal activity, including price-fixing, on the part of executives and board members at ADM and that it had tape recordings of meetings during which the illegal activity occurred. The response to these allegations by ADM's chairman and chief executive officer, Dwayne Andreas, and board members was incredibly arrogant. Instead of cooperating with Justice Department investigators and initiating an independent investigation of its own, the company battened down the hatches and assumed a defensive posture.

Alarmed by the company's response, institutional investors holding millions of ADM shares initiated a shareholder revolt and attempted to oust the board. Their efforts failed, but questions about the propriety of ADM board members and executives remain. According to John Nash, president and CEO of the National Association of Corporate Directors, "The problem is that the board of directors of Archer Daniels Midland is all basically inside directors, they're affiliated directors, or they're relatives of the company, or major investors in the company, so you have to question how independent are these boards with respect to the issues at hand. I view the Archer Daniels Midland board as the CEO's board. It's the theory of 'My company, my board,' and the CEO has selected all of those members. They're friends of the CEO, so you have to question their independence."[19]

Finally, in mid-January 1996, months after the issue drew national attention, Andreas announced that ADM would replace several current board members with directors who are free of any ties to the company. As of the date of Andreas's announcement, 10 of ADM's 17 board members were current or former executives of the company, and the other 7 had close personal or financial ties to top managers at ADM.[20]

The problems IBM, GM, and ADM encountered occur in every organization in every country, even in Japan. After Japan's Daiwa bank experienced stunning losses in 1995, investors learned that the company and Japan's Ministry of Finance knew about the bank's problems and tried to hide them from U.S. bank regulators. "Driving the criticism [of the Ministry of Finance] is the disclosure that the ministry heard of the losses from Daiwa in early August, but took no action on its own to verify them and kept American regulators in the dark for six weeks. Statements by ministry officials that they merely followed the trust-based Japanese way of doing things have run into ridicule."[21]

BUSINESSES ARE BEGINNING TO CATCH ON

Slowly, firms are catching on, and corporate giants are beginning to realize that they cannot continue to operate the way they have since the end of World War II. The world is far too competitive for that. For firms to grow and prosper, leaders must cut through the bureaucratic red tape and remove the obstacles that make it difficult for entrepreneurs to create and innovate. We will have more to say later about bureaucracies and the people who run them, or bureaucrats as they are called with some degree of contempt.

Ford Motor Company had to deal with these problems in the early 1980s, and they are a strong organization today because they did. But there are other examples to consider, like AT&T. On September 20, 1995, AT&T Chairman Robert E. Allen announced a strategic restructuring that divided the company into three separate companies—communications services, communications equipment, and transaction-intensive computing—and sold off AT&T Capital Corporation.

According to Allen, AT&T took this step to increase the value of the company to shareholders, to be more responsive to customers, and to better focus on growth opportunities in individual markets.[22] The company's actions will go a long way to help accomplish these objectives. But there were other reasons for this decision as well—the most important ones being that AT&T was simply too big to be managed effectively and too slow to compete with its increasingly fleet-footed competitors.

To be effective, organizations of all types and sizes must be able to move quickly into areas where opportunities emerge and to react with dispatch to solve problems. But at AT&T, things were not working exactly the way they were supposed to. Divisions and departments were "bumping into one another," and there was too little cooperation between them. Also, the company's bureaucracy was too large and too powerful, thus reducing the firm's ability to innovate and respond quickly.

In November 1995, AT&T announced it was offering buyouts to 80,000 of its management personnel, about half its management staff. This move was aimed at further reducing costs and the power of the company's bureaucracy. Additionally, it was designed to improve the company's ability to respond to market shifts.

In January 1996, AT&T announced that 40,000 of its 300,000 workers would be laid off in the first part of the year and that most of the layoffs would involve managers. Amazingly, half of AT&T's employees at the time were considered managers.[23] Talk about inefficiency. That means that for every person working, there was a person paid to supervise the activity. No wonder the company was less responsive than it needed to be.

Associated with this problem, internal politics were intense, and the company was diverting too many resources and too much time and energy away from critical issues facing the company (like protecting and improving its competitive position in industries that had become intensely competitive as firms like MCI developed strength and quickness).

Nonprofit organizations are learning about the importance of entrepreneurship as well. For example, the National Institutes of Health (NIH) recently announced that "the federal AIDS program needs to rely more on the curiosity of individual scientists, and less on the wisdom of committees, as it doles out research money."[24] This change in policy represents a radical departure from the ways of the past in which "central planning was deemed essential for research progress."[25] As William E. Paul, head of the Office of AIDS Research at NIH, wrote, "A turning point has been reached. Simple continuation of the policies of the past is likely to bring us only slow, fitful progress."[26]

Not only do organizations need entrepreneurs to be successful in developing new products and services, they also need to learn to develop their own sources of capital. This should be obvious by now. Our welfare system has proven that merely doling out money does not inspire the kind of creative energy that leads to self-sufficiency or long-term prosperity. Welfare for businesses produces similar results. "The first comprehensive survey of the Washington [D.C.] area's high-technology sector reveals a verdant seedbed of 2,331 companies stocked with promising technologies, but as a whole, still too small and underfunded to capitalize on them . . . But after decades of dependence on government contracts, most have not found the entrepreneurial nerve, investment capital or consumer appeal to make the leap into commercial prominence."[27] Unless organizations develop internal strength in critical areas, including product development and financing, they are not adequately equipped to compete in today's rapidly changing world.

BUREAUCRACY: AN IMPEDIMENT TO ENTREPRENEURSHIP, CREATIVITY, AND CHANGE

Managers in most organizations, large and small, are reluctant to hire and develop creative and innovative people because they are thought to be more trouble than they are worth. Their constant questioning and unwillingness to accept the status quo is threatening to the people who make up bureaucracies, and the disharmony they inspire can make bureaucrats feel very uncomfortable. However, the scarcity of creative people has the unintended side effect of virtually cutting off the supply of new ideas that inevitably determine the long-term prosperity of any organization.

Furthermore, the lack of creative people can disable an organization by blocking the flow of creative juices that inspire us to pursue challenging goals. Entrepreneurs stimulate us to raise our sights and search for new ideas that can transform an organization from a mediocre firm with modest profit potential to one with the capacity to produce huge profits. They also have the capacity to improve the quality of our lives by inspiring us to develop new products and services that help us in so many ways. Therefore, abolishing organizational resistance to change, and the entrepreneurs who inspire it, is imperative.

Bureaucrats make life unbearable for entrepreneurs, and they drive off the most talented ones. The problems they create are difficult to solve because managers in most organizations are not just part of the bureaucracy; they are the leaders of it. While they may adopt the terminology used today about teamwork, decentralization, total quality, and empowerment, their actions show clearly that they do not understand what these words mean. Instinctively they resort to centralization of decision making and exertion of control as preferred methods for solving problems, and most of them would not recognize the inconsistencies between their words and actions. Their behavior is deeply rooted, having evolved over many years of experience. Thus, changing their behavior is extremely difficult. Replacing the people in charge is likely to produce more positive short-term, and long-term, results than struggling to change their behavior.

Dr. Barry J. Marshall, a scientist at the University of Virginia Medical Center in Charlottesville, Virginia, is a good example of an entrepreneur who won out over the bureaucrats, but he is an exception to the rule. More than a decade ago, he challenged the medical community simply by suggesting that peptic ulcers are caused by a bacterium instead of stress or stomach acid, as most physicians believed. Eventually his colleagues' efforts to demolish his hypothesis helped to prove it, and he won the prestigious Albert Lasker Clinical Research Award.[28] The "skepticism and derision" he endured as they ridiculed his work could have destroyed his confidence and soured his attitude. Instead, he prevailed, and society is better off because he did. But most people are not that strong. They succumb to intense pressure to conform to accepted theories and practices in highly bureaucratic organizations, and we are denied important advances as a result. Bureaucratic resistance to change must be abolished.

EXAMPLES OF CORPORATE ENTREPRENEURSHIP

Minnesota Mining and Manufacturing (3M) is one of the most entrepreneurial companies in the United States. 3M engineers are expected to devote 15 percent of their time to independent projects that result in the creation of new product ideas that are the hallmark of the company's success.[29]

Their approach combines the best of Japanese-style teamwork and American maverickism to produce an uninterrupted string of successful product innovations. As one 3M executive said, "We want individual thought . . . because innovation is the key to survival."[30] At 3M, small groups are given total responsibility for product engineering and development, and their projects need not be justified or even revealed to supervisors. This is done to protect those who are coming up with new ideas from those who would attempt to destroy them.

Although less than half of the new ideas introduced ever become salable products, 3M continues this practice because it is the only way to ensure continued innovation and risk-taking on which the company is so dependent. The 3M strategy for encouraging entrepreneurship is similar to the creation of "skunk works" that were heralded by Tom Peters and Bob Waterman in their best-selling book, *In Search of Excellence*. Skunk works are "small, off-line groups not subject to the disciplines (or the bureaucratic pressures) of the corporation as a whole."[31] The reason firms like 3M use them is that they work.

The payoff for their commitment to entrepreneurship is a steady flow of new product ideas, many of which have no apparent market when they are first developed. As Clyde Hause, manager of the New Products Department for 3M's Industrial and Electronics Sector, says, "Two-thirds of the world's greatest inventions were market driven. The other third came from smart people who invented something and then found a use for it."[32] Post-it notes are a wonderful example of a product created by 3M scientists that had no apparent market at the time of creation, but which later produced hundreds of millions of dollars in revenues.

3M initiated a program called Genesis that grants funds to 3M engineers with good ideas that do not fit in with their division's strategic plans. Charles Murray, talking about the 3M way of doing business, says, "Creativity, the logic goes, is very much an individual experience, a process that resists the corporate approach—particularly the grinding bureaucracy so often present in huge companies."[33] 3M managers expect 25 percent of the company's sales to come from products introduced in the last five years. At 3M, "Engineers do not have to fit into any particular corporate mold. Nor are they forced to dress or look a certain way; they are not even expected to wear suits or ties."[34] According to Dr. Lester Krogh, vice president of research and development, "Typically, large companies expect all their scientists to behave a certain way. That's what we are trying to avoid. We want individual thought."[35]

Quad Graphics, a printing company in Pewaukee, Wisconsin, is another great example of a company that has learned how to innovate and has made innovation a part of its everyday life. Harry Quadracci, founder and president, describes the company's culture as "a circus with continuous performances by highly creative troupes."[36] In his 1984 "President's Letter" he wrote, "Clowns are a perfect symbol of the Quad Graphics philosophy of management, because, unlike so many others, they are not wedded to conventional wisdom. They retain their childlike ability to be surprised, and the flexibility to adapt to, or even thrive on, change."[37]

Quadracci thinks "all management is an experiment,"[38] and he believes that freedom and trust are the twin companions of control. The strength of his belief was revealed in 1974 when he initiated the annual "spring fling." One day a year, all the company's managers leave for a retreat of sorts and leave the company in the hands of its employees. Although the risks inherent in this approach are obvious, its effects on employee morale and commitment have been extremely positive. "Harry manages by letting people manage themselves and, through that responsibility, achieve things they never thought themselves capable of achieving."[39] Quad Graphics does not tolerate laggards, but it rewards risk-taking. Everyone is expected to work constantly to find new and better ways to do business. Sometimes things work; sometimes they do not. But they never stop trying. If they do, it is time for them to seek employment elsewhere.

To say Quadracci breaks with tradition is an understatement. The guiding theory he uses, called Theory Q, has two basic tenets: be informed and don't bother to make plans. His business thrives on ART (active risk-taking). He wants his people to take risks and to be responsible. He employs this belief every day. He tells about the time in 1985 when he purchased John Blair Marketing, a firm that publishes color advertising-coupon inserts for newspapers. Quadracci went to see the president late one afternoon and agreed on the spot to buy the company. A few weeks later, the deal was consummated. As Quadracci said about a year later, "One year ago, owning this company was the farthest thing from my mind. And here I am, sitting in the geographic center of all my dreams—Rockefeller Center, across the street from the Time-Life Building. And it was not in my plans."[40]

Quadracci believes in ART for everyone in the organization. He says, "I'd rather have 50 people out there all thinking independently—being in conflict with ideas without conflicting in personality—and working together independently to develop an operating policy that I can validate, than for me to sit up here from the top down and say, This is the way we are going to do it."[41]

He believes in hands-on management and staying in touch with the market. He is not a believer in planning and budgeting, though. The market changes too rapidly for that, and locking into plans and budgets has the adverse effect of thwarting the company's ability to respond to change. He uses his father-in-law's philosophy—MPYPIDK (My plan, your plan, I don't know. Let's just see what happens).[42] Using this approach, he encourages his people to takes risks and make things happen. They see an opportunity, and they seize it. One opportunity then leads to another. Says Quadracci, "So why sit there in November or October and try to develop a budget for the following year based upon something that happened the first six months of this year? That's what a budget is. It is so far removed from the reality of the market that the decisions aren't being made immediately. Those decisions are being made in a vacuum, they're not being made in a live environment."[43]

Does Quadracci's approach work? The facts speak for themselves. In 1976, Quad Graphic had 100 employees and plant and equipment worth $3.7 million. In 1985, the company had 20 presses in four plants worth $154 million and more than 1,800 employees. The company did $145 million in business that year. In 1986, Quad Graphics had 24 presses producing $265 million in business. In 1987, they added another plant, had 30 presses rolling, and sales climbed to $345 million.[44]

CREATING A HEALTHY ENVIRONMENT FOR ENTREPRENEURS

As we have said before, entrepreneurs are a rare breed. They do not think or act like other employees in most organizations. They thrive on new and exciting ideas, and they welcome change. The humdrum of day-to-day business bores them, since they prefer to take risks and extend their boundaries.[45] Thus, it is difficult for entrepreneurs to prosper in the typical corporate environment with its hierarchy, chain of command, formal reporting relationships, and politics. To create healthy environments for entrepreneurs, leaders must be willing to change everything. From reconfiguring boards of directors to reward systems, nothing should be sacrosanct.

Boards of Directors Must Be Informed and Involved

We have talked with hundreds of executives and board members, and we have no doubt that most organizations fail to utilize their boards properly. Many executives believe strongly that board members should not become involved in the details of day-to-day business operations and that they should refrain from creating the impression that they disagree with management on fundamental issues so as to avoid undercutting management in the eyes of employees. Clearly, if board members are too involved in day-to-day activities, they interfere and probably cannot do the critical job of establishing broad company policy that they are elected to perform.

However, having little on no knowledge of day-to-day operations leaves board members at the mercy of executives. Although they may think they always act in the best interests of the companies they manage, executives have agendas and biases that influence the decisions they make and the information they provide to board members. To do their jobs well, board members should be encouraged to ask questions and to seek answers from people involved with the companies they serve other than executives (i.e., employees, suppliers, customers, shareholders, and others).

Boards of directors must be well informed and involved to do their jobs correctly. They should *never* be rubber stamps for management, although many of them are. Instead, they should get to know and understand the products the company sells, the customers it serves, and the people in the company who are responsible for producing results. If they are too busy to do these things, they should not be asked to serve. If they already serve as board members, but cannot make this level of commitment, they should be asked to resign. Additionally, the performance of board members should be evaluated regularly, and those who fail to do their job properly should not be asked to serve again.

Too often, executives try to shield board members from information they should have and from people in the company whose opinions differ from those of corporate executives. In a bureaucratic environment, executives might attempt to orchestrate everything board members see and hear to make themselves look good and to get the board to do what they want. Thus, board members should be prepared to take the initiative themselves if necessary to arrange private, confidential meetings with people whose insights, although different from those of management, can assist them in doing the critical job of protecting the interests of shareholders (which may be different from the interests of executives).

It is conceivable that executives will resist this level of involvement by board members at first, but in the long run it is best for everyone involved with the company. If board members, the group sitting at the pinnacle of the corporate hierarchy, are not free to ask questions about company activities and to disagree with company policies and practices, it is highly unlikely that employees lower in the organization will feel free to do these things. Ultimately, to be competitive with the best firms in the world everyone must look constantly for new and better ways to do things and to question anything that stands in the way of improved performance.

Depose Dictators

A dictator is an absolute ruler; a tyrant; a despot.[46] Organizations headed by dictators feel almost like prisons in which managers are wardens or guards and employees are inmates. Dictators do not lead; they impose their will on others by force or coercion. They do not listen; they tell. Although they may be able to produce good short-term financial results, they sap the creativity, energy, enthusiasm, and zeal from their employees and destroy their spirit. In the long run, they will ruin an organization.

It is especially difficult for dictators to lead entrepreneurial organizations because entrepreneurs will not tolerate them for long. If they feel trapped in a dictatorial environment, good entrepreneurs will simply leave. Less talented people with few options are the ones most likely to endure dictators, and they are the ones who should be weeded out to make our businesses more competitive.

Ironically, many entrepreneurs have dictatorial styles, and therefore cannot lead. They may be creative and innovative in developing new product and service ideas, but their ability to inspire that same high level of performance from others is limited. Therefore, great care must be taken in appointing leaders to ensure that they are not dictators. If dictatorial leaders are already in place, they should be deposed.

Inject Excitement and Enthusiasm into the Organization

In bureaucratic organizations, "good managers" are calm, cool, and collected at all times. They go about their jobs with a sort of detached, impersonal, emotionless objectivity that is about as exciting as watching grass grow and about as motivating as a long swim in ice water. They may be professionals, but they display a complete lack of passion for the product or service they produce and hope to sell. Leaders must support their people and display enthusiasm, or they must be replaced by more entrepreneurial types who radiate excitement and inspire people.

Managerial support, excitement, zeal, and enthusiasm are essential for success in competitive markets. As Tom Peters has said, "I have discovered there are two sorts of corporate bosses: those who are gung-ho about management per se, and those who are obsessed with the product or service they deliver. Talk with the former for an hour, and you may still have no idea what they make. Hang around the others for 15 seconds, and you'll be regaled (like it or not, and it can get old for the innocent bystander) by tale after tale of the product, how it's being improved and changed, why it's great, etc."[47] The latter are far more likely to lead their organizations to success in competitive markets than the former.

Decentralize and Empower

Restructuring organizations to reduce the number of management levels as much as possible and to reduce the number of managers creates more autonomous units that allow people to make decisions and improve organizational performance. Therefore, this is a critical step in the process of empowering people so they can be entrepreneurial. Decentralizing decision making and eliminating unnecessary management positions puts the responsibility for performance where it belongs: in the hands of people at the lowest level possible in the organization. The underlying philosophy is different in decentralized firms. Instead of thinking about how many managers are needed, the focus is on how few of them are required to get the job done.

Decentralizing decision making has the side effect of reducing needless bureaucratic obstacles that hinder progress. There are fewer managers to filter information and to second-guess decisions, so people are freer to act. People need freedom to explore possibilities and room to make mistakes if they are to have any hope of achieving world-class performance.

Empowering people, and encouraging them to use their creativity and ingenuity, is essential for success in today's rapidly changing and competitive markets.

Dave Duffield, founder of PeopleSoft (a rapidly growing and profitable firm specializing in client server applications), put it very well when he explained his philosophy for growing a successful business. He said, "Find the best people in your industry, treat them well, give them a piece of the 'action' in the form of stock, be a coach rather than director, expect miracles, minimize bureaucracy, and fire people who start building fiefdoms."[48]

Encourage Hard Work, Experimentation, and Risk-Taking

Leaders need to give their people the time, resources, and freedom they need to do their jobs effectively. However, too often they are consumed with the desire to stay informed at the expense of the hard work, experimentation, and risk-taking that are fundamental to successful entrepreneurial activity. Insecure about the whole process of entrepreneurship, they saddle their people with unnecessary red tape and lengthy meetings, and they force their people to defend themselves and their ideas constantly without cause.[49] At best they slow the entrepreneurial process down to a snail's pace, and at worst they drive off their most talented entrepreneurs.

The inclination of managers to schedule frequent, lengthy meetings in hopes of overcoming their insecurity, in particular, can demoralize and discourage entrepreneurs. They must take precious time away from their important work to engage in these meetings, which consume 70 percent, or more, of their time in most organizations, and little or nothing of significance is accomplished. "As companies push for efficiency and give employees more say, many people are meeting more and accomplishing less, management experts say. 'We're having too many meetings called to deal with trivia under the pretense of collaboration,' said Sharon Lippincott, a Pittsburgh-based consultant."[50] According to Mitchell Nash, a partner in Interaction Associates Inc. in Cambridge, Massachusetts, about half the time people spend in meetings is an absolute waste.[51]

The excessive amount of time spent in meetings by most managers is nothing new. It was well documented by Neil Snyder and William Glueck more than 15 years ago.[52] This problem must be solved. A good first step is to require managers to keep a time log for a couple of weeks to give them an idea how much of their time, and the time of their subordinates, they consume in meetings. Next, you should ask them to identify the contributions each meeting made to the company's well-being and the cost of each meeting in terms of salary and benefits and lost opportunities. Ultimately, managers must begin to think in terms of the value added by each meeting and its cost. If they do not, they will continue to waste a great deal of time and frustrate your most productive people in the process.

In the absence of hard work, experimentation, and risk-taking by entrepreneurs, organizations die a slow death as their competitors eventually catch up with them and take their customers. Leaders must do everything in their power to ensure that entrepreneurs have the time and resources they need to do their jobs. Earlier we used 3M and Quad Graphics as examples of firms that have organized to encourage entrepreneurial activity. They are great examples to be emulated.

Accept Mistakes As the Cost of Progress

To succeed in today's rapidly changing global market, leaders must be willing to continually challenge the premises of their businesses. Additionally, they must be restless and discontented with the status quo, willing as we have said before to change everything about their businesses.[53] When they adopt this philosophy, they will find that entrepreneurs will take risks, and along with risks come mistakes.

The instinctive response to mistakes by most managers is to eliminate them and to create processes designed to guarantee they do not recur. In stable environments, this approach might work, but the world in which we live is not stable. It is changing so quickly only the most talented people can keep up. Thus, attempting to eliminate mistakes (which in reality cannot be accomplished) has the side effect of thwarting progress. Leaders must accept mistakes as a cost of doing business and teach everyone in their organizations to do the same.

Set High Expectations

While leaders must learn to accept mistakes, they must establish high expectations for all their people. Mistakes are tolerated, but not trying and mediocre performance are not. People have a tendency to live up to, or down to, the expectations set by leaders. Thus, expectations should be set at a level high enough to challenge people to excel.

Reward Performance

There is a great deal of personal risk associated with entrepreneurial activity in most firms. Try and fail, people suffer. Try and succeed, they get a pat on the back and a thank-you, maybe. Remember, it is extremely easy to assess the performance of people who develop and implement the ideas on which businesses build their organizations, because costs and progress are observable and measurable. If leaders want people to take risks and develop new ideas, the rewards for those who succeed must be commensurate with the risks taken. If they fail to adequately reward risk takers, then people will not take risks.

Leaders must develop a philosophy toward rewards that is incredibly simple: Reward performance and only performance. People should not be rewarded for the color of their skin, their gender, their family ties, or anything except what they have done.

MOVING ON

In the next three chapters, we will present outstanding examples of leaders in action. In chapter 10, we will look at Ted Turner, and in chapter 11, we will focus on Jack Welch. Then, in chapter 12, we will examine the changes at Ford Motor Company that have taken it from near bankruptcy in the early 1980s to an industry leader today.

ENDNOTES

1. "When These Gurus Preach, Business Bosses Listen," *U.S. News & World Report*, December 2, 1985, p. 7.
2. Elizabeth Corcoran, "Java Jumps Into the Net," *Washington Post*, December 10, 1995, p. H-1.
3. Ibid., p. H-1.
4. Tom Peters, "Still Leadership," *Forbes ASAP*, October 9, 1995, p. 184.
5. Kenneth Labich, "Kissing Off," *Fortune*, February 20, 1995, p. 44.
6. Kara Swisher, "Independent-Minded Manzi," *Washington Post*, October 12, 1995, p. D11.
7. Swisher, p. D14.
8. *Washington Post*, October 14, 1995, p. H1.
9. Peters, p. 184.

10. C.K. Prahalad and Vladimar Pucik, "Can Entrepreneurs Find a Home in Big Business?" *Business and Society Review,* Winter 1989, p. 11.

11. Ibid., p. 12.

12. Judith H. Dobrzynski, "IBM's Board Should Clean Out the Corner Office," *Business Week,* February 1, 1993, p. 27.

13. Thomas McCarroll, "How IBM Was Left Behind," *Time,* December 28, 1992, p. 27.

14. Jolie Solomon, "Brave New Directors," *Newsweek,* March 1, 1993, p. 59.

15. Ibid. p. 60.

16. John Greenwald, "Are America's Corporate Giants a Dying Breed?" *Time,* December 28, 1992, p. 28.

17. Solomon, p. 60.

18. Greenwald, p. 44.

19. Transcript from "Business Day" on Cable News Network, October 19, 1995, p. 1.

20. Associated Press, "Archer Daniels Midland Shuffles Board," *Washington Post,* January 16, 1996, p. D3.

21. Sandra Sugawara, "Daiwa Scandal Hits Japan with a Rare Form of Anger," *Washington Post,* October 26, 1995, p. D11.

22. AT&T News Release, "AT&T Announces Strategic Restructuring to Capture Opportunities of the 21st Century," September 20, 1995.

23. Kirstin Grimsley, "AT&T Promises Aid to Laid-Off Workers," *Washington Post,* January 3, 1996, p. C-1.

24. David Brown, "NIH Official Urges Shift in AIDS Policy to Scientist-Initiated Research," *Washington Post,* February 3, 1995, p. A9.

25. Ibid., p. A9.

26. Ibid.

27. Peter Behr and Kara Swisher, "Local Technology Firms Face Problems Going Commercial," *Washington Post,* May 10, 1995, p. F1.

28. "U.VA. Scientist Wins Award for His Research on Ulcers," *The Daily Progress* (Charlottesville, Virginia), September 27, 1995, p. A2.

29. Charles J. Murray, "Why 3M Values 'Intrapreneurship,'" *Design News,* July 4, 1988, p. 112.

30. Ibid., p. 112.

31. Prahalad and Pucik, "Can Entrepreneurs Find a Home in Big Business?" p. 10.

32. Murray, p. 112.

33. Ibid., p. 111.

34. Ibid.
35. Ibid., p. 112.
36. Daniel M. Kehrer, "The P.T. Barnum of Printing," *Across the Board,* May 1989, p. 53.
37. Daniel M. Kehrer, "The Miracle of Theory Q," *Business Month,* September 1989, p. 47.
38. Ibid., p. 53.
39. Ibid.
40. Ibid., p. 46.
41. Ibid., p. 47.
42. Ibid., p. 54.
43. Ibid.
44. Ibid.
45. Kevin McDermott, "Going It Alone," *D&B Reports,* March/April 1989, p. 35.
46. *The American Heritage Dictionary of the English Language,* 3rd ed., (Houghton Mifflin, 1992), p. 518.
47. Peters, p. 184.
48. Dave Duffield, Information provided for a presentation on his firm, People-Soft, in a strategic management class at the McIntire School of Commerce in November 1995.
49. Ibid.
50. Knight-Ridder, "We've Got to Stop Meeting Like This," *Washington Post,* December 31, 1995, p. H-2.
51. Ibid., p. H-2.
52. Neil H. Snyder and William Glueck, "How Managers Plan—The Analysis of Managers' Activities," *Long Range Planning,* February 1980, pp. 70–76.
53. Greenwald, p. 28.

10

CHAPTER

Ted Turner: The Building of an Empire

"Lead, Follow, or Get Out of the Way"

—Ted Turner's motto[1]

"I never quit. I've got a bunch of flags on my boat, but there ain't no *white* flags. I don't surrender."

—Ted Turner[2]

"Turner knows how to capture every market, even if there isn't even a market there."

—Ted Kavanau, CNN[3]

"I am the right man, in the right place, at the right time."

—Ted Turner[4]

The story of Turner Broadcasting's rise to the forefront of the communications industry starts with the dreams and the drive of one man who relentlessly pursued his vision through a constantly changing environment. The key to Ted Turner's success lies in his persistence and dedication to follow his dreams even in the face of adversity.

Turner's vision was simple: to build an empire in the telecommunications industry. From the first day he took over his father's billboard business,

---

This chapter was contributed by Kim Toppin, a McIntire School of Commerce alumnus who is with Paine Webber in New York.

Turner was constantly looking forward, envisioning new and as yet unimagined ways of combining his assets to give him an edge over his competitors. Turner is hailed as one of the most prominent entrepreneurs of the decade, one of the truly great magnates of this age. In spite of his highly visible escapades and inescapable notoriety, Turner is one of the most important men in television today. He has founded seven networks, the most significant of these from an influence perspective being CNN. Through CNN, the world is able to watch what is happening around the globe in real time. As the eyes of the world, CNN has achieved influence far beyond that of any other news-reporting organization in the world.

The power Turner wields through the empire he controls is considerable, and his influence is felt around the world. As a child, Turner thought of himself as a new Alexander the Great, and today he runs a $7.5 billion empire he created from a small, rundown local television station in Georgia. Turner's life is an epic, filled with exceptional drama, exhilarating highs, and disheartening lows. Those who know him well once thought the odds of his achieving success were quite limited, given what they believed was his penchant for taking enormous risks without adequate consideration for the consequences.

But remarkably, Turner has managed to come out on top despite the odds. His impressive achievements and his single-minded determination have taken him to a position of dominance in the television industry. The dedication, perseverance, vision, determination, and creativity that are so vital to Turner's character have carried him through many difficult periods in his life. Even his adversaries must admit that Ted Turner never gives up. He is a survivor, and to use his own words, he doesn't surrender.

THE BUILDING OF AN EMPIRE

Ted Turner was born in Georgia in 1938, to a father who was hard and demanding, sometimes distant, sometimes cruel. Beginning at age six, Ted spent most of his time at boarding schools, rarely even coming home for summer vacations. After completing the seventh grade, he returned home to Savannah for the summer to work for his father at Turner Advertising, his father's billboard business. He was paid $50 a week, and his father charged him $25 a week for room and board.[5] Although it may seem unusual for a 12-year-old boy to pay room and board to his parents, doing it convinced Ted he had the capacity for hard work.

His endurance, energy, and determination impressed his fellow workers, and set the stage for his later successes. When Ted was 22 years old, his only sister, Mary Jean, died of lupus. The suicide of his father just two years later devastated Ted and intensified his compulsion to achieve. After his father's death, Ted inherited Turner Advertising and started a journey that would bring him wealth, fame, influence, and power in the rapidly developing telecommunications industry.

THE EMERGENCE OF A LEADER

Turner took control of his father's business when he was 24 years old. Just before he died, his father arranged to sell off a large part of his business, leaving Ted only a small portion of the original company. "Ed [Ted's father] thought Ted was too young to run the business," said Bob Naegele, an old friend of the family.[6] Determined to hold on to his father's business in its entirety, Turner sold off real estate, including the plantation, and took on a great deal of debt. Irwin Mazo, who worked with Ted for the next eight years as his financial adviser and accountant, describes Turner as a man driven to succeed.[7]

Ted's passion was his work, and his dream of creating an empire consumed him. The billboard business was simply a vehicle to help him realize his dream. According to his first wife, Judy Nye, "The dream was just to build on the dream, till you can't go any further."[8]

From the first day he took the reins of his father's business, Turner was constantly looking for expansion opportunities. Although the billboard business was successful and was generating strong cash flow, Turner recognized the outdoor advertising industry was mature and offered very little room for growth. His first move away from outdoor advertising was into radio, but quickly after entering the radio industry, he purchased two television stations. Ultimately, television would provide Turner with the platform he needed to pursue his big dreams.

BUILDING THE FOUNDATION

Peter Drucker wrote:

> Successful entrepreneurs find innovative ways to seize unoccupied niches or carve out new niches of their own. Combine this ability with a contrarian

nature, and you have a powerful force for change. True entrepreneurs learn as much from their failures as their successes. But when they finally prevail it is the conventional wisdom which is most often proven wrong.[9]

As soon as Turner realized he could not fulfill his dreams in the billboard industry, he began to look elsewhere. He saw television as the industry in which he could build an empire. Like nearly all of Turner's decisions, the decision to move into television was made on the spur of the moment, with minimal thought about the likelihood of failure. Typical of gifted entrepreneurs, Turner felt the need to move forward aggressively to establish his position so he could compete. He did not allow the fear of failure or ridicule to stop him, and he was widely ridiculed each time he made a move.

In 1970, Turner bought Channel 17, a UHF television station in Atlanta that was losing $50,000 a month, for next to nothing.[10] A few months later, he purchased another UHF television station in Charlotte, North Carolina. At the time, his managers advised him against the project. In fact, Irwin Mazo was so upset about the Charlotte acquisition that he resigned, and convinced the board to veto the Charlotte acquisition, forcing Turner to buy it on his own. Jim Roddey, former president and chief operating officer of Turner Communications, left soon thereafter, beginning a long chain of employees who found Turner too difficult to work for.[11]

With the acquisition of the two UHF stations, Turner showed a visionary quality that moved him ahead of his competitors in the industry. Like many others, he had foreseen the rapid growth potential in the television industry. But more importantly, he realized he could use his empty billboards to advertise his own stations and that the two stations could share programming and equipment. This was an early indication of Turner's knack for combining his resources to create a whole that was larger than the sum of its parts. Turner's ability to see how combinations of assets can be used effectively, an ability most businesspeople have not developed to a significant extent, enabled him to accomplish his goals and to become a powerful force in telecommunications.

Although he initially had trouble keeping the stations on the air, Channel 17, renamed WTCG (Turner Communications Group), proved to be extremely successful. Using old movies and baseball (the Atlanta Braves) as programming staples, he turned the small UHF station into a profitable Atlanta television station, gaining a 15 percent market share, almost unheard of for a UHF station.[12]

THE BIRTH OF THE FIRST SUPERSTATION

In 1972, Turner expanded his horizons yet again. Building a television empire of great proportion requires a large audience, and Turner realized that he had to expand his distribution outside the Atlanta area. The easiest way to accomplish that was to expand into the cable business. In those days, cable was simply a way for viewers to receive basic network programming with a clear, static-free picture. Teleprompter, an Alabama cable service, wanted to offer its viewers a bonus for subscribing, so the owner approached Turner with a subscription proposition. Although he received none of the $4.95 subscription fee, WTCG was being seen by an additional 250,000 viewers, thus enabling him to raise more advertising revenue.[13] Suddenly, WTCG went from being an Atlanta television station to a regional channel, and Turner had found a way to make Channel 17 make money.

In 1974, Turner faced another critical decision, one that would change the scope of his business forever. The addition of 250,000 viewers was only the tip of the iceberg, and it opened up a world of interesting possibilities for Turner Broadcasting. Looking into the future, Turner saw his regional channel becoming a national channel, and he started looking for ways to make it happen.

At the time, satellites were the latest in technology. Although some observers thought it was foolish for a small regional television station to subscribe to a satellite service, it made sense to Ted Turner. He realized that it would become increasingly practical and efficient to broadcast his signal to markets across the country using satellite transmissions than by using the traditional approach, which involved building broadcasting towers in each television market in the country.[14]

Characteristically, Turner's mind was instantly made up. He acted quickly, signed on with RCA, and applied for FCC approval. This haphazard method of doing business has been Turner's trademark throughout his career. Once he is sold on an idea, nothing can stop him from carrying out his plan of action. Although his plans always seem to work out in the end, many people who have worked for him, whose tolerance for risk is lower than his, thought he was acting recklessly.

It was his "damn the torpedoes" philosophy that made it both exciting and infuriating to work for Turner. The dizzying pace of his work and his explosive personality were a combination few could abide for long. But for those who could tolerate his style, the Turner empire provided more opportunities than they could imagine.

THE TURNER WAY

Many of Turner's employees did not care for his sporadic management style, which was characterized by long absences followed by "bursts of hyperactivity when he returned and began stirring up the pot."[15] He was tolerant of his employees, but only if they could produce and pull their own weight. Turner made all of the major decisions, but he expected his employees to carry out all of the logistical details while he was away.

Although Turner's management style is unusual, he is successful in motivating his employees. His extraordinary energy level fosters a stimulating work environment and provides an example for his employees to follow. He is constantly looking ahead for the next opportunity, often seeing potential in his ventures that is not easily seen by others in the industry.

TURNER MOVES AGGRESSIVELY INTO SPORTS

In January 1976, Turner took another step toward solidifying the foundation for his empire by acquiring the Atlanta Braves baseball team. Although he had an exclusive contract to carry Braves games on Channel 17, the team was not winning, and Turner was concerned about losing viewers.

Convinced he could turn the Braves around and increase his audience share as a result, Turner decided to buy the Braves. He also thought it was important to buy the team to keep it in Atlanta.[16] With the purchase, Turner guaranteed the availability and cost of important programming for his station. At a press conference announcing the sale, in his usual rambling style, he promised that he would bring a World Series to Atlanta in five years, a promise that he would not fulfill until 1991.[17]

Although Turner knew almost nothing about baseball, his enthusiasm was boundless. "You know, baseball isn't complicated like football. One guy throws the ball, another guy catches it. Then you got squeeze plays, bunts, and all that stuff, but it isn't hard. And if I didn't know what to do, I would ask the players," Turner explained on a plane ride back to Atlanta from a yacht race.[18]

Despite Turner's lack of experience in professional sports, his expertise in marketing was applied to selling his new team to an ever expanding audience. And he did this successfully, applying his own special brand of publicity. Both the Braves and the Atlanta Hawks, the basketball team he purchased in 1977 for $4 million, served to increase the Superstation's viewership by nearly 100,000 new cable households per month.[19] However, by the end of a very busy summer in 1977, Turner was losing momentum. His usual 16-hour workdays became more difficult to fill, and he began looking for a new challenge to hold his attention.

CREATING A NEWS CHANNEL: CNN

> Although Turner likes to be known as a visionary, he is probably best understood as a borrower and a builder rather than an originator, more Roman than Greek.[20]

Once Turner had proven the value of satellite distribution with his Superstation, he knew he had to develop his strategic advantage in this area before the rest of the world caught on. He saw the news industry as ripe for a new entrant, and he started planning a 24-hour news service offered from Atlanta, Georgia, and distributed by satellite to the rest of the world.

Although several other firms had toyed with the idea of establishing an all-news cable channel before Turner started CNN, no action was taken until December 1978, when Turner pitched his idea to cable operators.[21] Characteristically, Turner planned to put CNN on the air in just 12 months.

By 1980, the three networks (ABC, CBS, and NBC) controlled virtually all of the news output, and television news was the primary news source for over two-thirds of American households.[22] Network news budgets had grown dramatically, as top personalities commanded anywhere from six-figure salaries to multimillion-dollar contracts. The networks were spending over $150 million per year just to produce the evening news, and no end was in sight.[23]

For his idea to work, Turner knew he had to find someone with knowledge and credibility to run his new organization. Reese Schonfeld, a man who shared Turner's passion for an all-news channel, was the man for the job. He was hired as the president of CNN, and the project was underway.

Schonfeld's first priority was to sign credible news announcers, and Dan Schorr, a respected newsman and legendary journalist, was the man he wanted to build the network on the air. Schorr agreed to do the job just 20 minutes before the press conference announcing the creation of CNN, under intense pressure from Turner. According to Schorr,

> So I looked at this guy, Turner, and saw that he understood what satellites could deliver. He understood cable and its potential. He had some idea of what kind of programming he wanted to put on: "If something's going on

anywhere," he said, "we're gonna bring it right in live. People want to see it happening in front of their eyes." Very bright. And, finally, he was a businessman. So he was doing right now what Bill Paley [founder of CBS] had done, by joining the knowledge of those key elements.[24]

Turner was under a great deal of pressure to sign Schorr before the press conference began. As a result, he agreed to a clause in Schorr's contract guaranteeing him complete editorial control at CNN. It gave Schorr enormous influence during the early development phase of CNN's history, and it precluded him from having to do anything he felt would compromise his professional standards.[25] This clause turned out to be a good deal for both Schorr and Turner. Schorr was able to participate in an important new venture in the industry he loved and had devoted his life to, and Turner got a highly regarded newsman who brought instant credibility to CNN.

In the early days, most analysts doubted CNN's ability to survive. It was nicknamed the "Chicken Noodle Network," and frequent technical mishaps and blunders gave them reason to believe they were correct. When CNN went on the air live with its "open newsroom" concept, the cameras caught everything from painters and electricians hanging from the rafters finishing their work to custodians emptying wastebaskets on the air.[26] Dan Schorr's clothes once caught fire while he was reporting the news, because a lightbulb exploded. When CNN cut from the story and returned to him, Schorr calmly provided viewers with a summary of the incident they had witnessed.[27] Here was the news, with all of its technical problems and missed cues, for all the world to see. But in spite of these "glitches," CNN caught the attention of many for its tenacity and spirit.

Almost immediately, CNN was engaged in a full-fledged battle with its first direct competitor: the Satellite News Channel. The new 24-hour news network, scheduled to go on the air in spring/summer 1982, was ABC/Westinghouse's attempt to crush CNN.[28] CNN moved quickly to the offensive, initiating plans for a new 24-hour news channel of its own called Headline News that would go on the air in January 1981, just four months after Turner conceived the idea. The new channel would offer a continuously updated summary of the day's events, recycled every half hour. Headline News was immediately successful, and SNC folded in 1983 after only 12 months of operation.[29] Turner arranged to buy SNC's 7.5 million subscribers for $25 million, and forged ahead with his network.[30]

CNN has become the most prestigious provider of world news in the broadcast industry. For most of the Gulf War, CNN was the prime source of news, information, and political intelligence for the U.S. government. The speed and accuracy of CNN's news gathering put the CIA to shame, and world leaders tuned in to CNN to find out what was going on instead of relying on their own agencies for up-to-the-minute information.

Time magazine relates a story that typifies CNN's global reach:

> On the night that the bombs began to fall on Baghdad, Gilbert Lavoie, press secretary to Canada's Prime Minister, Brian Mulroney, telephoned his counterpart Marlin Fitzwater at the White House. Marlin said, "Hi, what are you doing?" Lavoie recalls, "and I said, I'm doing the same thing you are—watching CNN."[31]

The key to CNN's success is its people and their penchant for being in the right place at the right time, with cameras, more quickly than anyone else. When the network first started, it had a staff of 300 and a newsroom in the basement of a converted country club in Atlanta. Today, the network has a staff of over 2,000, a budget that is continually growing even as major networks are cutting back, and a global presence dwarfing that of its rivals. More importantly, though, CNN is regarded by world leaders as the best source of breaking news in the world, and they tune in frequently to watch what is happening along with millions of other viewers.[32]

Just like other Turner companies, CNN is not satisfied with having achieved success. CNN executives continually look for ways to expand their viewer base. Whether they are supplying a news-feed service to broadcast stations or news and features packages tailored for airports and supermarket checkout lines, they keep their programming in front of receptive viewers. Advertisers have come to realize the value of their ads run on CNN, and the network has become very profitable.[33]

Just as he had done several times before, Turner had to leverage everything he owned to launch CNN. He was willing to lose everything—his television stations, the sports teams, his yachts—if the network failed. But it did not fail. Instead, it became a resounding success and established the standard against which other news organizations are measured.

AN ABORTED ATTEMPT TO TAKE OVER CBS

By early 1985, Turner was in a secure position financially, and he was beginning to look ahead to his next big move. He foresaw the consolidation in the broadcasting industry, and he wanted to be one of the big players.

Turner had discussed the possibility of merging with one of the three major networks in the early 1980s, but had been unable to reach an agreement. In 1981, he had a secret meeting with two CBS executives, who had flown to Atlanta to discuss the possibility of acquiring CNN. Turner offered to sell them less than 49 percent of the network, but CBS wanted complete control. As the CBS executives were preparing to leave, Turner told them something that was interesting and revealing. "You CBS guys are something," he said. "Someday I'm gonna own you. You bet I am. Remember I told you so. Hey, some terrific plane! Wanna sell it to me? What's the difference? I'll own it anyway, one of these days."[34] There was no doubt about the fact that Turner wanted to be a big player in the big game, and he was not in awe of any hot shot executives from CBS.

Four years later, in March 1985, Capital Cities acquired ABC for $3.5 billion, and Turner's juices really started flowing. In April 1985, with the aid of E.F. Hutton & Co., he announced a hostile takeover bid for CBS.[35]

The ABC takeover clarified the various regulatory agencies' positions on takeovers, and the time seemed ripe for Turner to go after CBS. On April 18, 1985, Turner announced the CBS takeover bid at New York's Plaza Hotel. To acquire CBS, Turner offered a variety of high-risk debt securities (junk bonds) in exchange for CBS stock. At the time of the offer, CBS's net worth was estimated at $7.6 billion, or $254 a share. The face value of Turner's offer was $175 a share in securities, but estimates of the market value of the offer ranged from $130 to $155 a share.[36]

If the offer had been accepted, he would have acquired the broadcast network and four of the five CBS-owned and -operated television stations. Turner planned to sell one station, the CBS records group, the CBS publishing group, radio stations, and various other holdings for $3.1 billion and use the proceeds from the sale to retire debt.[37] The reaction to Turner's offer was negative, and CBS prepared to launch a counterattack. They decided to take a "poison pill" (i.e., buy back roughly 21 percent of their stock for $960 million and incur a heavy debt load in the process), thus making CBS unattractive as a takeover target.[38]

Turner filed suit to prevent CBS from moving forward with its repurchase plan, but both the FCC and a federal judge in Atlanta ruled that the board had acted in a reasonable manner and in the best interests of the stockholders. The cost of the failed takeover attempt was very high for CBS. Since the struggle ended, CBS has had serious financial difficulties, and several members of the company's top management group at the time have been dismissed.[39]

Although TBS spent $18.6 million in legal and other fees on the takeover attempt, the loss had its compensations. Turner had successfully portrayed himself as a major player in the television industry, and he established himself as one of the leaders in the industry.

TURNER ACQUIRES A FILM LIBRARY

Since 1980, Turner had been discussing the prospect of purchasing MGM/UA from Kirk Kerkorian. When Kerkorian hinted that the Fayad family in Egypt was ready to make an offer to buy the company, Turner dropped all other interests and rushed to Hollywood to hammer out a deal.[40] He needed access to lots of films for programming on his Superstation so he could protect and expand his audience. The Superstation accounted for over 80 percent of TBS's profits, and it was costing Turner increasingly large amounts of money to license films, while some studios, MGM included, refused to license to TBS at any price.

The *New York Times* pointed out:

> Mr. Turner had begun to have problems buying movies for the Atlanta Superstation. In many cases, he was still paying the low rates for films that he had been charged in the 70s, when WTBS was just beginning to develop a national audience. That irritated Hollywood, and MGM even refused to lease films to WTBS. By 1985, Mr. Turner was worried that profit margins were beginning to erode as ad revenues failed to keep pace with costs at the Superstation, which accounts for 80 percent of the operating profits of Turner Broadcasting's core businesses."[41]

There was another important reason why Turner wanted to buy MGM/UA. The trend toward consolidation in the entertainment industry meant that in order for TBS to be a long-term player in the big game, he had to either "increase [his] distribution base—that would have been the CBS transaction—or acquire some software—that was the MGM deal."[42]

Kirkorian introduced Turner to Michael Milken, of Drexel Burnham Lambert, to arrange the $1.5 billion in financing he needed to consummate the deal. The arrangement was highly unusual, since Milken acted both as Turner's financier and MGM's banker, but he was the only one knowledgeable enough about MGM's balance sheet to structure the deal quickly.

By early 1986, the MGM/UA purchase had started to put tremendous pressure on Turner. New movie releases by MGM/UA bombed at the box office, and the studio was in trouble. Additionally, Turner owed nearly $2 billion, more than any individual in history,[43] and he had to find a way to get out from under the heavy debt load. In June 1986, Turner agreed to perhaps the only option he had: to sell almost everything back to Kirk Kerkorian, for $300 million, substantially less than he had paid for it less than three months earlier. He was left with only the film library, for which he still owed nearly $1 billion. In essence, Turner had paid $1.2 billion for the

MGM film library, at least $200 million more than it was worth according to so-called industry experts.

THE CABLE INDUSTRY COMES TO THE RESCUE

By 1987, Turner realized he was in serious financial trouble. However, considering TBS's enormous value to the cable industry, he believed he still had some leverage. In June 1987, a deal was announced: A group of 31 cable companies would purchase a 37 percent stake in TBS for $562.5 million, and they were given 7 of the 15 seats on a newly organized TBS board.[44] But more significantly, Turner was required to get a "supermajority"—affirmative votes from 12 of the 15 directors—for budget approval for any expenditure of $2 million or more.[45]

Although Turner thought he was losing control of his company, he had the good fortune to bring a valuable and influential group of investors into his company. It was clear, however, that Turner and his new board had different agendas. The board wanted TBS to look more like a corporation and less like a seat-of-the-pants, one-man show. But Turner wanted to retain control of the company. The board was also pressuring Turner to relinquish his daily activities to a CEO, something he did not want to do. It was obvious the board thought Turner was a good person to build a company, but not necessarily to run it. But Turner refused to relinquish operating authority, and the board backed down. The board did not want to stifle Turner's creativity, and he was not willing to give up control of the company.

After the dust settled, the new board and their arrangement with Turner turned out to be very positive for all concerned. The cable operators on his board had a significant stake in TBS, and they were eager to see Turner succeed. With advice from leaders in the industry and the clout each member of the board possessed, Turner was in a position to be extremely successful introducing new channels and building his network.

EXPANSION AT TBS EXPLODES IN THE 1990s

The benefits of Turner's new alliance with cable industry leaders became apparent in the early 1990s. First, he introduced a new cable channel called TNT (Turner Network Television). It combined the MGM film library with NBA and NFL events, and the audience response was phenomenal. The TBS board lent its support to the effort by distributing TNT through its networks, and it became the most successful launch of a new channel in cable industry history.[46]

Finally, many of the business decisions that had been questioned by skeptical observers in the industry (such as the decision to purchase the MGM film library for supposedly $200 million more than it was worth) were proving that Turner was, indeed, a broadcasting genius. He controlled approximately one-third of all cable viewing, with TNT, WTBS, CNN, and Headline News; his company was worth over $5 billion; and he was once again financially secure. Additionally, he had ventured further into international markets by broadcasting TNT and CNN in Europe, Latin America, and Asia. To top it off, Turner was named *Time*'s "Man of the Year" for 1991. There was even talk about Turner running for president of the United States.

In 1992, restless again, Turner was looking for ways to expand. He started the Cartoon Network and TCM (Turner Classic Movies, another cable channel broadcasting movies that are part of the supposedly overpriced MGM film library), and he prepared to become a player in Hollywood. In 1993, he finally achieved his objective when he purchased New Line Cinema and Castle Rock Entertainment, a movie studio and a production company.

MOVING INTO THE BIG LEAGUES

In September 1995, Time Warner announced a $7.5 billion stock deal to acquire Turner Broadcasting System Inc. Gerald Levin and Ted Turner made the announcement at a press conference, where Turner jokingly called Levin "boss" after announcing his intention to become vice chairman of the new organization (with Levin as CEO).[47] This combination made Time Warner the largest media company in the world, dwarfing ABC/Capital Cities/Disney and Paramount/Viacom.

The merged company combines TBS with Time Warner's vast holdings of media properties, including *People, Time*, HBO, and Warner Brothers cartoons, among others. The deal made Ted Turner the single largest shareholder of Time Warner stock, with a stake of 10 percent. Seagram's is the second largest shareholder with an 8.8 percent ownership interest.[48]

The Time Warner/TBS combination created the largest collection of assets in the entertainment industry. Turner's cable television empire combined with Time Warner's vast film libraries and distribution capabilities opened the door to possibilities still unimagined. Immediately, questions started to surface about how long Turner would be satisfied as the number two man in the company. Many observers predict Turner will eventually take over as chairman, and with the assets of the new company to play with, turn it into a multimedia conglomerate the likes of which the world has never seen.[49]

THE FUTURE

We can only speculate about what the future holds for Ted Turner, but it is a safe bet that he will continue to push forward in various ventures. While doing research for this chapter, we found an interesting comment Turner made back in 1977, and it is worth repeating:

> I don't think winning is everything. It's a big mistake when you say that I think trying to win is what matters. Be kind and fair and make the world a better place to live, that's what's important . . . I've made a lot of money, more than I ever thought I would . . . But if I continue to be successful, I would like to serve my fellow man in some way other than doing flips at third base . . . People want leadership, somebody to rally around, and I want to be a leader.[50]

ENDNOTES

1. Porter Bibb, *It Ain't As Easy As It Looks* (New York: Crown Publishers, 1993), p. 154.
2. Hank Whittemore, *CNN: The Inside Story* (Boston: Little, Brown, 1990), p. 5.
3. Bibb, p. 220.
4. William A. Henry, "History as it Happens," *Time,* January 6, 1992, p. 23.
5. Robert Goldberg and Gerald Jay Goldberg, *CitizenTurner* (New York: Harcourt Brace & Company, 1995), p. 41.
6. Bibb, p. 40.
7. Bibb, p. 51.
8. Goldberg, p. 116.
9. Peter Drucker, *Business Monthly*, September 1989, p. 43.
10. Bibb, p. 73
11. Goldberg, p. 129
12. Bibb, p. 84.

13. Goldberg, p. 135.

14. Ibid., p. 161.

15. Ibid., p. 158.

16. Ibid., p. 177.

17. Ibid., p.178.

18. Roger Vaughan, *The Man Behind the Mouth* (Boston: Sail Books, 1978), p. 34.

19. Bibb, p. 136.

20. Goldberg, p. 224.

21. Bibb, p. 158.

22. Ibid., p. 151.

23. Ibid., p. 152.

24. Whittemore, p. 49.

25. Bibb, p. 164.

26. Whittemore, p. 156.

27. Ibid., p. 157.

28. Goldberg, p. 279.

29. Ibid., p. 295.

30. Ibid., p. 295.

31. Henry, p. 24.

32. Richard Zoglin, "How a Handful of News Executives Make Decisions Felt Round the World." *Time,* January 6, 1992, p. 31.

33. Ibid., p. 32.

34. Goldberg, p. 337.

35. Ibid., p. 342.

36. Neil Snyder, "An Aborted Takeover Attempt," *Turner Broadcasting System (B),* 1986, p. 1.

37. Goldberg, p. 345.

38. Bibb, p. 283.

39. Snyder, p. 3.

40. Goldberg, p. 350.

41. *New York Times,* March 30, 1986, p. A-27.

42. Ibid.

43. Goldberg, p. 361.

44. Ibid., p. 379.

45. Ibid., p. 379.

46. Ibid., p. 397.

47. Eben Shapiro and Jeffery Trachtenberg, "Time Warner's Levin Finally Gets Respect, but at What Price?" *The Wall Street Journal*, September 14, 1995, p. A1.
48. Ibid., p. A3.
49. Ibid., p. A1.
50. *The Atlanta Constitution,* January 8, 1977, p. A-12.

11 CHAPTER

Jack Welch: Making GE Competitive

"Leaders—and you take anyone from Roosevelt to Churchill to Reagan—inspire people with clear visions of how things can be done better . . . The word *manager* has too often come to be synonymous with control—cold, uncaring, buttoned-down, passionless. I never associated the word *passion* with the word *manager*, and I've never seen a leader without it."[1]

—Jack Welch

Nonmainstream, nontraditional, countercultural, unorthodox, change oriented, maverick, excitable, active, bold, courageous, and passionate are all words which are commonly used to describe John Francis Welch Jr. More commonly referred to by his nickname "Jack," the chairman and chief executive officer of General Electric is considered by many to be one of the greatest business leaders of our time. These positive words which are used to describe him each contribute, in some measure, to understanding the complete Jack Welch.

However, words like cold, arrogant, egotistical, confrontational, intimidating, and even mean have also been used to describe Welch. When

This chapter was contributed by Amir Iskander, a McIntire School of Commerce alumnus who is with Bain and Company in Dallas, Texas.

he first became chairman at GE, Welch was referred to as "Neutron Jack" in a prominent business publication, because he made the decision to rightsize GE. His willingness and ability to confront the difficult choices leaders must make contribute to a complete image of Jack Welch, and they help to reinforce the notion that to be a great leader, you do not have to be very popular all the time. On the contrary, most leaders who leave a significant mark are wildly unpopular with many constituencies at least for a while, and especially at the beginning of their leadership careers when they first challenge the status quo.

Jack Welch's record of leadership didn't unfold much differently. When he first took over as GE's CEO in 1981, the company seemed to be doing incredibly well with an amazing $28 billion backlog of orders.[2] The last thing anyone expected was that Welch would shake things up or pursue radical change. Unfortunately for those who were content with the status quo and for those who feared change, that's exactly what he did.

THE FASHIONING OF CORE VALUES

What was it about Jack Welch that set him apart from the average business executive? Was it his tremendous intellect combined with his powerful charisma? Was it his political savvy, which led him to often be at the right place at the right time? While all these characteristics significantly contributed to Welch's leadership potential, almost all of them are found in men who never progress to the top position, and none of them are determining factors in one's ability to be a leader. While charisma is found in almost any leader of historical significance, charisma is a symptom of something greater—it is an inevitable result of a leader's religious adherence to a core set of values and beliefs.

Welch was blessed to have his beliefs developed throughout his childhood. The single most important influence in the cultivation of Welch's values was his mother, Grace Welch. Said Welch about his mother, "She always felt that I could do anything. She was always positive, always constructive, always uplifting."[3] It was clearly Welch's mother who taught him to believe in his ability to do extraordinary things, regardless of the circumstances. The belief that a person can accomplish anything he or she is willing to work for is one of Jack Welch's defining characteristics. It was a belief Welch would undoubtedly call upon in his rise to the top of GE.

It was also Grace Welch who nurtured in the future CEO a fierce determination and a virtually unshakable confidence in himself. A little known fact about Jack Welch is that he has had a stammer since childhood. Traces of it remain to this day. Likely because of his mother's encouragement, Welch never let it stand in his way. Rather than make young Jack feel insecure and always conscious of his speech impediment, his mother turned his adversity into an advantage. She told him that his stammer was no defect in him. Rather, she insisted, it simply signified that his mind operated so fast that his speech couldn't keep up.[4] As a result Welch never felt inferior; rather, he prized his intellect and developed it. Welch's intellect is considered to be his most extraordinary characteristic.

A deep rooted self-confidence also enabled Welch, who was not an exceptional athlete, to become the captain of his high school hockey and golf teams. He seemed to believe strongly that he could do anything and that he could control his own destiny. Welch gives his mother credit for developing this trait in him.[5]

Welch admits that he has always had an easy life. As an only child he was able to command the sole attention of both of his parents. He remembers his father as kind, but passive, calm, and quiet.[6] Since he was working during much of Welch's childhood, Jack's father had significantly less influence on him than did his mother. However, Welch's strong relationship with his mother was more than adequate in fashioning within the young Welch the seeds of greatness: self-confidence, faith that all things are possible, and an unconquerable courage to take action.

THE DEVELOPMENT OF CORE BELIEFS

The core beliefs that help Jack Welch lead General Electric did not suddenly spring forth when he took over at GE. They were beliefs he had developed throughout his childhood and during his early career at General Electric. These beliefs are *simplicity, speed, self-confidence,* and *constructive conflict.* These beliefs helped Jack Welch transform General Electric into a world-class company with a bright future.

Simplicity

A sharp intellect and a curious mind led Welch to pursue advanced degrees after high school. He earned his B.S. in chemical engineering from the University of Massachusetts, and his M.A. and his Ph.D. in chemical engineering from the University of Illinois. His Ph.D. thesis was on condensation in nuclear steam-supply systems.[7] Perhaps more interesting for Welch than the subject of his thesis was the process of developing it, which helped him to forge a personal belief in and a management philosophy of *simplicity* that has remained with him until this day. Said Welch, "I'm a firm believer that simple is the most elegant thing one can be. One of the hardest things for a manager is to reach a threshold of self-confidence where being simple is comfortable."[8]

Immediately after receiving his Ph.D. Welch began his career with General Electric. In 1960, with a new wife, a new Volkswagen Beetle bought for him by his father, and a new baby on the way, Welch moved 160 miles away from his hometown to Pittsfield, Massachusetts. GE's plastics division offered Welch his first full-time job as an engineer. His starting annual salary was $10,500.[9]

Welch's belief in simplicity may have been a significant hindrance to his ability to climb the corporate ladder in the excessively traditional and bureaucratic General Electric of 1960. However, in a stroke of fate, Jack Welch happened to be assigned to GE's tiny plastics division, which didn't get much attention from headquarters. As a result, the division was allowed to operate free of much of the stifling bureaucracy and red tape that marked the rest of GE.[10]

When he became chairman, Welch decided that for General Electric simplicity meant eliminating bureaucracy, inefficient practices, and redundant procedures. Simplicity in practice oftentimes meant the elimination of many jobs whose sole function it was to approve, deny, or slow down production processes. This elimination process came to be known at General Electric as "delayering." Welch saw layers upon layers of management as nothing more than obstacles in his pursuit of speed and simplicity. "Layers insulate," said Welch in describing his disdain for bureaucracy. "They slow things down."[11]

Speed

Welch never had the patience to wait around for formal reports or lengthy memos; he valued speed far too much to give in to traditional yet inefficient patterns of conduct. If he needed information he went directly to the person who had it, be it a chemist or an engineer or an executive, and he got it. Said Welch later in his career about the importance of speed, "Speed exhilarates and energizes. Whether it be fast cars, fast boats, downhill skiing, or a business process, speed injects fun and excitement into an otherwise routine activity . . . Speed helps force a company 'outside of itself' and prevents the inward focus that institutions tend to develop as they get bigger."[12]

Self-Confidence

The result of Welch's quest for speed and simplicity was not only that many bureaucrats lost their jobs but also that many producers would be forced to become more confident in their ability to make decisions without a rubber stamp of approval. This is exactly what Welch wanted: a lightning-fast, beautifully simple, and powerfully confident organization made up of individuals with the self-confidence to make their own decisions, to take the initiative to improve productivity in their departments, to have the courage to confront their inefficient managers, and most importantly to have a company in which the employees had the authority to respond quickly to customer concerns.

Self-confidence was a central theme to Welch's evaluation of his managers. He believed that it was one of the most important elements in transforming GE's executive team from mere managers to true leaders. He went so far as to attribute most of the organization's inefficiencies to a lack of confidence. "Insecure managers create complexity. Frightened, nervous managers use thick, convoluted planning books and busy slides filled with everything they've known since childhood. Real leaders don't need clutter."[13]

Constructive Conflict

In his early years at the plastics division, Welch developed the controversial concept of "constructive conflict."[14] Still used to this day by Welch, constructive conflict embodies fierce, loud, and sometimes angry debates about which direction the company or the division should take. Welch still engages managers from around the company at Crotonville, GE's management education and development center in New York State.

These exchanges are at times very confrontational, fierce, emotional, yet always open and honest. This is Welch's most controversial belief and it often draws powerful criticism from both the media and from former employees of GE. The labels "mean," "confrontational," "intimidating," and "overpowering" are mainly a result of Welch's episodes of constructive conflict. Some of his most severe criticism was lodged by a *Fortune* magazine story crowning Welch "the undisputed premier" of America's toughest chief executives.[15]

Why is it so important for Welch to attack the ideas of his managers in a confrontational manner? According to Welch, if an idea can't survive a spirited argument then it surely could not survive in the marketplace.[16] It is not Welch's intention to intimidate people for the sake of intimidation;

indeed, Welch was deeply hurt and offended by the *Fortune* article as well as the media's labeling of him as "Neutron Jack." His intention is to use this tool of confrontation as a wake-up call, as a way to change a 100-plus-year-old company.

Additionally, constructive conflict is not a tool Welch reserves for himself to use against his managers; Welch fully expects his managers to engage him in the same aggressive way when they disagree with his ideas. Obviously this requires that those around Welch have a tremendous amount of self-confidence if their ideas are ever going to be heard.

Regardless of the criticisms, Welch's style continues to work well for him. Welch has produced fabulous results in an organization that values results. In 1963 he was put in charge of one of GE's newest inventions, a tremendously durable, virtually unbreakable plastic called PPO (polyphenylene oxide). Welch quickly converted the plastic into a blend that was easy to mold and use in product applications. The resulting substance was named Noryl. With this change, GE Plastics had a product that was very marketable. Welch led the product from the time it had no market recognition, no known application, and no sales to $50 million in sales by 1973.[17]

In 1968 Welch was put in charge of both Noryl and Lexan, another virtually unbreakable plastic substance.[18] The two were big enough by then to create a department of their own. The Welch-managed department was exciting, fast-paced, always moving, and very different from what most people at GE were used to. Robert Wright, the president of GE-owned NBC who worked with Welch at plastics, described it as being "like a high flier, a little business which was run by this fellow who had a very odd reputation, boisterous, demanding. Welch took a lot of chances. He *believed* that the business would be successful" (italics added).[19]

Wright described the process of working for Welch as very exciting. Welch was able to make people believe, the way he did, that they could do anything. In 1968, at the age of 33, Welch's beliefs in himself, in his ability to achieve anything, in the values of speed, simplicity, and self-confidence, made him GE's youngest general manager and put him on a clear path to the chief executive office.

THE WILL TO LEAD

A core of strong values and beliefs was the essential ingredient to Jack Welch's rise to the top of General Electric. It created within him an immovable inner strength. This inner strength generates self-confidence and the will to lead even in the face of stiff competition. Confidence and will are extremely appealing to those who want to be led. They relish the conviction; they marvel at the certainty; and they are drawn to the truth that exudes from a man or woman who has the courage to act.

When Jack Welch became chairman and CEO of GE in 1981, he had a tremendous conviction that his beliefs were founded in the truth, and accordingly he had the extraordinary courage to face the fierce opposition to his plans to bring GE in line with his beliefs. Welch doesn't only have courage, he demands courage in his executives, in his managers, and in all of the employees at General Electric.

It took a great deal of courage to launch the assault that Jack Welch leveled against General Electric's corporate culture. Welch assembled GE's 120 corporate officers in October 1981 and began laying out his game plan for a revolution. To put it mildly, many of his ideas were not warmly received. Most of the senior executives in the organization were very proud of GE and the results it had achieved thus far. Now Jack Welch began talking about being number one or number two in every industry in which GE competed. This was shocking news to an organization consisting of hundreds of different companies (150 business units in 1981) competing in dozens of different industries, many of which were profitable, but not the first or second in their industry.

Jack Welch's "one or two" policy meant that many businesses would not survive in the new GE. In practice that was translated into a policy of "fix, close, or sell." Every business that was not first or second in its market would either become first or second through a fierce and focused pursuit of market share, or that business would be terminated. Those businesses that were clearly too valuable either in assets, market recognition, or market share to be closed would be sold. This clearly gave the leaders of business units that weren't first or second in their respective markets a tremendous incentive to improve their market position, regardless of how profitable they were. Many wondered why Welch was acting like the sky was falling when everything seemed to be going just fine. Needless to say, Welch's policy made him tremendously unpopular with some people at a time when it would have been far easier and vastly less painful for him to not pursue radical change.

It was, and it continues to be, easy to disagree with Welch's focus on being number one or two in every market. Many people do. Tom Peters, well-known management theorist and author of the best-selling book *In Search of Excellence*, is just one of the many experts who disagree with Welch's philosophy. Peters believed that the policy stifled creativity.[20] Many others believed that Welch was afraid of competition. Still others wondered why it was important to be first or second if a business unit was producing cash for the company. However, Welch saw a future in which GE would have to be far more financially sound than it had to be in the 1960s and 1970s. He believed that the key to that financial security was the fat margins and massive revenues that are a product of being in first or second place in every market and being able to benefit from economies of scale and superior levels of accumulated experience.

Said Welch about the number one or two philosophy, "Some people say that I'm afraid to compete. I think one of the jobs of a businessperson is to get away from slugfests and into niches where you can prevail. The fundamental goal is to get rid of weakness, to find a sheltered womb where no one can hurt you. There's no virtue in looking for a fight. If you're in a fight, your job is to win. But if you can't win, you've got to find a way out."[21]

While Jack Welch was courageously trying to light a fire under his executives, General Electric was posting record financial results. Net income in 1980 was up 9 percent, making GE the 10th most profitable business in America. Even though Welch understood this, and though he expected most to dislike his message, he also expected them to see what he saw, the way he saw—he expected them to see the tremendous advantages of starting the revolution now and not waiting until they had no choice. At GE, the resistance to change was more deeply rooted than he had anticipated. Adhering to his policies over the next few years would turn out to be a true test of his will to lead.

In 1981, there were already clear signs of the coming clash with fiercely competitive international corporations. Additionally, there were considerable signs of GE's weakness in 1981. Those who were willing to face reality and those who weren't too busy patting themselves on the back to take action noticed those signs. Only a very few of GE's 150 business units were number one or two in their markets, and almost two-thirds of GE's sales depended on aging businesses that were growing slowly or not at all. Many of GE's most rapidly growing businesses were using more cash than they produced, and GE's bureaucracy seemed too content with itself to notice.[22]

Perhaps the most threatening problem facing GE was the increasing Japanese dominance in the auto industry. Welch was fully cognizant of the fact that the tide of the nation was inextricably linked to the fortune of the automakers. One out of every five American workers was employed either directly or indirectly in the making, servicing, or selling of cars.[23] With the advent of the 1980s, American industry and the American economy were looking weaker and weaker as the Japanese economy and Japanese companies looked more and more powerful.

Welch was well aware that by the end of the 1980s General Electric would compete on a global scale in almost every one of its businesses. He was determined that the company be ready to compete with the far more efficient international producers. Welch's stated goal was that General Electric become "a company known around the world for its unmatched level of excellence. We want General Electric to be the most profitable highly diversified company on earth, with world-quality leadership in every one of its product lines."[24]

In his first three years as the CEO of General Electric Jack Welch cut over 70,000 jobs. Remarkably, this downsizing took place during a time of relative prosperity at GE, with earnings increasing from $1.65 billion in 1981 to $2.28 billion in 1984. But Welch's next move was even more dramatic. He decided to sell GE's housewares division. What seemed like a relatively simple decision from a financial and managerial perspective was a far more complex matter from the perspective of the average GE employee. The outrage which ensued was truly remarkable and quite unexpected by Welch.

Why such an uproar? Until 1984 when the housewares division was sold, the average American associated General Electric with the GE logo that adorned dozens of household appliances and the top of light bulbs. While the logo would remain in the American home via the light bulb, the household appliances, a rich cultural tradition at General Electric, would no longer bear the GE emblem. It was clear by now to everyone both inside GE and out that everything, as well as everyone, was fair game. Jack Welch was determined enough to do absolutely anything necessary to make GE the world's most competitive company.

THE CHANGE MAKER'S VISION

Jack Welch said:

> The competitive world of the 90s will make the 80s look like a walk in the park . . . To win we have to find the key to dramatic, sustained productivity growth.[25]

Jack Welch saw what many around him could not, or would not, see. Welch will undoubtedly go down in history as a visionary. Regardless of the criticisms that have been lodged against him, almost everyone agrees that he displayed tremendous vision in preparing General Electric for a full-scale global confrontation with the Japanese and Europeans far before it seemed evident that any such confrontation was imminent.

"Visionary" is generally the first word that comes to mind when one talks about effective leadership. It evokes fuzzy, warm feelings about great men who address large audiences and speak about things that make the heart beat faster and the mind race about the possibilities of the future. These popular visionaries speak with confidence and certainty about something that seems like a mere dream to their audience, but to them it seems like an inevitable reality, a forgone conclusion about the sequence and magnitude of events in the future.

What people sometimes miss is that the visions of these great leaders are birthed from their core values and beliefs. Their visions are an expression of what they perceive to be the truth. Jack Welch's vision for the future of General Electric was a leaner, more competitive organization that operated with speed, simplicity, and self-confidence. His vision was, in essence, a corporate-scale expression of the values that burned on the inside of him.

According to Noel Tichy, author of *Control Your Destiny or Someone Else Will*, an exhaustive study of Jack Welch's reign at General Electric, "During 1983 and 1984 . . . Welch struggled to articulate his vision guiding his actions. While he made rapid progress in the technical realm, he had little impact on GE's politics and culture . . . The CEO kept trying to explain his thinking, but his early efforts often failed to convey his ideas."[26]

In an attempt to clarify his vision for GE's future, Welch laid down the following four objectives in 1985:

1. Market leadership.
2. "Well-above-average real returns" on investments.
3. Distinct competitive advantages.
4. Leverage on GE's strengths.

Market leadership meant being number one or two in every market in which GE competed. "Well-above-average real returns" on investments was reflective of Welch's hesitancy to set inflexible, uniform, numerical goals for his business units. Instead, each investment would be evaluated individually based on the average return for an investment of its kind.

Distinct competitive advantages meant that GE would only compete where it could provide a value that no competitor could match, be it a lower-priced product or a product with superior technological advantages. This goal was also an expression of one of Welch's core beliefs—that GE should only get into fights that it can win. Leverage on GE's strengths translated into being involved in businesses that required intense capital expenditures and large-scale pursuits that required staying power.

Welch needed a forum to continue spreading his message. He wanted his people to continually be thinking about getting faster, getting better, and getting more productive. Welch developed his own forum in a companywide program called *Work-Out*. Work-Out consists of periodic large gatherings of GE employees and managers in groups of 100 or so people at a time. In these meetings employees have the opportunity to speak candidly to business leaders and to express how they feel about their jobs, the company, and what they can do to be more productive. Employees can also tell managers what they don't like about their management styles. Jack Welch regularly attends Work-Out sessions himself and he encourages employees to take him on as well as other managers.

According to Welch, "Work-Out has a practical and an intellectual goal. The practical objective is to get rid of thousands of bad habits accumulated since the creation of General Electric . . . The second thing we want to achieve, the intellectual part, begins by putting the leaders of each business in front of 100 or so of their people, eight to ten times a year, to let them hear what their people think about the company, what they like and don't like about their work, about how they're evaluated, about how they spend their time."[27]

Finally Welch realized he had to do more to institute the changes he wanted for GE. To accomplish his objective, he formulated what became known as Jack Welch's Six Rules.[28] They are based on his wisdom and experience, and they have helped Welch to bring about the changes he desired. They are:

1. Face reality as it is, not as it was or as you wish it were.
2. Be candid with everyone.
3. Don't manage, lead.
4. Change before you have to.
5. If you don't have a competitive advantage, don't compete.
6. Control your own destiny, or someone else will.

RESULTS OF EFFECTIVE LEADERSHIP

Effective leaders always make a difference. Be it in the business world, or the political arena, or in the field of religion, effective leaders always produce noticeable results. Jack Welch is certainly no exception. Regardless of how you feel about him, whether you are a critic or a supporter, you cannot argue with the dramatic quantitative and qualitative improvements he has produced at General Electric.

Quantitatively, Jack Welch has produced remarkably. In 1981 when he took the helm, General Electric's revenues and profits were $24.959 billion and $1.514 billion respectively. By 1991 revenues had reached $60.236 billion, a compound average annual increase of 9.2 percent. Profits had increased by an average rate of 11.3 percent per year to an incredible $4.435 billion in 1991.[29] The price of GE's stock rose an amazing 19 percent per year from 1981 to 1986 alone. In 1986 it was selling at around $44 per share, in July 1993 it was selling at around $100 per share.

The qualitative results are just as remarkable. While they are more difficult to articulate, their long-term contributions to GE's success are far more valuable than the dollars and cents. The will to lead and the courage to act that Jack Welch has instilled in GE's corporate culture have the ability to draw from people the best they have to offer. His assault on bureaucracy and boundaries freed people to think, to challenge their leaders, to become more productive, and at the same time to feel like they are a part of something bigger than themselves.

There is no doubt Welch has devoted his time and effort during his tenure at the helm of GE working to involve every GE employee in the company to make it a world-class competitor. His reason is simple. Said Welch, "I think any company that's trying to play in the 1990s has got to find a way to engage the mind of every single employee. Whether we make our way successfully down this road is something only time will tell—but I'm sure it's the right road."[30]

ENDNOTES

1. Robert Slater, *The New GE: How Jack Welch Revived an American Institution* (Homewood, IL: Business One Irwin, 1993), p. 167.

2. Noel M. Tichy and Stratford Sherman, *Control Your Destiny or Someone Else Will* (New York: Doubleday, 1993), p. 73.

3. Cynthia Hutton, "The Mind of Jack Welch," *Fortune*, March 27, 1989, p. 39.

4. Slater, p. 29.
5. Tichy and Sherman, p. 47.
6. Ibid., p. 46.
7. Ibid., p. 48.
8. Slater, p. 28.
9. Tichy and Sherman, p. 49.
10. Ibid., p. 50.
11. Slater, p. 260.
12. Ibid., pp. 260–61.
13. Noel Tichy and Ram Charan, "Speed, Simplicity, Self-Confidence: An Interview with Jack Welch," *Harvard Business Review*, September–October 1989, p. 114.
14. Tichy and Sherman, p. 49.
15. Ibid., p. 86.
16. Ibid., p. 75.
17. Ibid., p. 50.
18. Ibid., p. 60.
19. Slater, p. 38.
20. Ibid., p. 90.
21. Ibid., p. 75.
22. Ibid., p. 75.
23. Ibid., p. 60.
24. Ibid., p. 67.
25. Ibid., p. 253.
26. Ibid., p. 88.
27. Tichy and Charan, p. 118.
28. Hutton, p. 50.
29. Tichy and Sherman, p. 261.
30. Ibid., p. 248.

12
CHAPTER

Rebuilding Ford Motor Company

Between 1980 and 1982, Ford Motor Company lost $3.3 billion.[1] As early as June 1980, *Fortune* magazine estimated that Ford had "no more than four years to turn its North American divisions around or face illiquidity."[2] To make Ford's plight even worse, in 1980 the quality of Ford automobiles ranked last among the Big Three automakers in the United States.[3] In February 1981, *Business Week* reported that Ford's financial condition was "rapidly deteriorating."[4] Ford's very survival was in jeopardy. The company had reached the point where it had no choice but to make drastic changes or face insolvency.

By 1983, Ford had turned the corner and was off and running again. The company earned $1.9 billion in 1983 and nearly $3 billion in 1984.[5] By 1987, Ford's $3.3 billion profit eclipsed GM's $2.9 billion profit for the first time since 1924—an amazing feat since GM's 37 percent market share was almost double Ford's 20 percent share of the market.[6] By 1990, an independent survey ranked Ford first in quality among the Big Three U.S. automakers.[7] The turnaround at Ford is unprecedented. This chapter tells how the leaders at Ford took an industry joke and made it into the shining example of quality and profitability in the U.S. auto industry in a few short years.

DEPRESSION IN DETROIT

In the late 1970s and early 1980s, the U.S. automobile industry was in a state of turmoil. Auto executives blamed most of their problems on Middle Eastern politics, the Organization of Petroleum Exporting Countries (OPEC), and rising oil prices. The oil crisis began in 1973 when Middle Eastern oil producers embargoed petroleum exports to the West for five months. During this time, fuel prices doubled, and for the first time U.S. consumers began paying attention to fuel economy.

Despite their problems and shifting consumer preferences, automakers continued to produce large gas guzzlers. They had experimented for a few years with compact cars by introducing cars like Ford's Pinto and Chevrolet's Vega, but the quality of these cars was poor. American consumers preferred the higher-quality, lower-priced foreign cars made by Toyota, Datsun, and Volkswagen. As a result of the oil crisis, the market share of cars imported to the United States increased from 15.3 percent in 1973 to 18.2 percent in 1975.[8]

By 1976, the shock of the oil embargo had begun to wear off. Also, the U.S. government developed policies which helped to keep fuel prices artificially low. Therefore, U.S. automakers continued to make big cars and to ignore quality. However, in 1978 and 1979, OPEC raised oil prices again—this time by over 50 percent, creating yet another oil crisis. Suddenly, fuel efficiency became the most important criterion for most American car buyers, and between 1979 and 1980, imported cars jumped from a market share of 21.8 percent to 26.7 percent.[9]

To make matters worse, U.S. automakers had to satisfy the demands of the United Auto Workers (UAW). Like other unions, the UAW aggressively pushed for higher wages and increased union control in the workplace—demands that made it virtually impossible for U.S. automakers to compete. By 1975, American autoworkers were making at least $20 an hour—much more than the average U.S. car buyer earned.[10] By 1982, U.S. automakers were in serious trouble. Imported cars took a whopping 27.9 percent share of the U.S. market, and interest rates approached 20 percent. These factors combined to devastate U.S. car manufacturers. Their sales plummeted, and they were forced to lay off more than 250,000 workers.[11]

PROBLEMS IN THE EXECUTIVE SUITES

While auto executives continued to ignore the needs of consumers and to turn out low-quality, gas-guzzling cars, foreign automobile manufacturers were making great progress in designing and producing attractive, economical cars with a wide variety of amenities. To put it bluntly, U.S. automobile manufacturers simply did not measure up to their foreign competitors,[12] and the blame rested squarely on the shoulders of the people in the executive suites.

Ford Motor Company was no exception. According to Anne Fisher from *Fortune,* "In Detroit's Dark Days of the early 1980s, many auto industry analysts saw Ford Motor Co. as a has-been, doomed to muddle along deep in General Motors' shadow."[13] The very survival of the company was questionable. In 1986, Eric Gelman from *Newsweek* explained Ford's predicament this way:

> Let's put the Ford Motor Co., circa 1980, on the couch: it's losing a billion dollars a year. The company, a collection of rival fiefdoms, boils with internal politics. Out of touch with its employees, and worse, its customers. Ford builds bland and stodgy cars. Quality is an afterthought. Prescription: change everything. Find a less destructive way to manage, design a whole new car that will bring customers back into the show-rooms, learn how to build quality cars.[14]

The magnitude of Ford's problems became evident when the company recorded a $1.8 billion loss in 1980. Executives at Ford knew something drastic had to be done to ensure the company's survival, but solving the problems and remaining viable would not be easy. They suffered from the same disease that plagued every U.S. auto manufacturer at the time—the "Don't Mess with Success Mentality." "Detroit was sleepwalking during the early 1970s. The Japanese were just a blip on the horizon. Although Ford and the other automakers had consumer research programs, they did not detect the consumer discontent that was building in the marketplace."[15] In addition, a long-standing division between management and labor at Ford had sapped the company's creative energy and led to worker cynicism and a poor work ethic.[16]

FORD'S FIRST NONFAMILY CEO

During the latter half of the 1970s, a power struggle at the top of Ford's management hierarchy prompted an unusual turn of events. Henry Ford II, chief executive officer of the firm, was on the brink of retirement. Most people assumed that his successor would be Lee Iacocca, Ford's dynamic president since 1970. But Henry Ford had developed a personal dislike for Iacocca, and Iacocca was fired in 1978. The way was clear for Philip Caldwell, Ford's handpicked successor,[17] to become CEO. Ford "wanted a conservator of the company and the family interest. Far from threatening to go outside the system, Caldwell *was* the system."[18] In March 1980, Caldwell became CEO.

Ford's decision did not receive unanimous and enthusiastic support. Many believed that Iacocca was a strong leader who could turn the company around. At the same time, Caldwell's abilities were questioned by those who believed his low-key personality could not carry the company through the hard times ahead.[19] But the decision was final nonetheless.

Others were willing to give Caldwell a chance. He had a good mind, and he could see the "big picture." In fact, he had proven his ability as an effective "turnaround manager" when he revitalized Ford's Philco Division earlier in his career. Caldwell's management techniques were nothing unusual; he merely used a down-to-basics, hard-nosed management style that was typical at Ford. What was unusual was his emphasis on product *quality*. The quality focus, which was understood quite well in Japan and Germany, was innovative at the time in the U.S. automobile industry, and it would prove to be vital to Ford's success.[20]

DRASTIC COST REDUCTIONS

When Caldwell took the helm at Ford, he was in charge of a sinking ship. The situation demanded swift action to ensure the firm's survival, and the first order of business was to cut costs. Fixed costs in particular needed trimming, because they represented a large portion of total costs. Despite workforce reductions at Ford before he became CEO, Caldwell further cut labor costs by drastically reducing hourly and salaried positions and by cutting executive salaries and other compensation. In the late 1970s, there were 190,000 hourly workers. By 1985, Ford had not only reduced the hourly work force by 80,000, but it had closed eight U.S. plants and trimmed the white-collar staff by 30 percent.[21] From 1980 to 1982, Caldwell cut fixed costs at Ford by approximately $3 billion.[22] By 1985, Ford's North American break-even point had been reduced by 40 percent, and worldwide operating costs had been cut by more than $1 billion a year.[23]

Cost-cutting measures were not the solution to Ford's problems, but they were a step in the right direction. According to Caldwell, "We had to think the unthinkable and achieve the seemingly impossible . . . But we had to do it to survive."[24] While Ford, like other U.S. automobile manufacturers, had been bloated and inefficient for years, it took the realization of cold, hard facts and the threat of the company's demise to force the company's leaders to address the problem. Having tightened operations, it was now time to change the ship's heading.

THE BIG PICTURE

Obviously, cutting costs is not "thinking the unthinkable or achieving the impossible." Anyone, with or without significant talent, ability, or experience, can order cost reductions, and accountants and finance people can literally rip costs out of any business. That is the way things have been done for decades in corporate America, and the result has been the progressive decay of our competitiveness in industry after industry. Something different was required at Ford.

What Ford needed, and what Caldwell had in mind, was nothing less than a revolution in the way cars were conceived and built. Learning to compete with Japanese and German automobile manufacturers would require a great deal of hard work. It was not enough to just catch up with them. Caldwell knew Ford had to surpass them. To do this, Ford had to make the best car ever produced, and that is exactly what he set out to accomplish. "Ford," he declared, "would become both a domestic and world leader in automotive styling, safety, engineering, construction, and durability."[25]

Two principles guided Caldwell as he pursued his vision. The first was that product quality is of paramount importance, and the second was that employee dignity was essential for success.[26] Product quality had never before been viewed as vital to the successful production of automobiles at Ford. In fact, quality had become an embarrassing subject for the company. In 1980, "Ford was rated lowest among the Big Three automakers in the quality and styling of cars."[27] Without a doubt, regaining competitiveness would require changing the attitudes, beliefs, and actions of every employee at Ford, including the executives who had allowed Ford to fall so far behind its competitors.

The decision to make quality a major issue at Ford was not easy to implement, but Caldwell continued to persist "on product quality and improved design in the 1980s."[28] Under his leadership, the company developed a new advertising slogan, "Quality is Job One." "Job One" is carmaking jargon for the first car of a new model to proceed down the assembly line. Hence, quality would be the first element to go into every new car. Caldwell summed up his stand on quality this way: "Quality is an ethic, a course of action to govern everything we do."[29]

According to David Halberstam, author of *The Reckoning,* "Ford had to prove to its workers and the public that quality was important at Ford."[30] Of course, workers did not initially believe that quality was important, because they knew Ford products were not top quality and that quality was never even an issue before. Thus, to implement real change it was important for Caldwell and the other leaders at Ford to communicate the quality message in everything they said and did. Otherwise, Ford's employees would not understand the new goal. Caldwell had his work cut out for him because the workers believed that increasing quality meant nothing more than increasing production.

ENTER DONALD PETERSEN: THE FORCE FOR CHANGE

Despite his many strengths, Caldwell was not a "people person." According to David Halberstam, "Caldwell was not an easy man for whom to work. Any project in which he was involved, no matter how simple, was attacked with infinite, painstaking thoroughness."[31] "Caldwell was old school, wedded to formal chains of command, but [he] is credited with sensing his approach was wrong and laying the groundwork for the reforms [at Ford]."[32]

When Caldwell was named CEO in 1980, Donald Petersen became president and chief operating officer. Petersen began his career at Ford in 1949. He joined the company after serving in the marines during World War II and going to Stanford to get his MBA. Brian Dumaine of *Fortune* tells the story of Petersen's first contact with Ford:

> Egged on by a Ford campus recruiter, [he] traveled to Dearborn for an interview. Petersen missed his bus stop, and the driver dropped him by the side of the highway. Undaunted, he hurled his suitcase and then himself over a fence and walked to the Ford administration building. Says he: "I was dusty, but they liked me." Ford hired Petersen at $300 a month, one of the highest salaries paid to a Stanford business school graduate that year.[33]

Petersen joined Ford as a product planner. In the 1950s he worked on the Thunderbird team, and he developed the Mustang and the LTD in the 1960s.[34] Petersen worked his way up through the product side of the business. He served as head of diversified products and international automotive operations before becoming president and COO in 1980.[35]

Petersen, like Caldwell, was a soft-spoken man. While Caldwell served as Ford's CEO and developed Ford's new vision, Petersen was responsible for implementing the management techniques that enabled the company to progress along the path to prosperity. Petersen was not afraid of change or the conflict associated with it. Instead, he realized that *real change* and continuous improvement would be the only way for Ford to pull itself out of its slump. Because of his success in making critical changes at Ford, Petersen became chief executive officer of Ford in 1985.

Known as Ford's "Smiling Cobra," Petersen was an engineer who was very demanding of employees.[36] He was known as a "car guy" because he turned every issue into a product issue. One Motor City observer said about the product expert, "Petersen has gasoline in his veins."[37] He knew the product well, and he understood that the product was the key to the company's success.

Petersen triumphed at Ford because he was able to work within the conservative organization while making significant changes. Halberstam said, "If anyone could run a top-heavy, overly bureaucratized company in the modern era and at the same time champion product, many believed, then it was Donald Petersen."[38] During his five years as chairman of the board and CEO, Petersen's "pioneering use of participatory management at Ford 'taught the elephant to dance' and resulted in the biggest comeback ever in the U.S. auto industry—he oversaw an increase in market share from 17 to 22 percent."[39]

FORD'S MISSION, VALUES, AND GUIDING PRINCIPLES

Petersen worked tirelessly as president and later as CEO of Ford to turn the company around. He invited Dr. W. Edwards Deming, a renowned statistician, management consultant, and quality guru, to assist him in developing a broad statement of the company's mission, values, and guiding principles. Stated simply, Ford's mission was "to continually improve products and services to meet customer's needs, allowing us to prosper as a business and to provide a reasonable return for our stockholders, the owners of our business."[40] This simple statement was to guide the company as it approached an uncertain future, and it would eventually lead to long-term improvement, customer satisfaction, and profitability.

To fulfill the mission, Petersen believed that everyone in the company had to recognize the value of people, products, and service. Believing that workers are the source of the company's strength, he valued teamwork and employee involvement. Realizing that the company would ultimately be judged by the quality of its products and the service provided after purchase, he emphasized the product itself. Finally, he understood that profits were vital to the company's survival.[41]

Five guiding principles went hand in hand with these beliefs:

1. Quality comes first.
2. Customers are the focus of everything we do.

3. Employee involvement is our way of life.

4. Dealers and suppliers are our partners.

5. Integrity is never compromised.[42]

DIVISION BETWEEN MANAGEMENT AND LABOR

Relations between management and labor at Ford were not good, and the unnecessary friction between the them made even simple problems difficult to solve. According to Bernard Clifford, a Ford employee hired in 1972,

> When I was first hired, the plant was run really badly. The workers felt like they were not part of the process and that nobody gave a shit about them, and management reinforced the feeling. It was like a war between management and the workers. For one side to get the other to do something, they had to bring out the guns and hold them to their heads.[43]

Clearly, this type of relationship between the work force and management could not continue to exist if real change was to be made.

EMPLOYEE INVOLVEMENT WAS ESSENTIAL TO FORD'S SUCCESS

The poor work climate at Ford contributed greatly to the company's overly bureaucratic structure, but things had to change. Ford's new direction required a new way of thinking and acting. Petersen knew precisely what would be needed. Jerry Flint, author of a 1990 *Forbes* article, says, "Petersen's goal was to replace the one-man rule with team participation throughout the company, from the factory floor to the executive suite."[44] Petersen had developed a positive view on teamwork from his experience in the truck operations, a division where the people were viewed as okay but not fast-trackers. He explains why his experience in truck operations was so fulfilling:

> They did leave us alone to a very large extent, and that meant we were able to work in a more informal atmosphere. It got rather hard to know who was the engineer and who was the financial guy and who was the personnel guy. Everybody spoke to the issue that was on the table. So that was an extremely good affirmation for me of how constructive it is when people work together and really believe they're part of the team.[45]

From his own experience in truck operations, Petersen was able to realize that a participative team structure would be vital to implement change at Ford.

Petersen consequently implemented a program called "Employee Involvement" (EI) in order to decentralize the company and to get employees more involved in running it. EI was a simple concept, but it worked. The basic idea was to form teams that would meet regularly to discuss methods of improving the workplace, increasing production, and facilitating communication within the organization. By encouraging creativity and participation at all levels, employees became actively engaged in their work, and they developed a sense of pride and a belief that their efforts made a real difference.

For example, as a part of the EI program, some assembly workers were asked for their advice before a car was about to be designed. The line workers suggested that the body panels should have fewer than eight pieces so they would be easier to assemble and that all bolts should have the same size heads so that one wrench could be used for the whole car. Ford implemented these suggestions, and the assembly workers were more than pleased to see their suggestions implemented because they felt that they had really made a difference.[46] In this manner, Petersen encouraged people to share their diverse perspectives, and he advocated constructive conflict that demands the best people have to offer. As a result, performance did increase.

Essentially, Petersen bet the success of his revitalization effort on the willingness and ability of Ford employees to respond positively to the EI initiative. It was later said that "Petersen [had] invested nearly all his moral capital in a labor relations reform program called employee involvement."[47] Although it worked out well in the end, Petersen's approach created a great deal of conflict, disbelief, and fear when it was first introduced.

BUILDING SUPPORT FOR EMPLOYEE INVOLVEMENT

In order to overcome anticipated resistance to changes associated with the EI program and to explain why it was important to involve employees more in the decision-making process, Ford's managers met with leaders of the United Auto Workers union. They took with them important financial information to reinforce their points. The result was that the union understood why the EI program was needed and why their support was vital to its success. Caldwell describes Ford's success in gaining union support:

> There has been a considerable amount of good will on the union side. What we call our employee involvement program does exactly what the words

say: involve everybody so they make a contribution. For example, we share our manufacturing cost data with the union, and we are bringing labor in when we look at a new manufacturing concept.[48]

Caldwell points out that Ford's cooperative relationship with the UAW has yielded very successful production results: "Ford in the U.S. hasn't lost the production of a single car or truck due to a strike in the last five years."[49] EI has been very successful at Ford because management was able to gain union support for the program.

Before Petersen's discussions with union leaders, however, he met with top management officials at Ford to explain the idea behind EI to them and to get their support as well. By working closely and directly with top management and labor, Petersen was able to involve employees at all levels of the company in an effort that would eventually save the company and lead it back to profitability and quality.[50] Petersen emphasized the importance of the Employee Involvement program when he said,

> The first step in revitalizing your workforce is to launch an employee involvement program, as we did at Ford. If any company, of any size, hopes to make significant improvements, it has to take advantage of the know-how of everyone in the company, not just the people at the top . . . At Ford, our employee involvement program started slowly and had its ups and downs, but ultimately it was one of the driving forces behind the company's come-back in the 1980's.[51]

MEASURING THE SUCCESS OF EMPLOYEE INVOLVEMENT

Experts have praised Petersen's EI program. For example, Director Keller of Furman Selz Mager Dietz & Birney has said, "Ford has opened channels of communication. You've got people sharing data and understanding each other's problems, decisions are being made with more and better information, which leads to better decisions."[52]

The best gauge of EI's success is employee feedback. Autoworker Bernard Clifford, for example, was much more positive about Petersen's ideas than about the earlier management style: "EI has improved things. There is a lot less animosity between workers and management. People feel more like they are a part of what is going on. They are not just tied to the machine. They are not peons. The EI program raises everyone's self-respect. I never had too much self-respect at work before I got involved with EI."[53]

Another worker's experience also demonstrates the power of EI. Kevin Doyle, author of a 1992 article in *Incentive*, tells the story:

> One man said he'd been with Ford for 25 years and hated every minute of it—until he was asked for his opinion. He said that question transformed his job. Petersen explains that, as part of the employee-involvement imperative, the man was asked to go to a plant that was designing new machinery he would be running. "He told me that it was wonderful to have people make changes, then and there, to meet his needs. He also said he came away from the whole thing feeling there was a real response to his needs as a human being."[54]

In 1983, Ford quantified its progress in EI by surveying employees. The results were impressive: 82 percent of the 750 employees surveyed said they were satisfied with their jobs; only 58 percent were satisfied before EI was instituted.[55]

EI had an impressive financial impact on the company as well. "A typical employee recommendation adopted under the EI program saved the company anywhere from $300,000 to $700,000."[56] Consider this example, which is just one of many. Workers at a Louisville plant discovered that the chrome trim coming from an outside supplier was wrinkled because of poor packaging. They visited the supplier to discuss the problem, and together came up with a better packaging method that produced both cost savings and improved product quality.[57]

THE LASTING IMPACT OF EMPLOYEE INVOLVEMENT AT FORD

Even after the initial turnaround in the 1980s, Ford has continued to successfully use employee involvement at all levels of the organization. For example, Petersen has since established a company conference center where executives from around the world meet to receive information and discuss basic strategies. In January 1987, the company's top 400 people met to discuss the strategic issues facing the company in the next two decades. The group then broke up into teams to discuss innovative ideas to address such issues.[58]

In a 1988 *Fortune* article, author Charles A. Riley II comments, "Such worker involvement was a major factor in the improved quality of Ford's cars in the eighties, which played a large role in its financial turnaround. Industry veterans who remember the company a decade ago say the change in attitude among employees is almost palpable."[59]

PARTICIPATIVE MANAGEMENT

Participative Management (PM), which went hand in hand with EI, is another program Petersen initiated to raise the level of performance and the profit level at Ford. It "allowed low-level managers to make essential decisions without having every one approved by a higher-up."[60] Nancy Badore, Ph.D. in industrial psychology, helped Petersen install the program. Petersen began implementing PM with seminars to explain its value. He then pushed responsibility down the hierarchy and rewarded participative managers. Petersen also visited factories to listen to what workers had to say and to convince them that Ford would actually adopt good ideas that came up from the rank and file.[61] Doug Frazier, head of the UAW at that time, was instrumental in making PM a success as he was very open to the idea.[62]

OVERCOMING RESISTANCE TO PARTICIPATIVE MANAGEMENT

As with any new program, initially there was a great deal of resistance to PM. According to Petersen, the most resistance came from older middle managers who found it very difficult to change the way they had been working for the past 25 or 30 years. Petersen says the following about the skeptics: "These people tend to have self-doubt and lack confidence because they see they are not continuing to grow. They tend to be more defensive in their thinking and more protective of what they do have . . . That's why we found it was critically important to spend time retraining people and discussing the power of teamwork and involvement."[63] Ford needed all employees to buy into PM for the program to be successful.

Middle managers were consequently encouraged to voice their opinions to departments that would have previously operated in isolation. For example, when the Aerostar minivan was being developed, Ford solicited advice from the marketing department—something that had never been done before. Beryl S. Stajich, Aerostar's marketing manager, says, "Five years ago the engineers would have built it to be the most cost-efficient and then told us to market it."[64]

PARTICIPATIVE MANAGEMENT YIELDED SUCCESSFUL RESULTS

Initially, only 6 out of 25 plants were willing to try PM. However, success stories at those plants helped to spread the idea throughout the company. Petersen recalls one case that stood out in his mind—a Richmond, California, parts depot. Having decided to give PM a try, the hourly employees suggested that the managers stay home for a week in order to let them run the operation. The hourlies wanted to demonstrate that they had the ability to perform extremely well on their own. The results were impressive: That week, the Richmond parts depot set several records for accuracy and timeliness in filling orders. Participative management not only improved the performance of that plant but also raised morale significantly at the Richmond parts depot.[65]

Caldwell reflects back on this dramatic change at Ford: "We stopped shipping products if an employee on the floor said they weren't right, and we stopped penalizing people if they didn't make their quotas because of worries about quality. That was a radical departure for Ford."[66] By decentralizing management, PM helped Ford generate new ideas, improve communications, and make better decisions in a more efficient manner.

USING EI AND PM TO PRODUCE QUALITY RESULTS

With programs like EI and PM, Petersen successfully changed the traditionally mechanistic structure of Ford into a more organic structure in which employees had a stake in the future. Greg Easterbrook said in a 1986 issue of *The Washington Monthly,* "Ford has reformed itself internally, changing itself from a notoriously rigid bureaucracy, where managers quaked at the sight of their own shadows, to decentralized mellow-land."[67] This change was essential for long-term success at Ford.

Petersen referred to the old vertical structure of Ford as one where "quality considerations fell between the cracks."[68] He felt that it was not possible for quality to become an issue in such a structure because it generated perverse incentives and warped motivations that hindered efforts to improve anything. But, the reorganization made possible by Employee Involvement and Participative Management made quality attainable as well.

STATISTICAL PROCESS CONTROL

To prevent quality breakdowns, Petersen implemented a program called Statistical Process Control, one of Deming's methods for charting defects. The theory behind the process was that carefully monitoring defects would allow their causes to be identified and eliminated.[69] Petersen further emphasized that it was the job of all employees—not just those in manufacturing—to make quality their first priority.[70]

To ensure that the quality of parts bought from the hundreds of outside suppliers met Ford's requirements, the "Q1 Award" was created and given to suppliers who put "quality first." Ford measured each supplier using a complicated system. Suppliers were accepted only if they scored above a certain level.[71] This process led to the implementation of a just-in-time (JIT) inventory system at Ford. And JIT led to more free space, reduced confusion, and less potential for damage to inventory.[72]

Quality had, in reality, become job one. According to a 1986 *U.S. World & News Report* article, "Ford [had] made the quest for quality nearly into a religion, arguing to workers, managers and suppliers that the cheapest way is to do things right the first time."[73]

CUSTOMER FOCUS RESULTED IN AN ENTIRELY NEW CAR

Petersen was not satisfied simply making a quality car. He wanted to create a car the customer would *desire,* one the customer would truly want to own and drive. In such a car, the driver and the car would be in perfect harmony.[74] Petersen went to consumers to find out what they were looking for in a car, and then he focused the company on providing it for them. Zeroing in on customers' wishes, Petersen was convinced, would make the difference between doing things correctly and incorrectly.

Since Ford had never before allowed customers to define quality, it was a difficult concept for employees to understand initially. For example, Petersen recalls a conversation with a transmission engineer who was confused about why a particular kind of transmission was receiving so many complaints. Petersen describes the engineer's experience in the following manner:

> He thought the way the transmission had been designed and manufactured would guarantee a quality product, but it wasn't until he went out driving with some customers that he understood what quality really meant. The customers would point out to him what they didn't like, maybe a little stumble or a little hitch. Then he understood that the customers' reaction was much more important to quality than the refinement of gear-tooth cutting.[75]

GETTING THE JOB DONE

The first step in revitalizing Ford was to bring about a change in the company at the philosophical level and then to take actions that produced positive results. Everyone in the organization had to be taught to focus on quality, employees, and customers. It was no easy task, but it had to be done if Ford was to survive and prosper.

According to a 1984 *Newsweek* article, "During the worst day of the auto slump, Ford executives concluded, somewhat belatedly, that the old way of doing business was dead . . . Ford would have to jump out ahead of the market."[76] At a time when Ford had no truly competitive cars, Caldwell realized that the company had to produce an entirely different product in order to survive.[77] One of the first steps he took as CEO was "to go for a look that would make Fords radically different from other American cars."[78] And that is precisely what Ford did.

David E. Davis, Jr., editor of *Automobile Magazine* noted that, "Ford rather audaciously went for a new kind of auto when the public had lost confidence in the old kind."[79] That product was to be the Ford Taurus. Because of past failures, it was essential for Ford to be cautious as it developed the Taurus. If the Taurus had followed the pattern of previous new cars the company had developed, the end result would have been an undistinguished product that could not help turn the company around.[80] But instead, the $3.5 billion Ford invested in the Taurus—at a time when it was losing more than a billion dollars a year—renewed the company's hopes and brought back *black* ink to their income statement.

A sequential process of specialization had destroyed many new Ford products in the past. Petersen described the structure that caused such disasters as "a collection of vertical 'chimneys.' Each chimney's managers usually didn't communicate very well with their counterparts in other chimneys."[81] Petersen's emphasis on teamwork was used to transform the old vertical structure and thereby prevent this problem from reoccurring. The new structure provided an excellent opportunity for Ford to create the Taurus.

EMPOWERING EMPLOYEES

"Sigma" was the name given to the original team of employees that was formed to work on the Taurus project. Lewis Veraldi, a man deeply dedicated to Ford, was selected to head the team that eventually adopted the name "Team Taurus" in the spring of 1980. Petersen made sure that Veraldi was given the independence to use his own knowledge to make important decisions about the Taurus. Petersen said, "We asked Lew Veraldi to head the group, but we were careful not to tell him what to do and to let him make all the day-to-day decisions."[82] The formation of

Team Taurus demonstrated the company's dedication to throwing out the traditional organization structure for the sake of quality.[83]

Jack Telnack was put in charge of product design for the car. Telnack was skeptical at first, because Ford executives had always been afraid to stray from convention. Telnack suspected that this team of highly skilled individuals had been formed simply to make another boxy car. Influenced by European cars, Telnack wanted to move toward a more rounded look, which was known as the Aero or eggshell look, but he was afraid he would not be given enough freedom to make such a drastic change.[84]

When Telnack was handed a clean sheet of paper and told to design something very different than before, he was extremely surprised.[85] Even more surprising to everyone at Ford was the fact that Caldwell supported the new Aero look. Although he spoke with Telnack early on to ensure that he was reaching far enough, Caldwell later kept his distance and seemed neutral about the Taurus. Halberstam noted in *The Reckoning* that "despite Caldwell's support of quality and of the . . . Taurus program, Petersen was considered more sympathetic to product, more innovative, and quicker to make decisions than anyone else in the upper echelons of the company."[86] It was Petersen who reassured Telnack that he was free to create a car that he himself would like to drive. Telnack relates, "When quality experts and participative management consultants began appearing around the plant, I said to myself, `My God, these guys really have a process that I've been looking for that I couldn't define.'"[87]

LEADER WITH A SMALL "I"

Lewis Veraldi was certainly a leader at Ford. He may not have been running the entire company, but he had a very specific vision for Team Taurus: "to build the very best mid-market car that anyone could build."[88] According to Petersen, "Lew Veraldi was a company officer and had the confidence and personality to convince those around him to buy into his vision and to support what he and his team were trying to do."[89]

Veraldi learned Petersen's management techniques and implemented them with his own style. He laid out goals that would lead Team Taurus toward realizing its vision. The first was to create a "world-class car" with superior quality, for product integrity would not be compromised. The next goal was to make customers the sole definers of quality. Finally, the team would involve people both "upstream" and "downstream" in order to accomplish the first two goals. That is, the team would include everyone from the CEO to the assembly line worker, the supplier, the customer, and so on in the process of developing the Taurus.[90]

This process enabled Team Taurus to implement Petersen's idea of replacing the conventional method of "sequential" development with "concurrent" development.[91] That is, Petersen made sure that the Taurus project was not passed from one specialist to the next. Veraldi and his team worked on the Taurus through to completion. This continuity was important, for it enabled employees to become truly involved in the project and to feel a real stake in both the final product and, as a result, in the company's future.[92]

Veraldi used many of the management techniques introduced by Petersen to make sure the team was successful. For example, he formed teams of employees from different departments so the ideas generated would incorporate different areas of expertise. Product and manufacturing engineers, designers, and marketing experts with different perspectives were all brought together so that problems could be solved early on—before a crisis occurred. For example, manufacturing suggested changes in design that would result in increased productivity and improved quality.[93] Although each team member brought a different skill set to the table, they all worked together to create one product—a car that was not only functionally superior but also appealing to the consumer.

A WORLD-CLASS CAR

The Taurus was to be the ultimate American midsize car. Modeled after European luxury cars and economical Japanese automobiles, Petersen declared that the Taurus would provide "tight handling, no mushy ride; exterior styling dictated by aerodynamics; interior styling dictated by ergodynamics."[94]

"Ford was ready to commit itself to a 'world-class' car, one in league with the best sold anywhere,"[95] reported Eric Taub in *The Making of the Car That Saved Ford*. To do this, Veraldi implemented a technique called "Best in Class" (BIC).[96] This was a method of competitive benchmarking in which Ford purchased and tore apart 50 of the world's best midsize cars to analyze various components and features deemed to be praiseworthy.[97] Ford bought such cars as the Honda Accord and Toyota Corolla in order to conduct reverse engineering and then to select the best features and improve on them for use in the Taurus. For example, Ford designers modeled the trunk of the Taurus after that of the Audi 5000, which was considered to be the world's easiest trunk to operate; they also copied the Audi's accelerator pedal, which had the best feel. In addition, Ford studied the Toyota Camry to develop a top-quality hood-balancing mechanism; the Supra was modeled for its accuracy in fuel gauging.[98] And, Ford found the BMW 528e to have the best tire and jack storage. In the end, Ford met or exceeded 80 percent of such best-in-class features.[99]

Following Petersen's principle that customers come first, Ford employees interviewed many customers to find out what typically went wrong with their cars so that these problems could be avoided in the Taurus. Using interview data, Veraldi created a Best-in-Class inventory of over 400 suggestions, from rear visibility to the number of turns on the handle required to lower a window.[100]

Veraldi was committed to the Best-in-Class program, and he was committed to perfection as a realistic objective. He said,

> Look, I'm a perfectionist . . . If you're going to work for me, I expect you to try to reach perfection. You'll find out that I've got a passion for perfection. There's no point in trying to reach for mediocrity, because then you'll just fall short of mediocrity. And don't tell me you can't do something. Everything's possible. Just figure out a way to do it. On this project, you'll be doing some pretty common things. But our success will come only if you do those common things uncommonly well.[101]

PRODUCT INNOVATION THROUGH CUSTOMER INPUT

It may come as a surprise to many people, but the automobile industry has traditionally not included the customer when making important design decisions. Yet, without the customer a company cannot prosper and grow. So Ford made extensive use of market research to find out what customers did and did not want in cars and what they did and did not like about them as well. As automobile industry standards went at the time, such change was a major innovation.[102]

Ford employees talked to thousands of potential customers. Focus groups were assembled for tests using Ford, Japanese, and European automobiles. Both general and specific questions were asked to determine precisely what the consumers wanted.[103] In some cases, Ford showed the Taurus to groups and then went back to let them drive prototypes of the model. After driving the prototypes, consumers were able to make further suggestions. This whole procedure was new to both Ford and the American automobile industry.[104] Yet this type of customer input was required if Ford was to develop a car that was tailored to suit consumer tastes.

Valuable information was gathered using this process. For example, customers suggested including a net for holding grocery bags upright in the trunk and painting oil dipsticks bright yellow for easy identification. Although these were minor suggestions, they mattered to customers, so Ford incorporated the new features in the Taurus.[105] Ford also made major changes based on customer research. For example, designers realized that Americans had come to want a slightly larger, more impressive car. The team made the necessary adjustments although they required a great deal of effort and money.[106]

ANTICIPATING FUTURE CUSTOMER NEEDS

Petersen was not satisfied with merely incorporating customers' present suggestions. He realized that for the Taurus to become the best in its class, Ford had to go even further than finding out what customers wanted and then making the necessary changes. He said,

> When you're developing a product or a service, you have to look beyond what the average customer says he wants to things that he doesn't even know he can have. He doesn't know he can have them because he hasn't seen or heard of them. Coming up with features like this is quite a challenge, but it's absolutely essential if you hope to stay ahead of the competition. If you deliver only what the customer wants at the moment, somebody else is going to blow you away with something that goes beyond your product or service in quality or innovation.[107]

Veraldi was able to make this jump with the Taurus by soliciting input from everyone who was affected by the Taurus project upstream and downstream. For example, when seats were being designed, employees tested an entire array of seats that engineers had developed. Petersen describes the process: "We had people of all sizes and shapes take long trips in these seats, and we used their reactions to zero in on the best kind of seats for the Taurus."[108]

Employee input was also used to test dashboard instruments and controls for ease of use and speed. People were timed using the various features on the dashboard in order to find the quickest and most comfortable way to do things such as turn on the headlights. For example, the team found that the quickest and easiest way to turn on lights was to turn a large round dial on the left side of the steering wheel.[109] And, indeed, this feature was incorporated into the Taurus. When planning all of the Taurus features, the team took suggestions from over 1,400 employees and incorporated at least 700 of these suggestions into the final product.[110]

Team Taurus also revolutionized the way manufacturers dealt with suppliers. Traditionally, manufacturers solicited supplier bids only after a car's design was fully complete. However, team Taurus decided to sign long-term contracts with suppliers and invite them to product planning sessions.[111] The "Must See Before" (MSB) program was instituted whereby suppliers were shown how their individual contributions would fit into the project so they could understand how to make quality improvements and make helpful suggestions. As part of the MSB program, the carpet supplier was able to align the carpeting in the Taurus so that the grain would match up correctly. And many other suppliers were able to make small, but vital, improvements that have made the Taurus a truly great car.[112]

After putting over five years of energy and over $3 billion into the Taurus project, Ford created a world-class car that was different from any other American car that had ever come out of Detroit. Petersen said the most important thing about the Taurus project was that "the whole effort validated the benefits of great communication and teamwork."[113] He was right, and the team included everyone who had anything to do with the car.

THE ULTIMATE TEST OF QUALITY: WILL IT SELL?

The Taurus was first released on December 26, 1985. What were the results? *Consumer Reports* said, "These new Ford products are the best-performing products we've tested."[114] *Motor Trend* awarded Taurus its Car of the Year award in 1986. *Forbes* stated that "Ford spent five years and $3 billion on these cars, and the money clearly wasn't wasted."[115] On the day of Taurus's release, a Nebraska Ford dealer commented, "This is the best response I've seen for a new car since the 1969 [Lincoln] Mark."[116] The Taurus was rated one of the world's top 10 cars by *Car and Driver* for the years 1986, 1987, and 1988.[117] In November 1986, *Newsweek* stated, "Ford has the hottest car on the market (the Taurus), the quality of its products is up and its profits are the best in Detroit—more than $2.5 billion so far this year."[118] A 1988 *Training & Development Journal* article reports, "Under Petersen's leadership, in 1986 Ford out-earned its archrival, General Motors, for the first time in 62 years, boosted profits by 40 percent in 1987, and showed the world that Americans can build a quality car."[119]

Ford also succeeded in capturing a group of customers whom they consider to be more influential than the customers who purchased the Ford LTD, the predecessor of the Taurus. For example, research conducted in the late 1980s showed that the average age of a Taurus buyer is 47, compared to 59 for the LTD. Taurus owners also have a higher average income at $38,000—$10,000 higher than LTD owners. And, 40 percent of Taurus owners have college degrees versus 29 percent of LTD owners. Consequently, Ford was successful in attracting young professionals to their new Taurus.[120]

What is even more impressive is the fact that the Ford Taurus remains one of the world's best cars. In May 1990, *Motor Trend* said the Taurus "represents the established standard in the class. If you're simply shopping for the best all-around four-door, the choice remains the same as it was five years ago: the Ford Taurus LX."[121] Furthermore, according to the November 16, 1992, issue of *Fortune,* the Economic Strategy Institute of Washington, D.C., reported that Ford is more cost-efficient in making small, four-cylinder cars than either Honda or Toyota. Alex Taylor III, author of the *Fortune* article, commented that "Ford . . . has built itself into an automobile manufacturer better than any in Europe and virtually the peer of the best in Japan."[122] When customers were asked, "Are you very or fully satisfied with your car? 9 out of 10 customers of both Ford and the best Japanese companies say, 'Yes, absolutely.'"[123]

In Petersen's own words, the Taurus was developed from scratch and became one of the best successes of the 1980s as a result of Ford's new mission and structure:

> The Taurus evolved as employees combined their suggestions and their expertise to give the final product the subjective look and feel of what I called the "driver's car." The Taurus actually got under way around 1980, when employee involvement, participative management, and multidepartmental teaming were just getting started at Ford . . . Six years later, when Taurus made its debut, the EI, PM, and teamwork programs had permeated the company. The Taurus project was a real test for these ideas. It showed what you can accomplish when you bring a team of talented people together and give them the freedom to do what they know is best.[124]

Petersen is quick to share the credit for success with his people. When he was once asked how he was able to turn around the company, he responded "There's an old saying in the Northwest—and it's one of my favorites—that if you see a turtle on top of a fencepost, you know it didn't get there by itself."[125]

FORD'S FUTURE IS BRIGHT

In December 1993, Ford's new CEO, Alex Trotman, went from thinking the unthinkable to actually saying it. He wanted to move his company from number two in market share behind General Motors to number one. While many scoffed at the likelihood of that happening, Trotman is more of a realist than a dreamer, and the statistics suggest that he has a good opportunity to achieve his objective. In 1978, GM had a 46.7 percent share of the U.S. market compared to Ford's 26.3 percent. In 1993, 15 years after the successful onslaught of the U.S. market by Japanese, German, and other European car manufacturers, Ford's share of the U.S. market had declined only slightly to 25.5 percent while GM's share fell to 33.4 percent. Clearly Ford's path could lead to dominance in the U.S. market.[126]

There are important changes at Ford that suggest the company will not soon develop the old "Don't Mess with Success" disease again. The 1996 Taurus was completely redesigned. "It has a rounded, sloping hood that disappears into elliptical head lamps. It has muscular, sculpted side panels; a gigantic, steeply slanted windshield; a more-oval-than-thou instrument panel; a very round rear window; and a rear-end that gives the illusion of flight."[127]

These changes were made at a time when the Taurus was the top-selling car in the United States. According to Jack Telnack, now Ford's vice president for design, "I don't want people to walk into a showroom and see an old friend. I want them to get excited."[128] He believes if they are totally comfortable with what they see, then the design is already obsolete.

When the 1996 Taurus came out, the immediate response was less enthusiastic than the leaders at Ford had hoped, and many industry analysts criticized Ford for "messing with a good thing." Ironically, these are the same people who criticized Ford in the early 1980s for lacking vision and courage and failing to develop new products consumers would want to buy. If over time consumers come around to the new styling and the new Taurus succeeds as expected, then we expect to see General Motors and other automakers follow the Taurus lead in short order. Already Mercedes-Benz has introduced a new car in its 1996 E series that looks remarkably like the new Taurus, and it is selling faster than they can manufacture it.

Even more exciting, Ford is moving rapidly to establish itself as a truly international company. This is part of a plan called Ford 2000, which is aimed at pushing the "world's second-largest industrial company to the next level of multinational corporations, the truly international corporation—a company without a country."[129] The company's goal is to become the "biggest, most efficient auto manufacturer in the world. At Ford these days, Job One is to become No. 1."[130] Ultimately, Trotman plans to make sure that all 1,800 of Ford's executives have international work experience, and he plans to move decision-making responsibility out of headquarters even more than it has been already to enable the company to seize opportunities quickly. If he succeeds, Ford and companies like it may be defining how business will be done in the world in the future.

ENDNOTES

1. Marilyn Edid, William J. Hampton, and Richard A. Melcher, "Now That It's Cruising, Can Ford Keep Its Foot on the Gas?" *Business Week,* February 11, 1985, p. 48.

2. Alton F. Doody and Ron Bingaman, *Reinventing the Wheels* (Ballinger Publishing Company, 1988), p. 24.

3. Donald E. Petersen and John Hillkirk, *A Better Idea: Redefining the Way Americans Work* (New York: Houghton Mifflin, 1991), p. 5.

4. Doody, p. 24.

5. Charles G. Burck, "Ford's Mr. Turnaround: 'We Have More to Do'," *Fortune,* March 4, 1985, p. 83.

6. Brian Dumaine, "A Humble Hero Drives Ford to the Top," *Fortune,* January 4, 1988, p. 23.

7. Peter Doyle, "The Motivators," *Incentive,* January 1992, p. 75.

8. Doody, pp. 14–17.

9. Ibid.

10. Ibid.

11. Ibid., pp. 17–18.

12. Ibid., pp. 14–17.

13. Anne B. Fisher, "Ford Is Back on the Track," *Fortune,* December 23, 1985, p. 18.

14. Eric Gelman, "Ford's Idea Machine," *Newsweek,* November 24, 1986, p. 64.

15. Warren Brown, "Ford Tinkers with Success," *Washington Post,* January 15, 1995, p. H1.

16. Patricia Galagan, "Donald E. Petersen: Chairman of Ford and Champion of Its People," *Training & Development Journal,* August 1988, p. 20.

17. Doody, pp. 25–26.

18. David Halberstam, *The Reckoning* (William Morrow and Company, 1986), p. 585.
19. Doody, pp. 26–27.
20. Ibid., pp. 27–28.
21. Fisher, p. 20.
22. Doody, pp. 30–31.
23. Burck, p. 84.
24. Doody, p. 31.
25. Ibid., p. 33.
26. Doody, pp. xv–xvi.
27. Petersen, p. 5.
28. Alex Taylor III, "U.S. Cars Comeback," *Fortune,* November 16, 1992, p. 55.
29. Doody, p. 33.
30. Halberstam, p. 643.
31. Ibid., p. 587.
32. Greg Easterbrook, "Have You Driven a Ford Lately?", *The Washington Monthly,* October 1986, p. 29.
33. Dumaine, p. 23.
34. Ibid.
35. Edid, p. 52.
36. "This Time, Ford Has a Better Idea," *U.S. News & World Report,* December 15, 1986, p. 54.
37. Edid, p. 52.
38. Halberstam, pp. 652–53.
39. Robert A. Luke Jr., "Ford Has a Better Management Idea," *Management Review,* January 1992, p. 27.
40. Petersen, p. 13.
41. Ibid.
42. Ibid.
43. Richard Feldman and Michael Betzold, *End of the Line: Autoworkers and the American Dream* (Weidenfeld & Nicolson, 1988), p. 44.
44. Jerry Flint, "We Need Manufacturing People at the Top," *Forbes,* August 20, 1990, p. 58.
45. Ibid.
46. Russel Mitchell, "How Ford Hit the Bull's Eye with Taurus," *Business Week,* June 30, 1986, p. 70.
47. Easterbrook, p. 24.
48. Burck, p. 84.

49. Ibid.

50. Petersen, pp. 25–47.

51. Ibid., p. 25.

52. Gelman, p. 66.

53. Feldman, pp. 44–45.

54. Doyle, p. 75.

55. Ibid., p. 82.

56. Ibid., p. 81.

57. Ibid., p. 80.

58. Galagan, p. 22.

59. Charles A. Riley II, "The Seven Keys to Business Leadership," *Fortune,* October 24, 1988, p. 59.

60. Eric Taub, *Taurus: The Making of the Car that Saved Ford* (Penguin Books USA Inc., 1991), p. 61.

61. Petersen, pp. 48–67.

62. Luke, p. 28.

63. Ibid.

64. Edid, p. 49.

65. Luke, pp. 28–29.

66. Dumaine, p. 24.

67. Easterbrook, p. 25.

68. Gelman, p. 65.

69. Taub, p. 221.

70. Petersen, p. 14.

71. Ibid., p. 160.

72. Doody, p. 95.

73. "This Time, Ford Has a Better Idea," p. 54.

74. Petersen, pp. 12, 14.

75. Galagan, p. 23.

76. Gelman, p. 64.

77. Doody, p. 38.

78. Halberstam, p. 646.

79. "This Time, Ford Has a Better Idea," p. 54.

80. Doody, p. 40.

81. Ibid., p. 42.

82. Petersen, p. 70.

83. Mitchell, p. 69

84. Halberstam, pp. 646–49.
85. Alex Taylor III, "The Stylist Who Put Ford Out in Front," *Fortune,* January 5, 1987, p. 82.
86. Halberstam, p. 651.
87. Gelman, p. 65.
88. Doody, p. 55.
89. Petersen, p. 77.
90. Doody, p. 45.
91. Ibid.
92. Petersen, p. 72.
93. Mitchell, p. 69.
94. Easterbrook, p. 27.
95. Taub, p. 13.
96. Ibid., p. 56.
97. Petersen, p. 72.
98. Easterbrook, p. 27.
99. Mitchell, pp. 69–70.
100. Taub, p. 57.
101. Ibid., p. 58.
102. Doody, p. 47.
103. Ibid., p. 51.
104. Ibid., pp. 51–52.
105. Mitchell, p. 70.
106. Doody, p. 50.
107. Petersen, p. 73.
108. Galagan, p. 24.
109. Mitchell, p. 70.
110. Petersen, p. 75.
111. Mitchell, p. 70.
112. Petersen, p. 76.
113. Ibid.
114. "This Time, Ford Has a Better Idea," p. 54.
115. Jerry Flint, "We're Going to Do Just Fine," *Forbes,* October 21, 1985, p. 38.
116. Taub, p. 249.
117. Doody, p. xii.

118. Gelman, p. 64.

119. Galagan, p. 20.

120. Rebecca Fannin, "The Road Warriors," *Marketing & Media Decisions,* July 1993, p. 64.

121. Taub, p. 250.

122. Taylor, p. 54.

123. Luke, p. 29.

124. Petersen, p. 69.

125. Galagan, p. 20.

126. James R. Healey, "Ford CEO's Better Idea: Pass GM In Sales," *USA Today,* December 15, 1993, pp. 2B and 7B.

127. Brown, p. H1.

128. Brown, p. H5.

129. Warren Brown and Frank Swoboda, "Ford's Brave New World," *The Washington Post,* October 16, 1994, pp. H1 and H4.

130. Ibid. p. H4.

INDEX